STEVE JOBS

/GENIUS BY DESIGN_

Disclaimer: Campfire Graphic Novels has published this book in its Campfire Heroes series, in pursuance of its mission, and in the good faith, that the story will inspire readers by recounting the life of an unforgettable person. This graphic novel has been conceived with the intent to tell the Steve Jobs story in an easy and accessible way. In doing so, for the sake of legitimacy, the publisher has shown trademarked logos and product images of Apple Inc. and other organizations with which Steve Jobs was associated. Also, some characters have been illustrated in the likeness of individuals who were part of Steve Jobs's life. The events that have been described in the narration of the story are based on known facts; liberty has been taken in composing these events for the interest of the reader and they are not always an exact reproduction of what transpired or was said. Further, the publisher has produced facts and figures from reliable published material and reportage. As the content has been produced using secondary sources, the publisher wishes to maintain the inadvertence of errors of omission or commission; and state that it has not intended to hurt, demean, or undermine the business prospects of, any individual, group, or organization. This book is not a complete biography. Rather, it covers certain aspects of Steve Jobs's life, and hopes to celebrate his legacy.

Acknowledgment of Trademarks and Copyrights: The publisher has used trademarked logos of Apple Inc., Hewlett-Packard (HP), Atari, NeXT, and Pixar. The publisher has used images of products such as the iMac, the iPod, the iPhone, the MacBook, and the iPad, as well as those of MacPaint and iTunes, all of which are trademarks of Apple Inc. The publisher has created an image in the likeness of the '1984' ad, has used the text and images of the 'Think Different' campaign, and used an image of an iPod ad, all of which are copyrights of Apple Inc. The publisher has used images of *Toy Story*, *A Bug's Life*, and *Toy Story 2*, which are copyrights of Pixar. The publisher has used an image of a Xerox graphical user interface, which is a trademark of Xerox Corporation. In addition, the publisher has used a selection of Bob Dylan lyrics with permission from the licensing department of the Bob Dylan Music Company. All trademarks and copyrights are the property of their respective owners. The publisher fully respects and does not claim any right to the trademarks and copyrights used, nor does it endorse or associate itself with any product or company mentioned in this book.

Published by Kalyani Navyug Media Pvt. Ltd.
101 C, Shiv House, Hari Nagar Ashram, New Delhi 110014, India

ISBN: 978-93-80028-76-7

Printed in India

Steve Jobs

/GENIUS BY DESIGN_

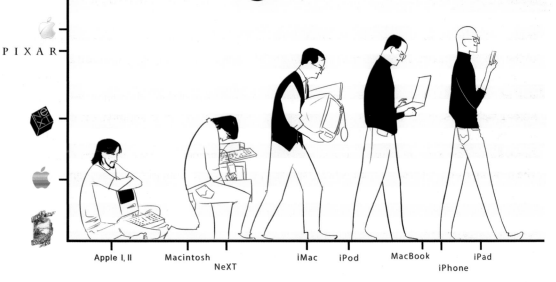

PIXAR

Apple I, II   Macintosh   NeXT   iMac   iPod   MacBook   iPhone   iPad

iVolution

CAMPFIRE

KALYANI NAVYUG MEDIA PVT LTD

New Delhi

Campfire Team

SCRIPT:
JASON QUINN

LINE ART:
AMIT TAYAL

'For ~~these~~ <u>those</u> of us lucky to have ~~written~~ <u>worked</u> ~~about~~ <u>with</u> him, it's been an ~~handsomely~~ <u>insanely</u> great ~~honour~~ honor.'

EDITS:
ADITI RAY
SUKANYA MEHTA

COLOR & DETAILING:
VIJAY SHARMA
PRADEEP SHERAWAT

DESKTOP PUBLISHING:
BHAVNATH CHAUDHARY

CREATIVE DIRECTION:
ANUJA THIRANI

About the author

Jason Quinn

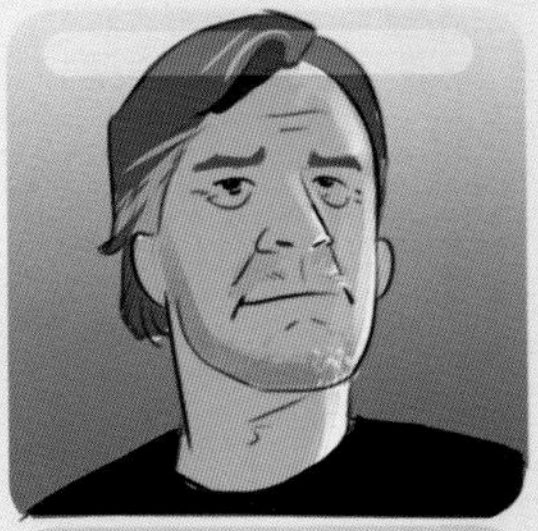

Comic books taught me how to read, and while most boys in my grade dreamed of becoming astronauts or firemen, I wanted to become a comic book artist. When I realized I couldn't draw to save my life, I decided to write instead. Since then, I've worked in radio, television, and publishing, but my first love has always been comics and graphic novels. I wrote my first stories on the Mac, and Steve Jobs is one of my all-time heroes. Working on this book has truly been an insanely great experience!

About the artist

Amit Tayal

Ever since I was nine years old, I knew I wanted to be an artist. But making a career out of it and establishing myself as a comic book artist in India didn't come easy. After a brief shot at accountancy and then animation, I found what I was looking for in my role as a graphic novel illustrator at Campfire. Steve Jobs was a design icon, so illustrating his graphic biography was a real challenge. Ultimately though, I decided on a simple, reader-friendly approach, and a style with clean lines.

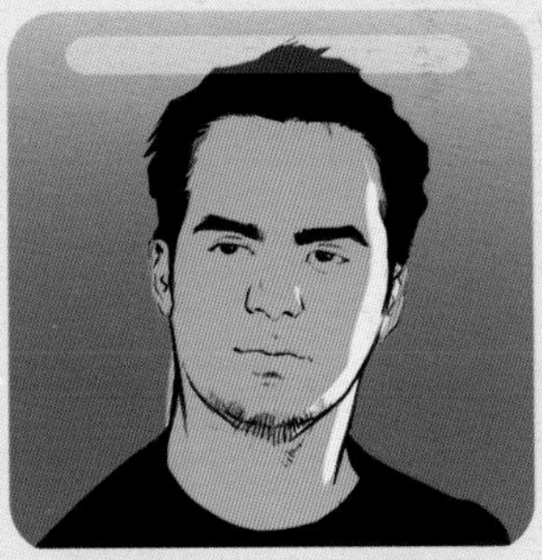

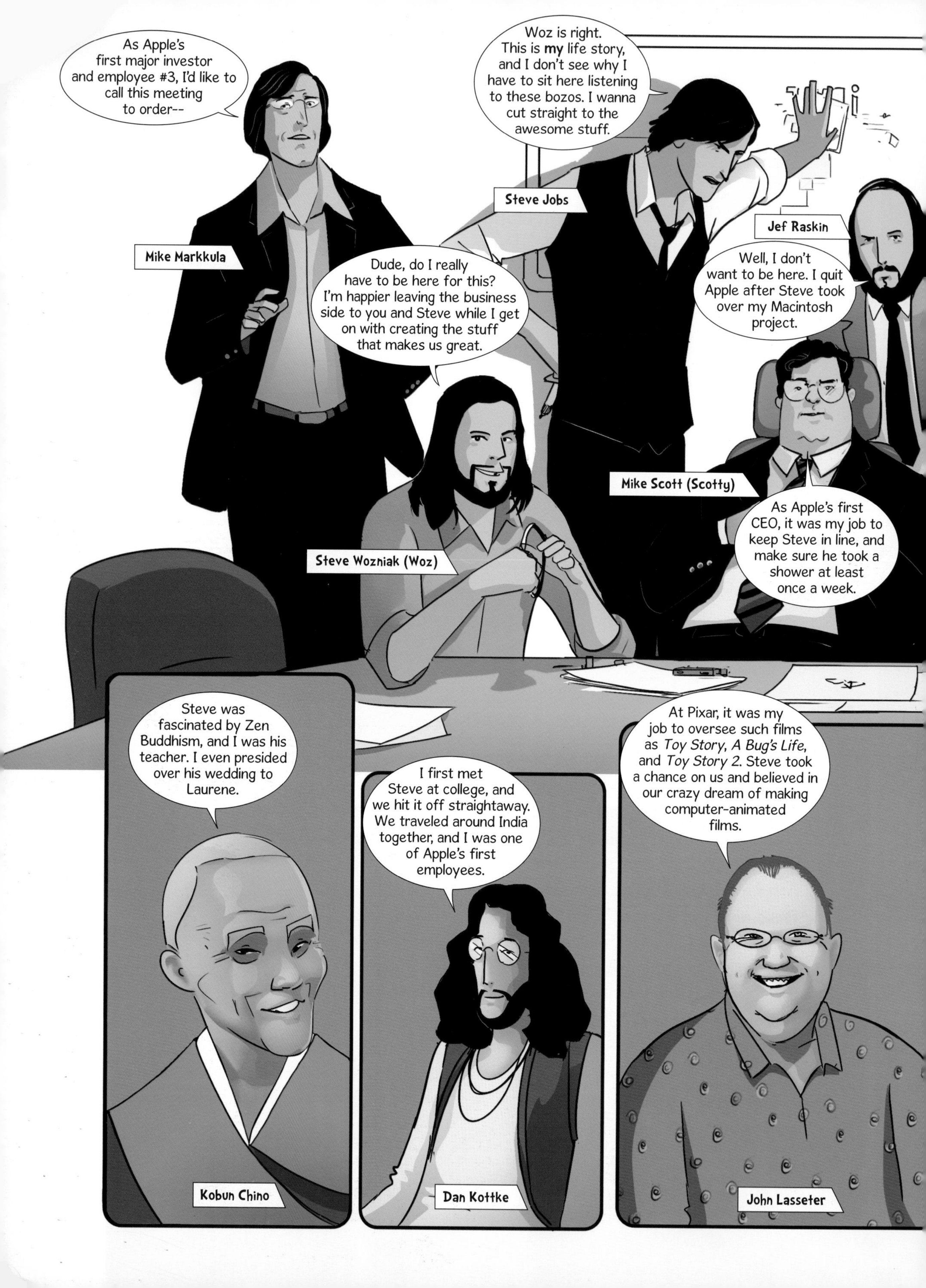
As Apple's first major investor and employee #3, I'd like to call this meeting to order--
Mike Markkula
Woz is right. This is my life story, and I don't see why I have to sit here listening to these bozos. I wanna cut straight to the awesome stuff.
Steve Jobs
Jef Raskin
Well, I don't want to be here. I quit Apple after Steve took over my Macintosh project.
Dude, do I really have to be here for this? I'm happier leaving the business side to you and Steve while I get on with creating the stuff that makes us great.
Steve Wozniak (Woz)
Mike Scott (Scotty)
As Apple's first CEO, it was my job to keep Steve in line, and make sure he took a shower at least once a week.
Steve was fascinated by Zen Buddhism, and I was his teacher. I even presided over his wedding to Laurene.
Kobun Chino
I first met Steve at college, and we hit it off straightaway. We traveled around India together, and I was one of Apple's first employees.
Dan Kottke
At Pixar, it was my job to oversee such films as Toy Story, A Bug's Life, and Toy Story 2. Steve took a chance on us and believed in our crazy dream of making computer-animated films.
John Lasseter

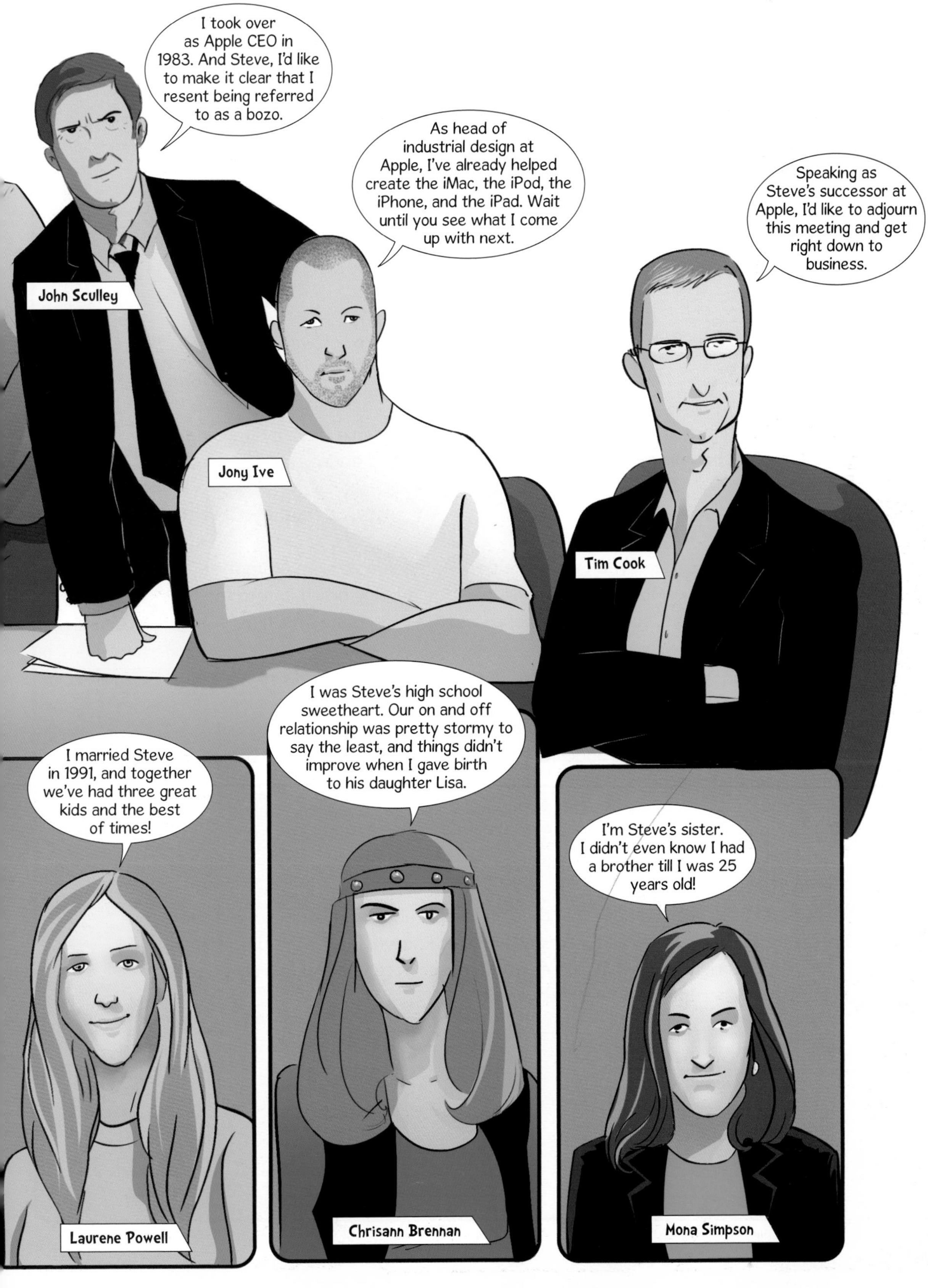
I took over as Apple CEO in 1983. And Steve, I'd like to make it clear that I resent being referred to as a bozo.
John Sculley
As head of industrial design at Apple, I've already helped create the iMac, the iPod, the iPhone, and the iPad. Wait until you see what I come up with next.
Jony Ive
Speaking as Steve's successor at Apple, I'd like to adjourn this meeting and get right down to business.
Tim Cook
I married Steve in 1991, and together we've had three great kids and the best of times!
Laurene Powell
I was Steve's high school sweetheart. Our on and off relationship was pretty stormy to say the least, and things didn't improve when I gave birth to his daughter Lisa.
Chrisann Brennan
I'm Steve's sister. I didn't even know I had a brother till I was 25 years old!
Mona Simpson

'Steve was among the greatest of American innovators—brave enough to think differently, bold enough to believe he could change the world, and talented enough to do it.'

Barack Obama

'We will all miss the Bob Dylan of machines, the hardware software Elvis.'

Bono

'I once said to him that he must be extremely proud of what he had done. He agreed but said he was even prouder of what he had not done.'

Paul McCartney

'We went into the garage when we were two young people with no money… Steve gets a reputation for being a strong leader and being brash, but to me he was just always so kind, such a good friend, and I'm just gonna miss him.'

Steve Wozniak

'Just as Steve loved ideas and loved making stuff, he treated the process of creativity with a rare and a wonderful reverence. You see, I think he, better than anyone, understood that while ideas ultimately can be so powerful, they begin as fragile, barely formed thoughts, so easily missed, so easily compromised, so easily just squished.'

Jony Ive

'Steve never followed the herd. He thought deeply about almost everything and was the most unconventional thinker I have ever known. He always did what he thought was right, not what was easy. He never accepted the merely good. He would only accept great—insanely great.'

Tim Cook

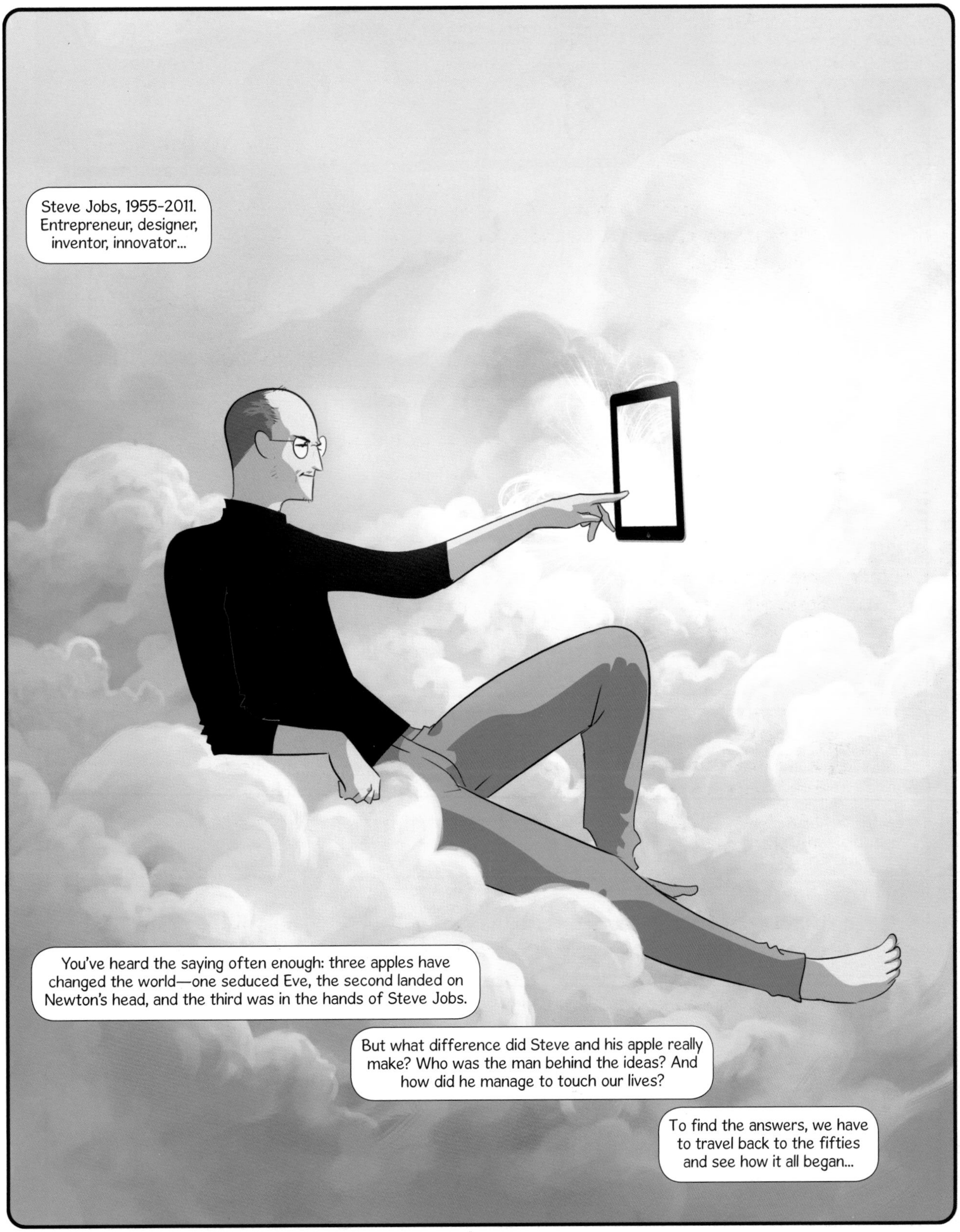
Steve Jobs, 1955-2011. Entrepreneur, designer, inventor, innovator...
You've heard the saying often enough: three apples have changed the world—one seduced Eve, the second landed on Newton's head, and the third was in the hands of Steve Jobs.
But what difference did Steve and his apple really make? Who was the man behind the ideas? And how did he manage to touch our lives?
To find the answers, we have to travel back to the fifties and see how it all began...

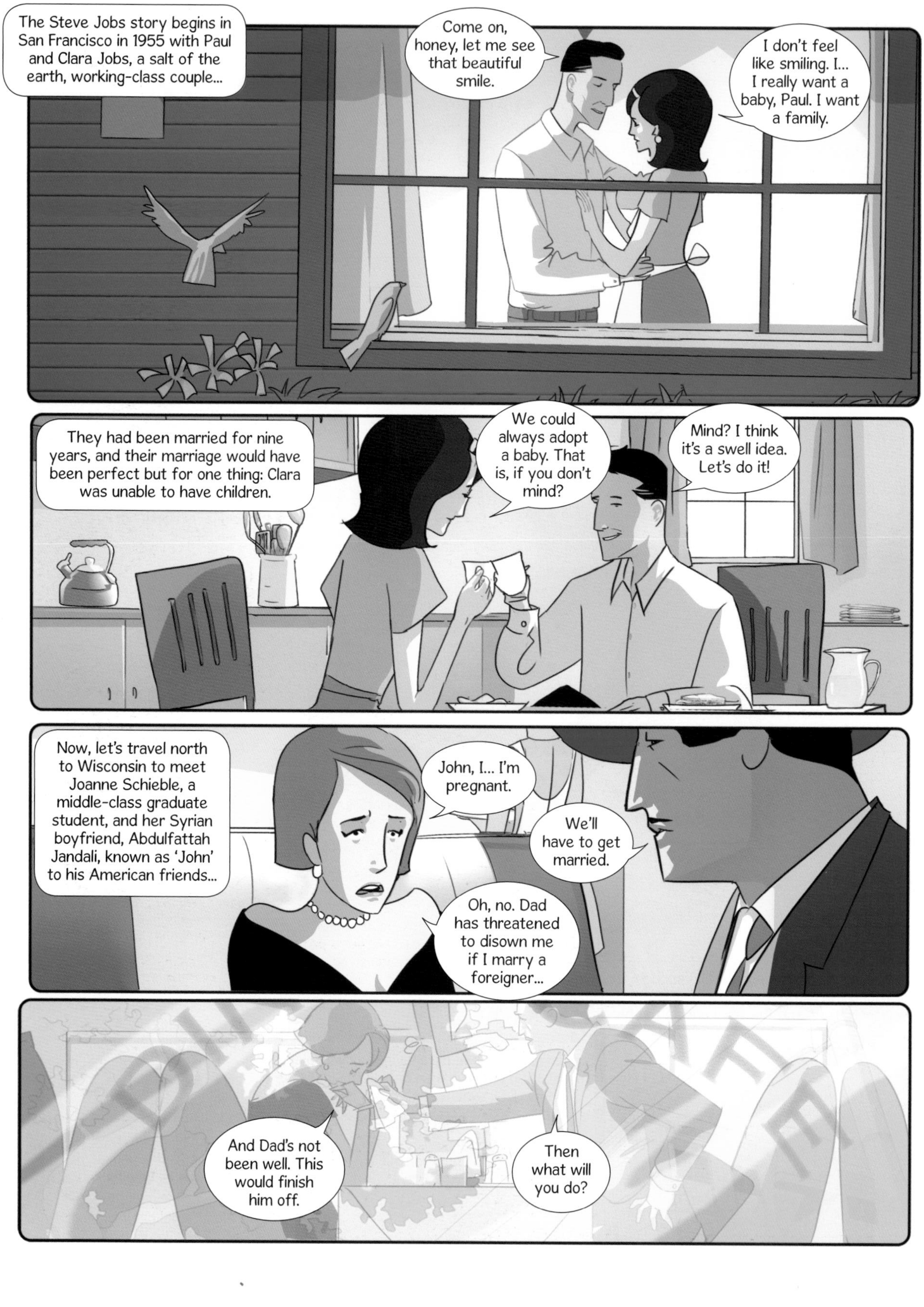
The Steve Jobs story begins in San Francisco in 1955 with Paul and Clara Jobs, a salt of the earth, working-class couple...
Come on, honey, let me see that beautiful smile.
I don't feel like smiling. I... I really want a baby, Paul. I want a family.
They had been married for nine years, and their marriage would have been perfect but for one thing: Clara was unable to have children.
We could always adopt a baby. That is, if you don't mind?
Mind? I think it's a swell idea. Let's do it!
Now, let's travel north to Wisconsin to meet Joanne Schieble, a middle-class graduate student, and her Syrian boyfriend, Abdulfattah Jandali, known as 'John' to his American friends...
John, I... I'm pregnant.
We'll have to get married.
Oh, no. Dad has threatened to disown me if I marry a foreigner...
And Dad's not been well. This would finish him off.
Then what will you do?

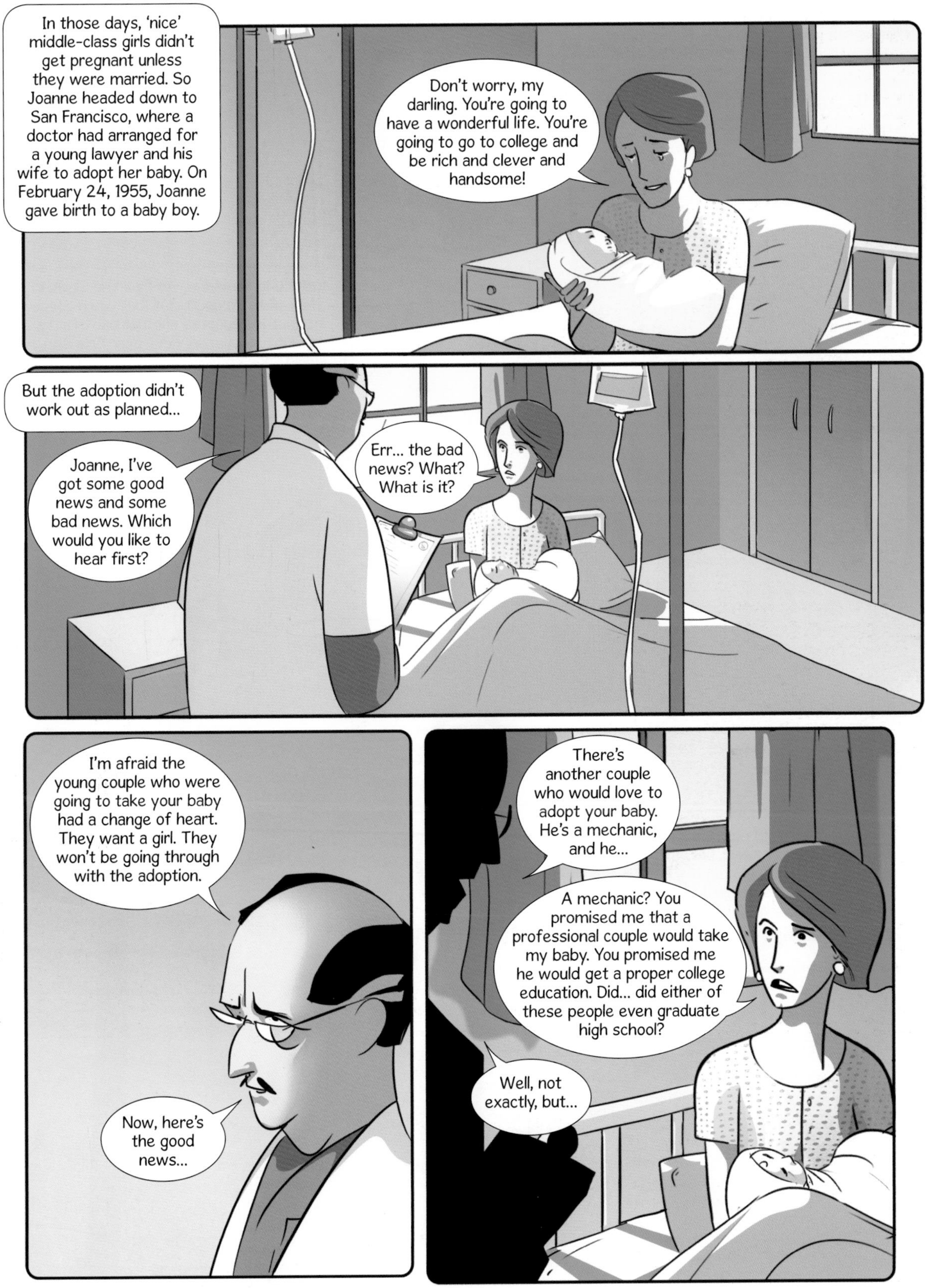
In those days, 'nice' middle-class girls didn't get pregnant unless they were married. So Joanne headed down to San Francisco, where a doctor had arranged for a young lawyer and his wife to adopt her baby. On February 24, 1955, Joanne gave birth to a baby boy.
Don't worry, my darling. You're going to have a wonderful life. You're going to go to college and be rich and clever and handsome!
But the adoption didn't work out as planned...
Joanne, I've got some good news and some bad news. Which would you like to hear first?
Err... the bad news? What? What is it?
I'm afraid the young couple who were going to take your baby had a change of heart. They want a girl. They won't be going through with the adoption.
Now, here's the good news...
There's another couple who would love to adopt your baby. He's a mechanic, and he...
A mechanic? You promised me that a professional couple would take my baby. You promised me he would get a proper college education. Did... did either of these people even graduate high school?
Well, not exactly, but...

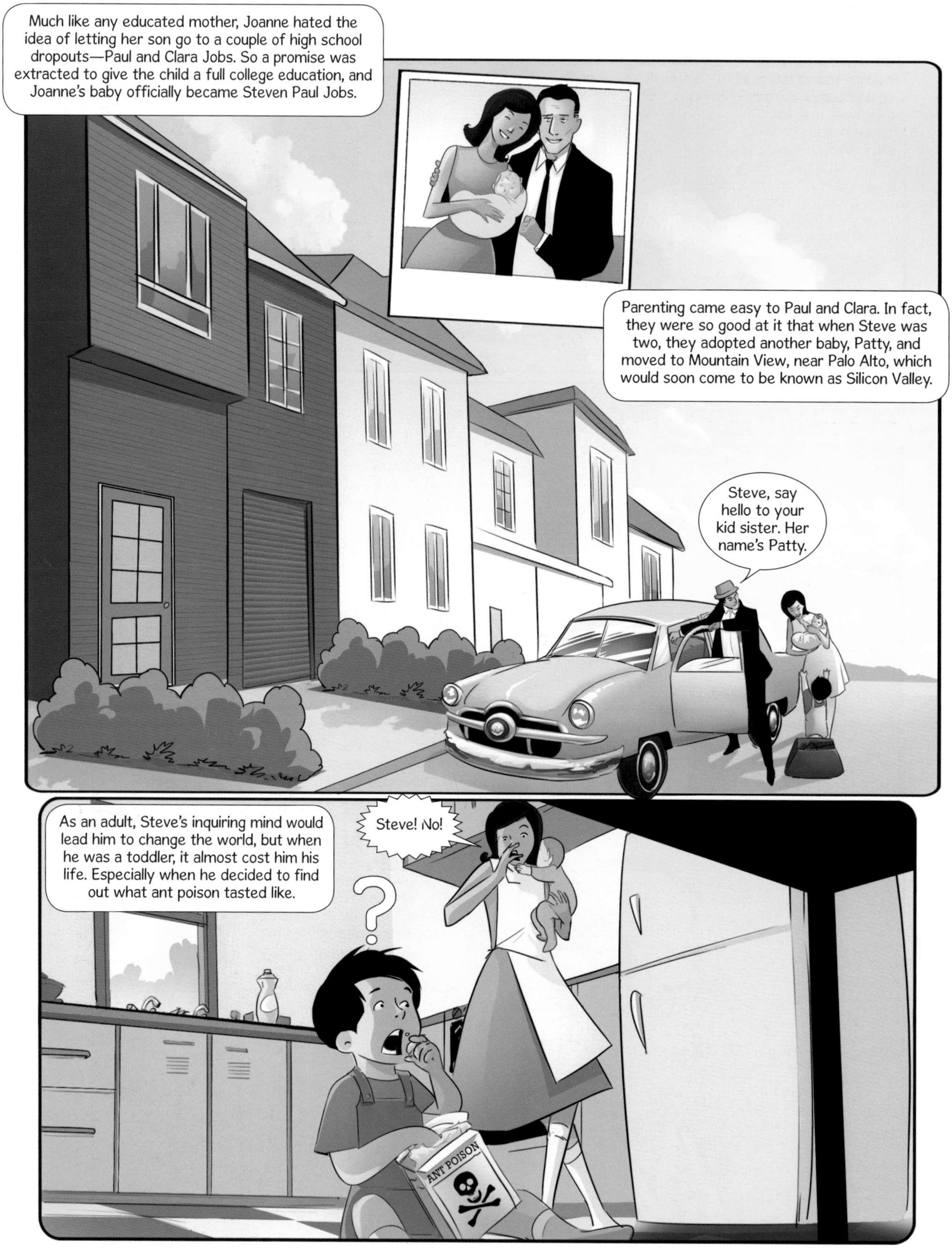
Much like any educated mother, Joanne hated the idea of letting her son go to a couple of high school dropouts—Paul and Clara Jobs. So a promise was extracted to give the child a full college education, and Joanne's baby officially became Steven Paul Jobs.
Parenting came easy to Paul and Clara. In fact, they were so good at it that when Steve was two, they adopted another baby, Patty, and moved to Mountain View, near Palo Alto, which would soon come to be known as Silicon Valley.
Steve, say hello to your kid sister. Her name's Patty.
As an adult, Steve's inquiring mind would lead him to change the world, but when he was a toddler, it almost cost him his life. Especially when he decided to find out what ant poison tasted like.
Steve! No!
?
ANT POISON

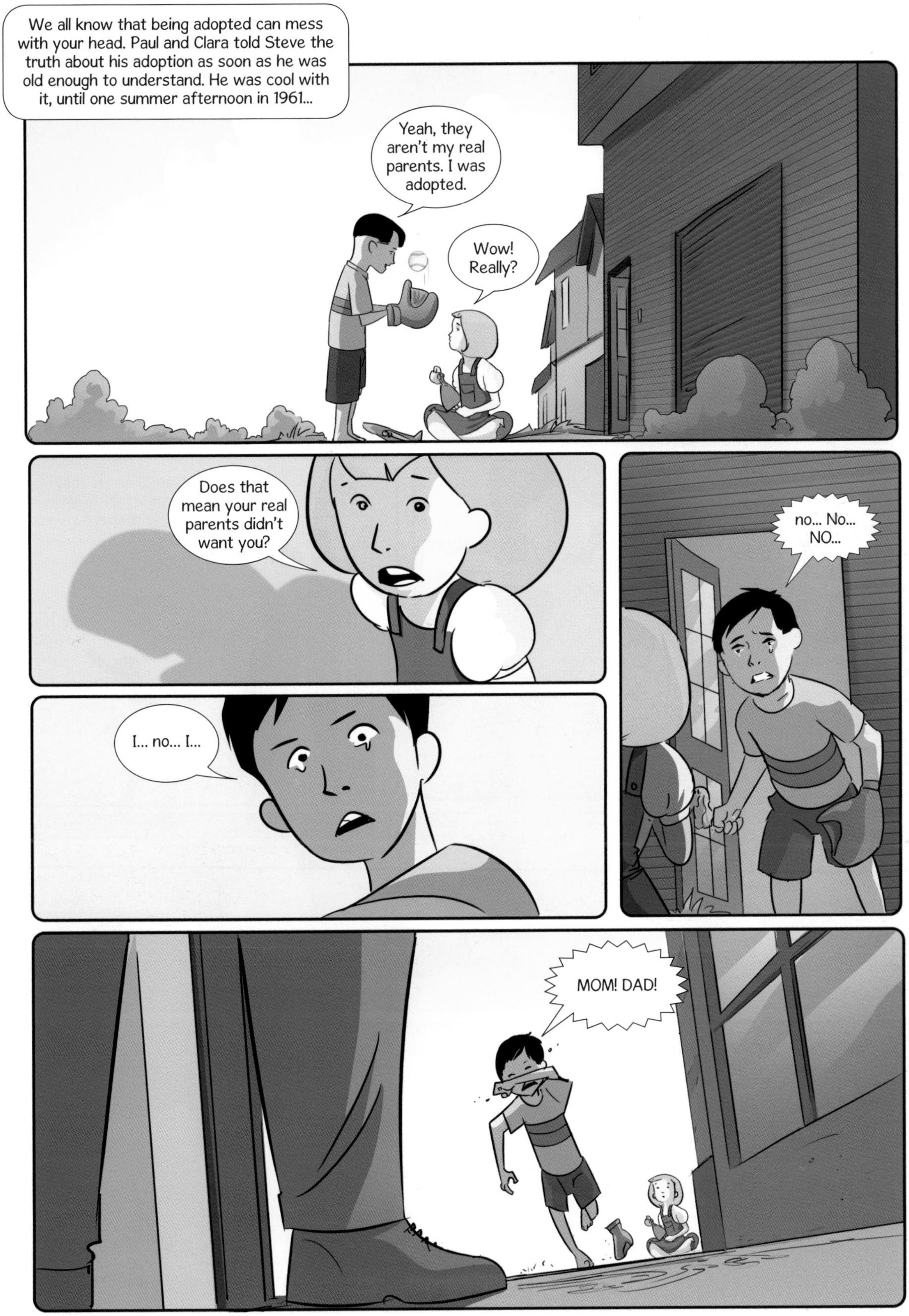
We all know that being adopted can mess with your head. Paul and Clara told Steve the truth about his adoption as soon as he was old enough to understand. He was cool with it, until one summer afternoon in 1961...
Yeah, they aren't my real parents. I was adopted.
Wow! Really?
Does that mean your real parents didn't want you?
I... no... I...
no... No... NO...
MOM! DAD!

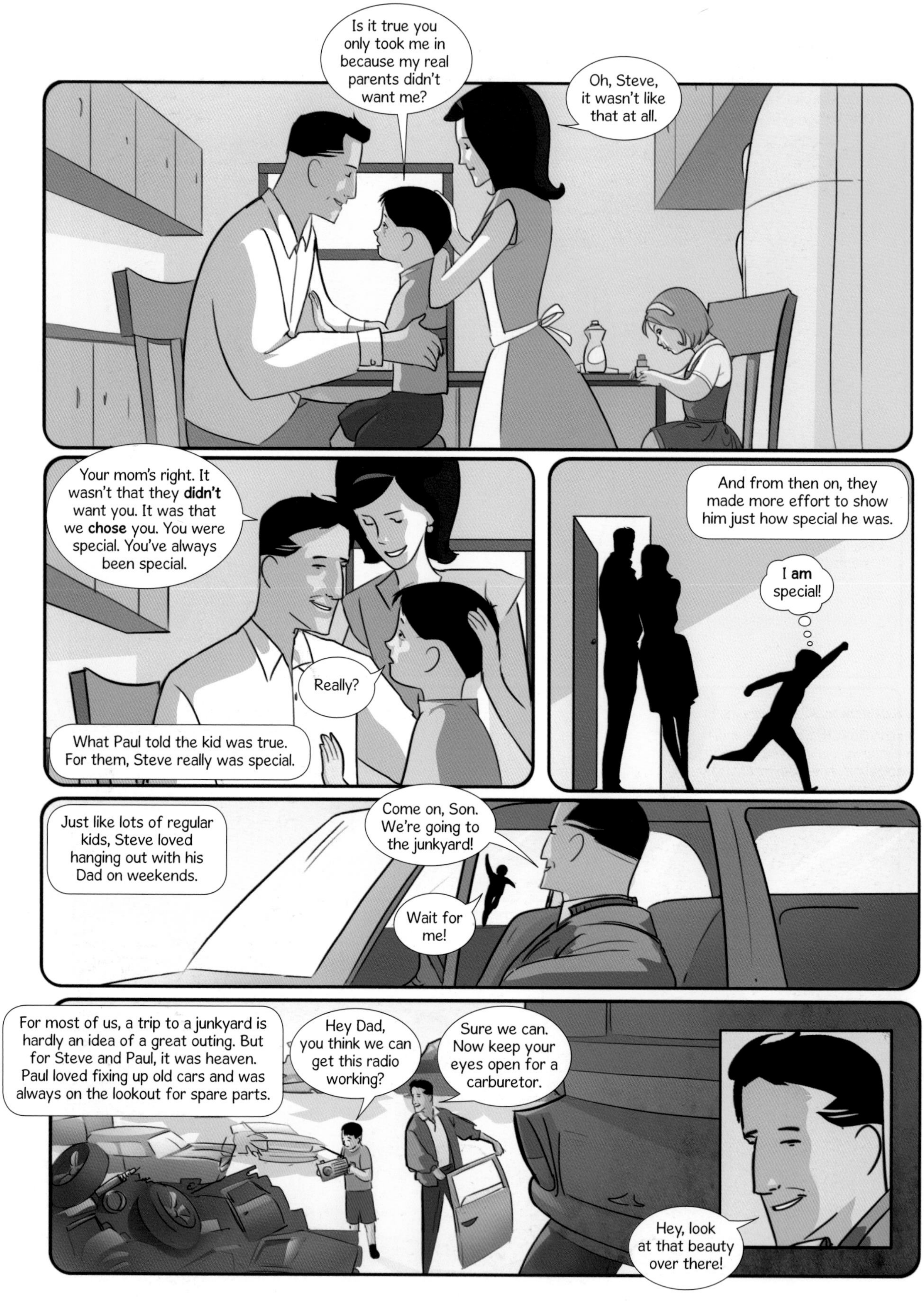
Is it true you only took me in because my real parents didn't want me?
Oh, Steve, it wasn't like that at all.
Your mom's right. It wasn't that they **didn't** want you. It was that we **chose** you. You were special. You've always been special.
Really?
What Paul told the kid was true. For them, Steve really was special.
And from then on, they made more effort to show him just how special he was.
I **am** special!
Just like lots of regular kids, Steve loved hanging out with his Dad on weekends.
Come on, Son. We're going to the junkyard!
Wait for me!
For most of us, a trip to a junkyard is hardly an idea of a great outing. But for Steve and Paul, it was heaven. Paul loved fixing up old cars and was always on the lookout for spare parts.
Hey Dad, you think we can get this radio working?
Sure we can. Now keep your eyes open for a carburetor.
Hey, look at that beauty over there!

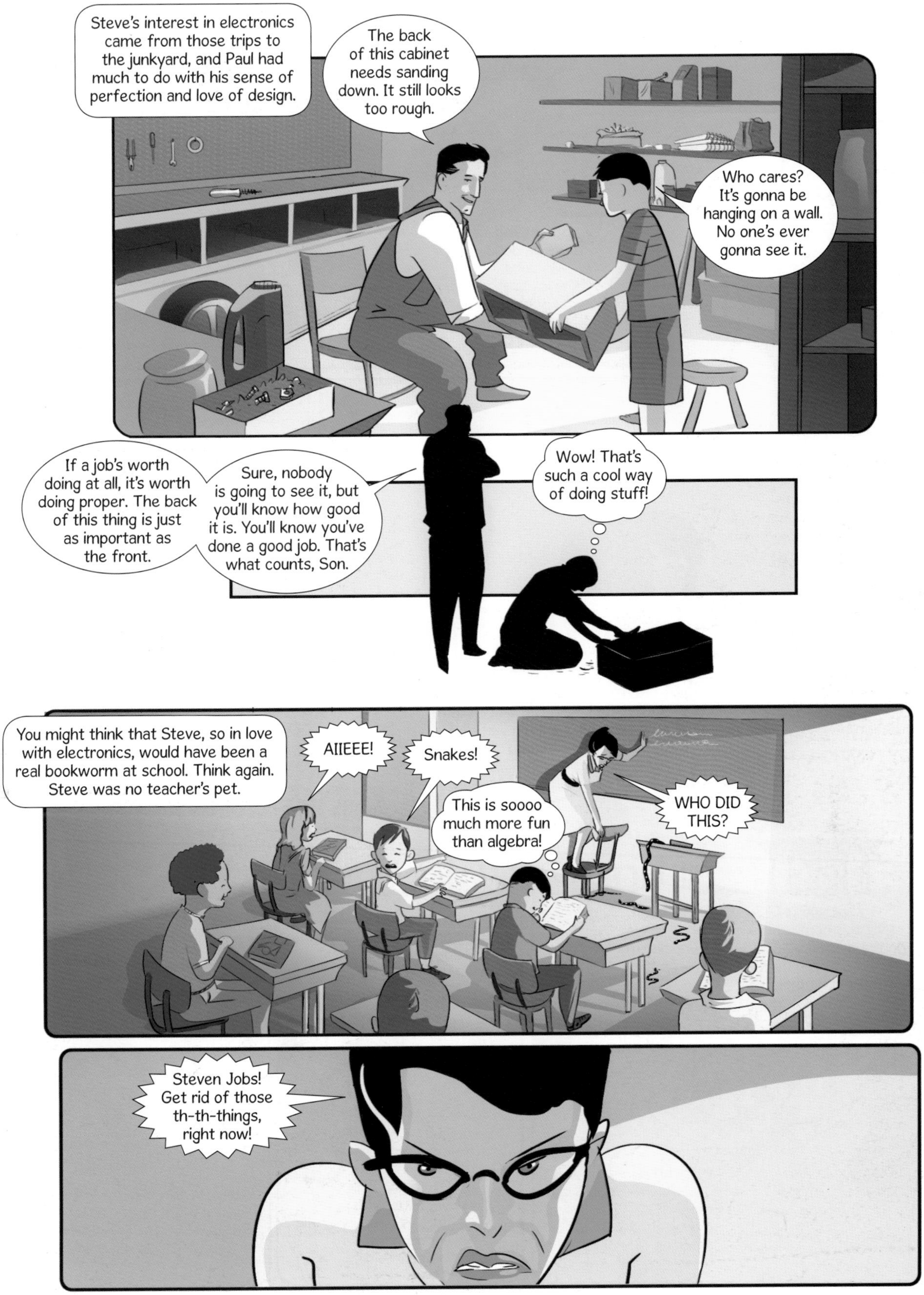
Steve's interest in electronics came from those trips to the junkyard, and Paul had much to do with his sense of perfection and love of design.
The back of this cabinet needs sanding down. It still looks too rough.
Who cares? It's gonna be hanging on a wall. No one's ever gonna see it.
If a job's worth doing at all, it's worth doing proper. The back of this thing is just as important as the front.
Sure, nobody is going to see it, but you'll know how good it is. You'll know you've done a good job. That's what counts, Son.
Wow! That's such a cool way of doing stuff!
You might think that Steve, so in love with electronics, would have been a real bookworm at school. Think again. Steve was no teacher's pet.
AIIEEE!
Snakes!
This is soooo much more fun than algebra!
WHO DID THIS?
Steven Jobs! Get rid of those th-th-things, right now!

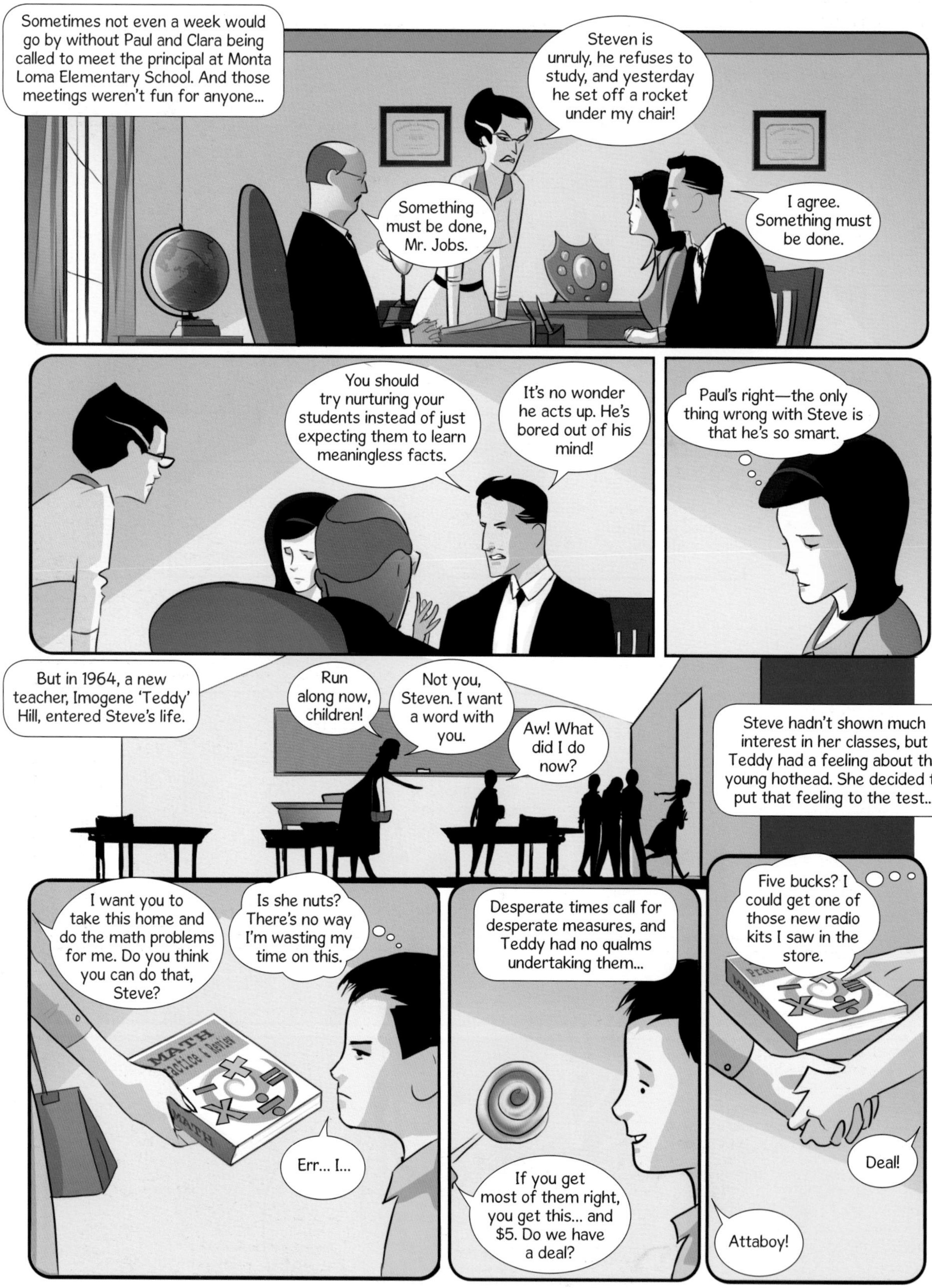
Sometimes not even a week would go by without Paul and Clara being called to meet the principal at Monta Loma Elementary School. And those meetings weren't fun for anyone...
Steven is unruly, he refuses to study, and yesterday he set off a rocket under my chair!
Something must be done, Mr. Jobs.
I agree. Something must be done.
You should try nurturing your students instead of just expecting them to learn meaningless facts.
It's no wonder he acts up. He's bored out of his mind!
Paul's right—the only thing wrong with Steve is that he's so smart.
But in 1964, a new teacher, Imogene 'Teddy' Hill, entered Steve's life.
Run along now, children!
Not you, Steven. I want a word with you.
Aw! What did I do now?
Steve hadn't shown much interest in her classes, but Teddy had a feeling about the young hothead. She decided to put that feeling to the test...
I want you to take this home and do the math problems for me. Do you think you can do that, Steve?
Is she nuts? There's no way I'm wasting my time on this.
Err... I...
Desperate times call for desperate measures, and Teddy had no qualms undertaking them...
If you get most of them right, you get this... and $5. Do we have a deal?
Five bucks? I could get one of those new radio kits I saw in the store.
Deal!
Attaboy!

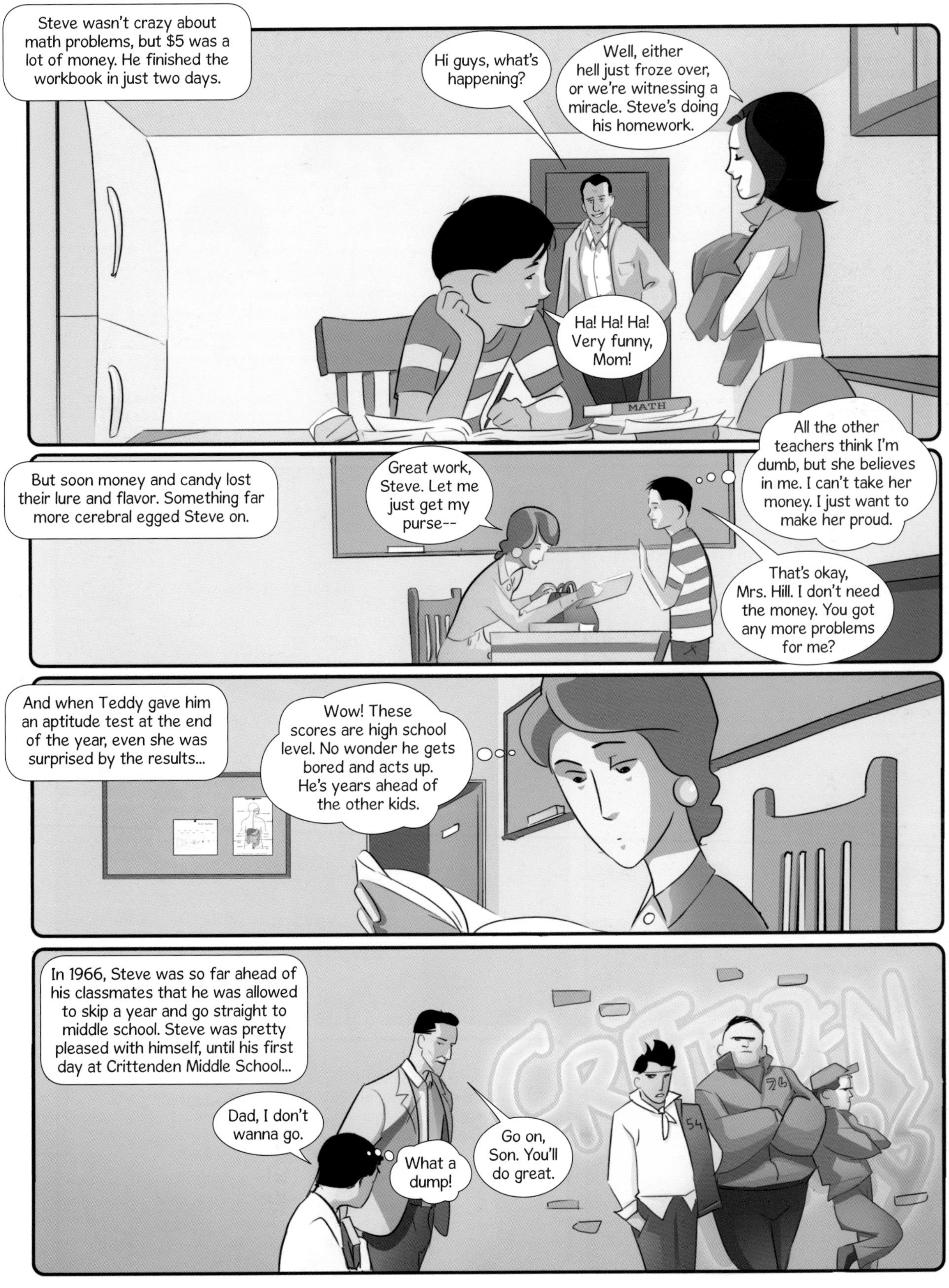
Steve wasn't crazy about math problems, but $5 was a lot of money. He finished the workbook in just two days.
Hi guys, what's happening?
Well, either hell just froze over, or we're witnessing a miracle. Steve's doing his homework.
Ha! Ha! Ha! Very funny, Mom!
MATH
But soon money and candy lost their lure and flavor. Something far more cerebral egged Steve on.
Great work, Steve. Let me just get my purse--
All the other teachers think I'm dumb, but she believes in me. I can't take her money. I just want to make her proud.
That's okay, Mrs. Hill. I don't need the money. You got any more problems for me?
And when Teddy gave him an aptitude test at the end of the year, even she was surprised by the results...
Wow! These scores are high school level. No wonder he gets bored and acts up. He's years ahead of the other kids.
In 1966, Steve was so far ahead of his classmates that he was allowed to skip a year and go straight to middle school. Steve was pretty pleased with himself, until his first day at Crittenden Middle School...
Dad, I don't wanna go.
What a dump!
Go on, Son. You'll do great.

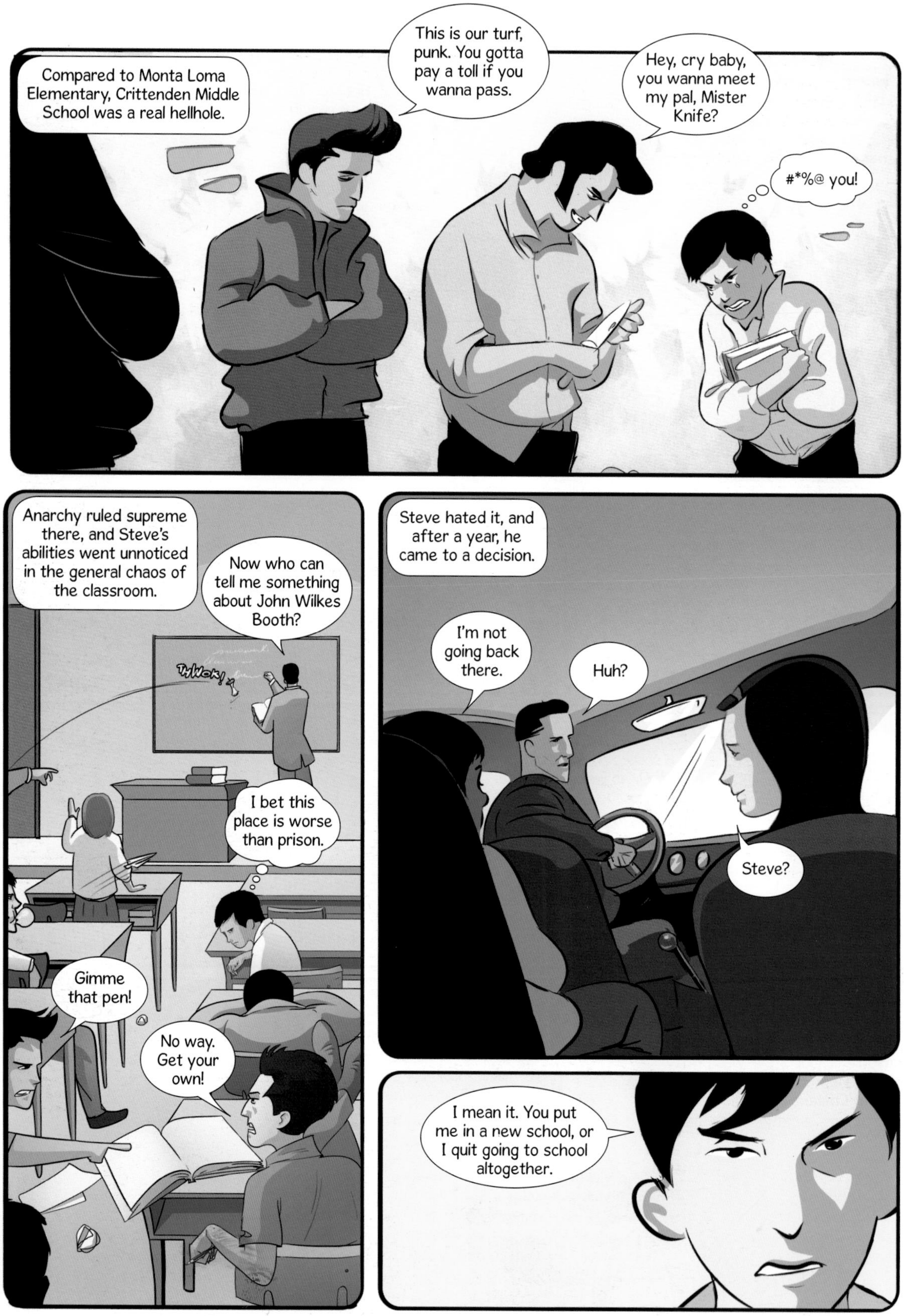
Compared to Monta Loma Elementary, Crittenden Middle School was a real hellhole.
This is our turf, punk. You gotta pay a toll if you wanna pass.
Hey, cry baby, you wanna meet my pal, Mister Knife?
#*%@ you!
Anarchy ruled supreme there, and Steve's abilities went unnoticed in the general chaos of the classroom.
Now who can tell me something about John Wilkes Booth?
THWOK!
I bet this place is worse than prison.
Gimme that pen!
No way. Get your own!
Steve hated it, and after a year, he came to a decision.
I'm not going back there.
Huh?
Steve?
I mean it. You put me in a new school, or I quit going to school altogether.

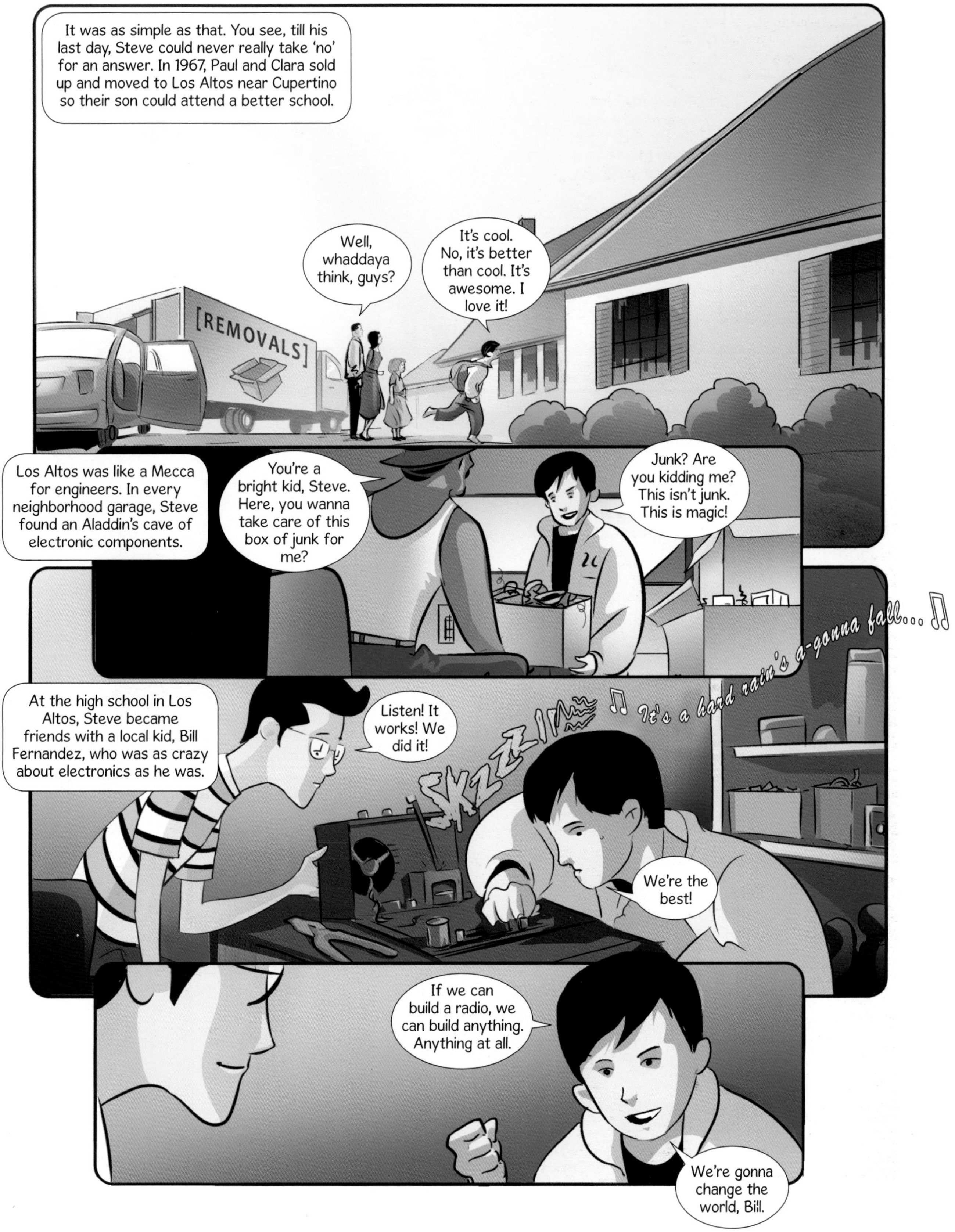

It was as simple as that. You see, till his last day, Steve could never really take 'no' for an answer. In 1967, Paul and Clara sold up and moved to Los Altos near Cupertino so their son could attend a better school.
Well, whaddaya think, guys?
It's cool. No, it's better than cool. It's awesome. I love it!
[REMOVALS]
Los Altos was like a Mecca for engineers. In every neighborhood garage, Steve found an Aladdin's cave of electronic components.
You're a bright kid, Steve. Here, you wanna take care of this box of junk for me?
Junk? Are you kidding me? This isn't junk. This is magic!
At the high school in Los Altos, Steve became friends with a local kid, Bill Fernandez, who was as crazy about electronics as he was.
Listen! It works! We did it!
SKZZZ!!
♫ It's a hard rain's a-gonna fall... ♫
We're the best!
If we can build a radio, we can build anything. Anything at all.
We're gonna change the world, Bill.

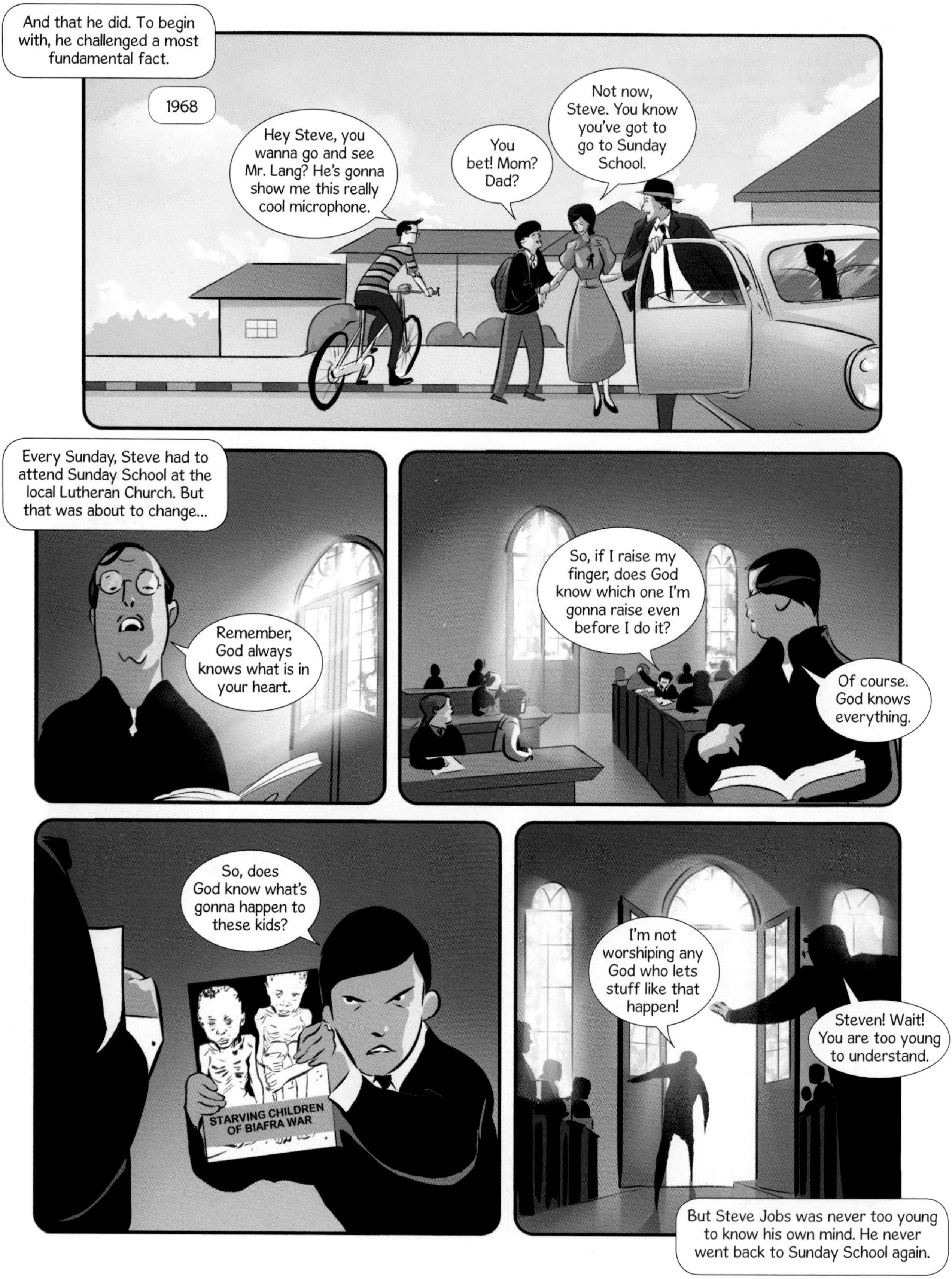
And that he did. To begin with, he challenged a most fundamental fact.
1968
Hey Steve, you wanna go and see Mr. Lang? He's gonna show me this really cool microphone.
You bet! Mom? Dad?
Not now, Steve. You know you've got to go to Sunday School.
Every Sunday, Steve had to attend Sunday School at the local Lutheran Church. But that was about to change...
Remember, God always knows what is in your heart.
So, if I raise my finger, does God know which one I'm gonna raise even before I do it?
Of course. God knows everything.
So, does God know what's gonna happen to these kids?
STARVING CHILDREN OF BIAFRA WAR
I'm not worshiping any God who lets stuff like that happen!
Steven! Wait! You are too young to understand.
But Steve Jobs was never too young to know his own mind. He never went back to Sunday School again.

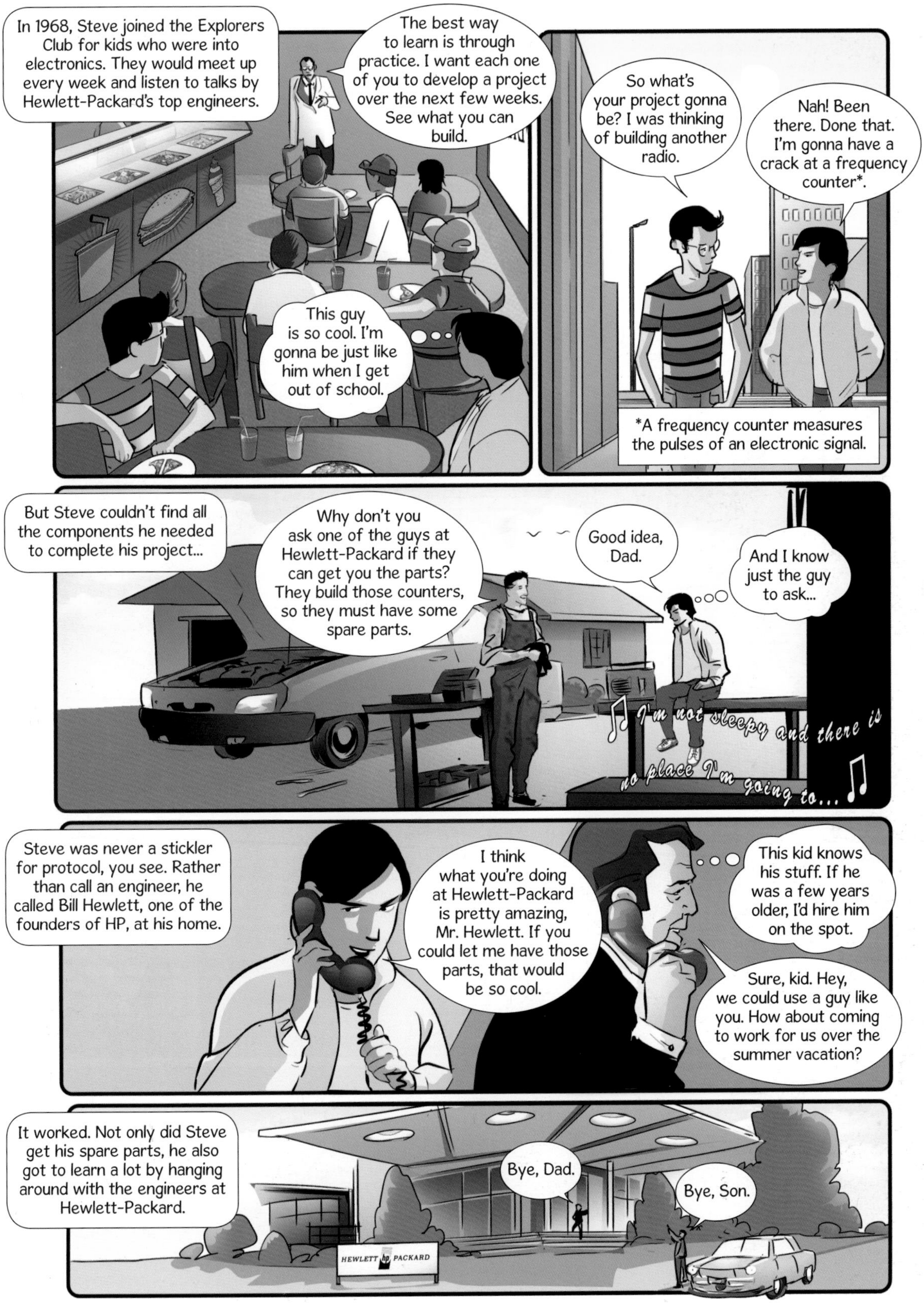
In 1968, Steve joined the Explorers Club for kids who were into electronics. They would meet up every week and listen to talks by Hewlett-Packard's top engineers.
The best way to learn is through practice. I want each one of you to develop a project over the next few weeks. See what you can build.
This guy is so cool. I'm gonna be just like him when I get out of school.
So what's your project gonna be? I was thinking of building another radio.
Nah! Been there. Done that. I'm gonna have a crack at a frequency counter*.
*A frequency counter measures the pulses of an electronic signal.
But Steve couldn't find all the components he needed to complete his project...
Why don't you ask one of the guys at Hewlett-Packard if they can get you the parts? They build those counters, so they must have some spare parts.
Good idea, Dad.
And I know just the guy to ask...
I'm not sleepy and there is no place I'm going to...
Steve was never a stickler for protocol, you see. Rather than call an engineer, he called Bill Hewlett, one of the founders of HP, at his home.
I think what you're doing at Hewlett-Packard is pretty amazing, Mr. Hewlett. If you could let me have those parts, that would be so cool.
This kid knows his stuff. If he was a few years older, I'd hire him on the spot.
Sure, kid. Hey, we could use a guy like you. How about coming to work for us over the summer vacation?
It worked. Not only did Steve get his spare parts, he also got to learn a lot by hanging around with the engineers at Hewlett-Packard.
Bye, Dad.
Bye, Son.
HEWLETT hp PACKARD

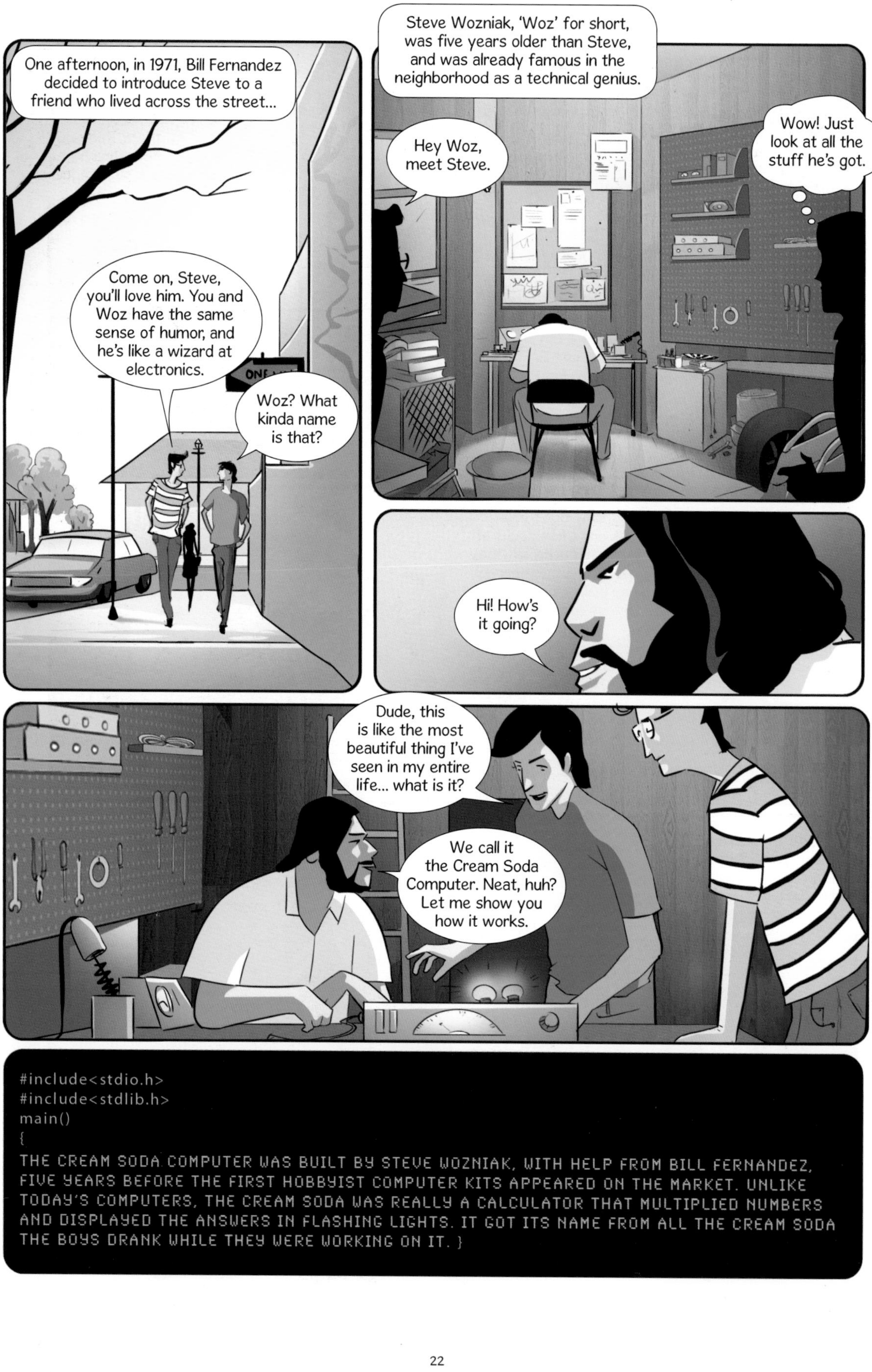
One afternoon, in 1971, Bill Fernandez decided to introduce Steve to a friend who lived across the street...
Come on, Steve, you'll love him. You and Woz have the same sense of humor, and he's like a wizard at electronics.
Woz? What kinda name is that?
Steve Wozniak, 'Woz' for short, was five years older than Steve, and was already famous in the neighborhood as a technical genius.
Hey Woz, meet Steve.
Wow! Just look at all the stuff he's got.
Hi! How's it going?
Dude, this is like the most beautiful thing I've seen in my entire life... what is it?
We call it the Cream Soda Computer. Neat, huh? Let me show you how it works.

```
#include<stdio.h>
#include<stdlib.h>
main()
{
THE CREAM SODA COMPUTER WAS BUILT BY STEVE WOZNIAK, WITH HELP FROM BILL FERNANDEZ,
FIVE YEARS BEFORE THE FIRST HOBBYIST COMPUTER KITS APPEARED ON THE MARKET. UNLIKE
TODAY'S COMPUTERS, THE CREAM SODA WAS REALLY A CALCULATOR THAT MULTIPLIED NUMBERS
AND DISPLAYED THE ANSWERS IN FLASHING LIGHTS. IT GOT ITS NAME FROM ALL THE CREAM SODA
THE BOYS DRANK WHILE THEY WERE WORKING ON IT. }
```

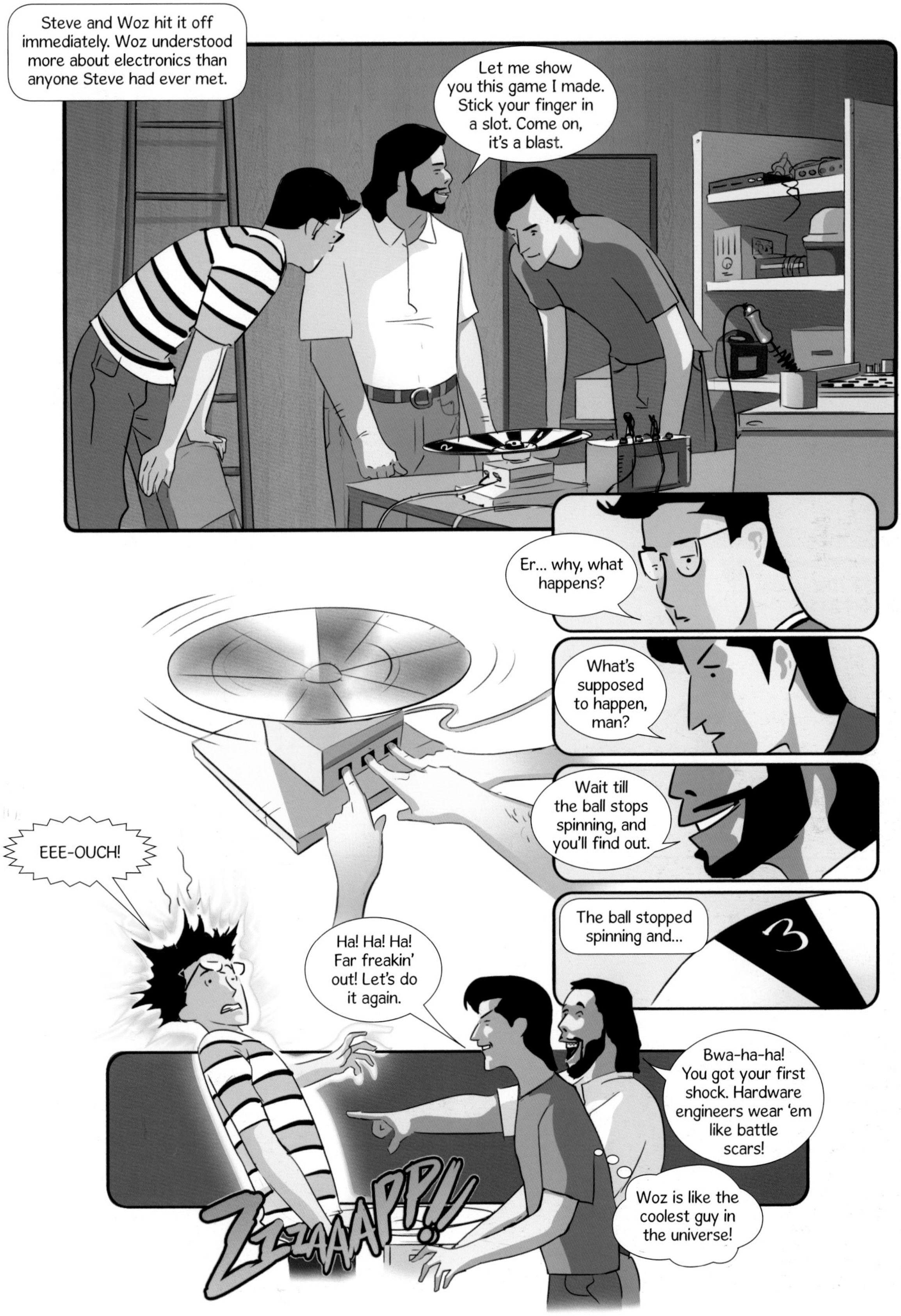
Steve and Woz hit it off immediately. Woz understood more about electronics than anyone Steve had ever met.
Let me show you this game I made. Stick your finger in a slot. Come on, it's a blast.
Er... why, what happens?
What's supposed to happen, man?
Wait till the ball stops spinning, and you'll find out.
The ball stopped spinning and...
3
EEE-OUCH!
ZZZAAAPP!!
Ha! Ha! Ha! Far freakin' out! Let's do it again.
Bwa-ha-ha! You got your first shock. Hardware engineers wear 'em like battle scars!
Woz is like the coolest guy in the universe!

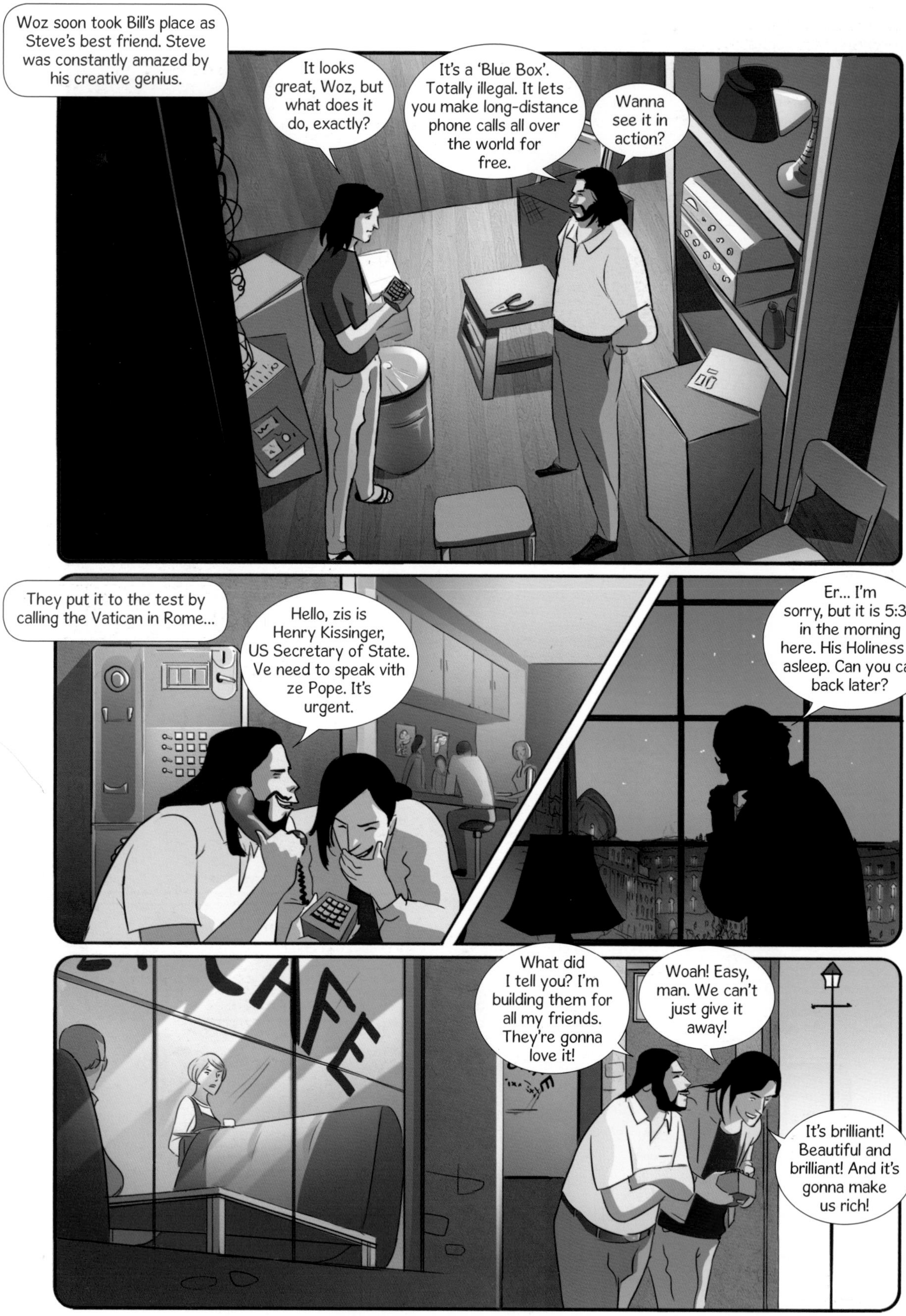
Woz soon took Bill's place as Steve's best friend. Steve was constantly amazed by his creative genius.
It looks great, Woz, but what does it do, exactly?
It's a 'Blue Box'. Totally illegal. It lets you make long-distance phone calls all over the world for free.
Wanna see it in action?
They put it to the test by calling the Vatican in Rome...
Hello, zis is Henry Kissinger, US Secretary of State. Ve need to speak vith ze Pope. It's urgent.
Er... I'm sorry, but it is 5:30 in the morning here. His Holiness is asleep. Can you call back later?
CAFE
What did I tell you? I'm building them for all my friends. They're gonna love it!
Woah! Easy, man. We can't just give it away!
It's brilliant! Beautiful and brilliant! And it's gonna make us rich!

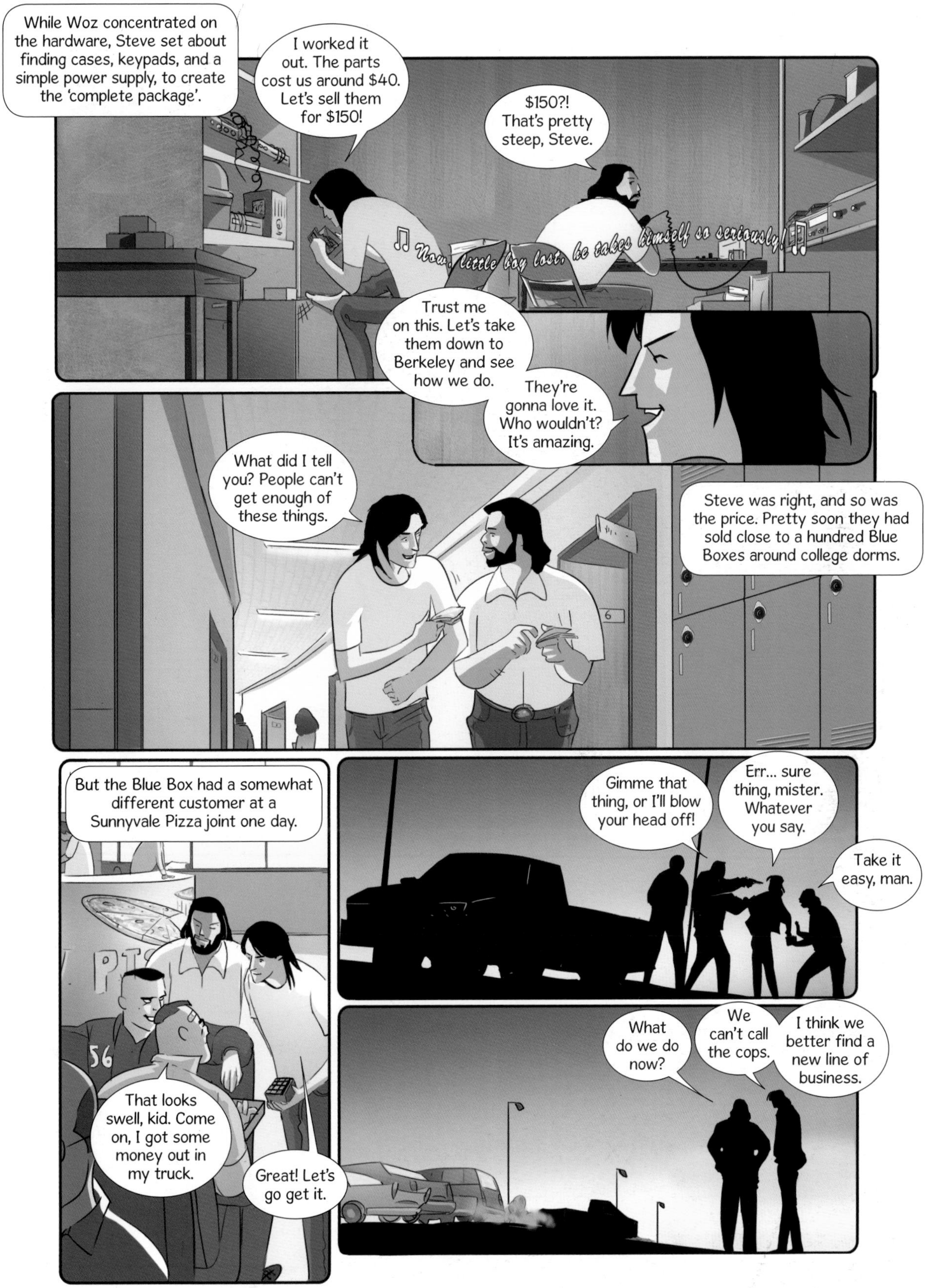

While Woz concentrated on the hardware, Steve set about finding cases, keypads, and a simple power supply, to create the 'complete package'.
I worked it out. The parts cost us around $40. Let's sell them for $150!
$150?! That's pretty steep, Steve.
♫ Now, little boy lost, he takes himself so seriously! ♫
Trust me on this. Let's take them down to Berkeley and see how we do.
They're gonna love it. Who wouldn't? It's amazing.
What did I tell you? People can't get enough of these things.
Steve was right, and so was the price. Pretty soon they had sold close to a hundred Blue Boxes around college dorms.
But the Blue Box had a somewhat different customer at a Sunnyvale Pizza joint one day.
That looks swell, kid. Come on, I got some money out in my truck.
Great! Let's go get it.
Gimme that thing, or I'll blow your head off!
Err... sure thing, mister. Whatever you say.
Take it easy, man.
What do we do now?
We can't call the cops.
I think we better find a new line of business.

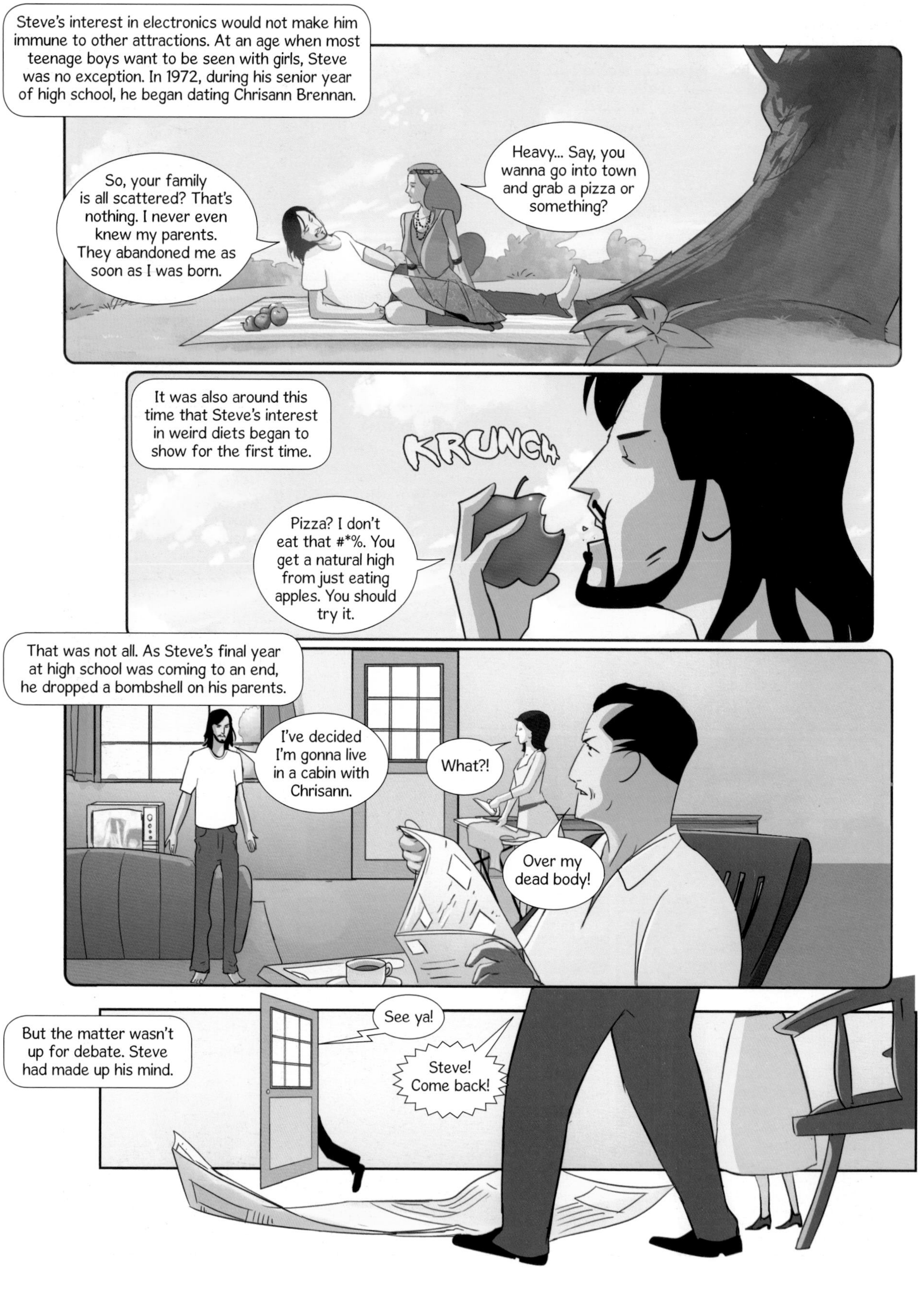

Steve's interest in electronics would not make him immune to other attractions. At an age when most teenage boys want to be seen with girls, Steve was no exception. In 1972, during his senior year of high school, he began dating Chrisann Brennan.
So, your family is all scattered? That's nothing. I never even knew my parents. They abandoned me as soon as I was born.
Heavy... Say, you wanna go into town and grab a pizza or something?
It was also around this time that Steve's interest in weird diets began to show for the first time.
KRUNCH
Pizza? I don't eat that #*%. You get a natural high from just eating apples. You should try it.
That was not all. As Steve's final year at high school was coming to an end, he dropped a bombshell on his parents.
I've decided I'm gonna live in a cabin with Chrisann.
What?!
Over my dead body!
But the matter wasn't up for debate. Steve had made up his mind.
See ya!
Steve! Come back!

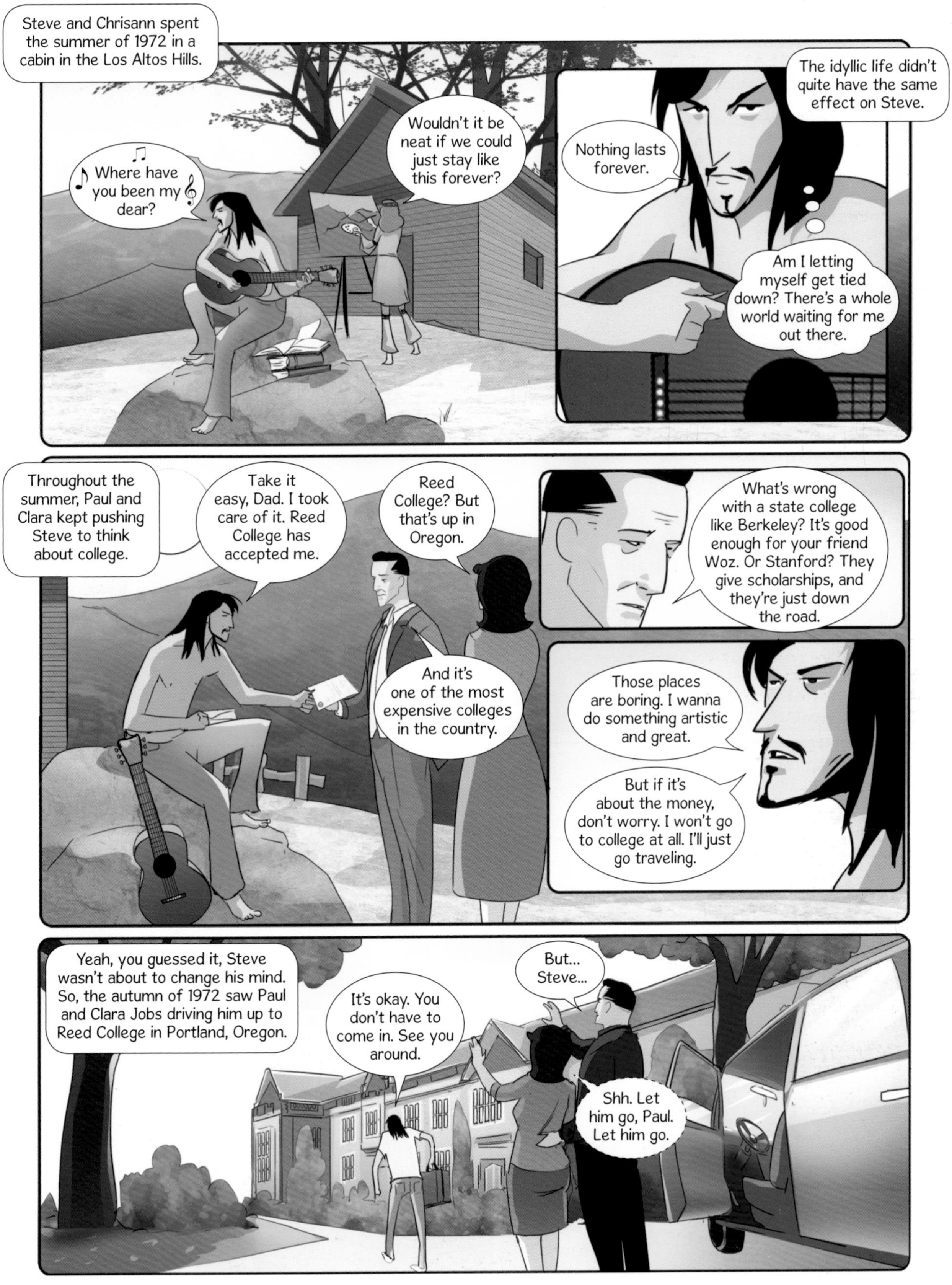

Steve and Chrisann spent the summer of 1972 in a cabin in the Los Altos Hills.
Where have you been my dear?
Wouldn't it be neat if we could just stay like this forever?
The idyllic life didn't quite have the same effect on Steve.
Nothing lasts forever.
Am I letting myself get tied down? There's a whole world waiting for me out there.
Throughout the summer, Paul and Clara kept pushing Steve to think about college.
Take it easy, Dad. I took care of it. Reed College has accepted me.
Reed College? But that's up in Oregon.
And it's one of the most expensive colleges in the country.
What's wrong with a state college like Berkeley? It's good enough for your friend Woz. Or Stanford? They give scholarships, and they're just down the road.
Those places are boring. I wanna do something artistic and great.
But if it's about the money, don't worry. I won't go to college at all. I'll just go traveling.
Yeah, you guessed it, Steve wasn't about to change his mind. So, the autumn of 1972 saw Paul and Clara Jobs driving him up to Reed College in Portland, Oregon.
It's okay. You don't have to come in. See you around.
But... Steve...
Shh. Let him go, Paul. Let him go.

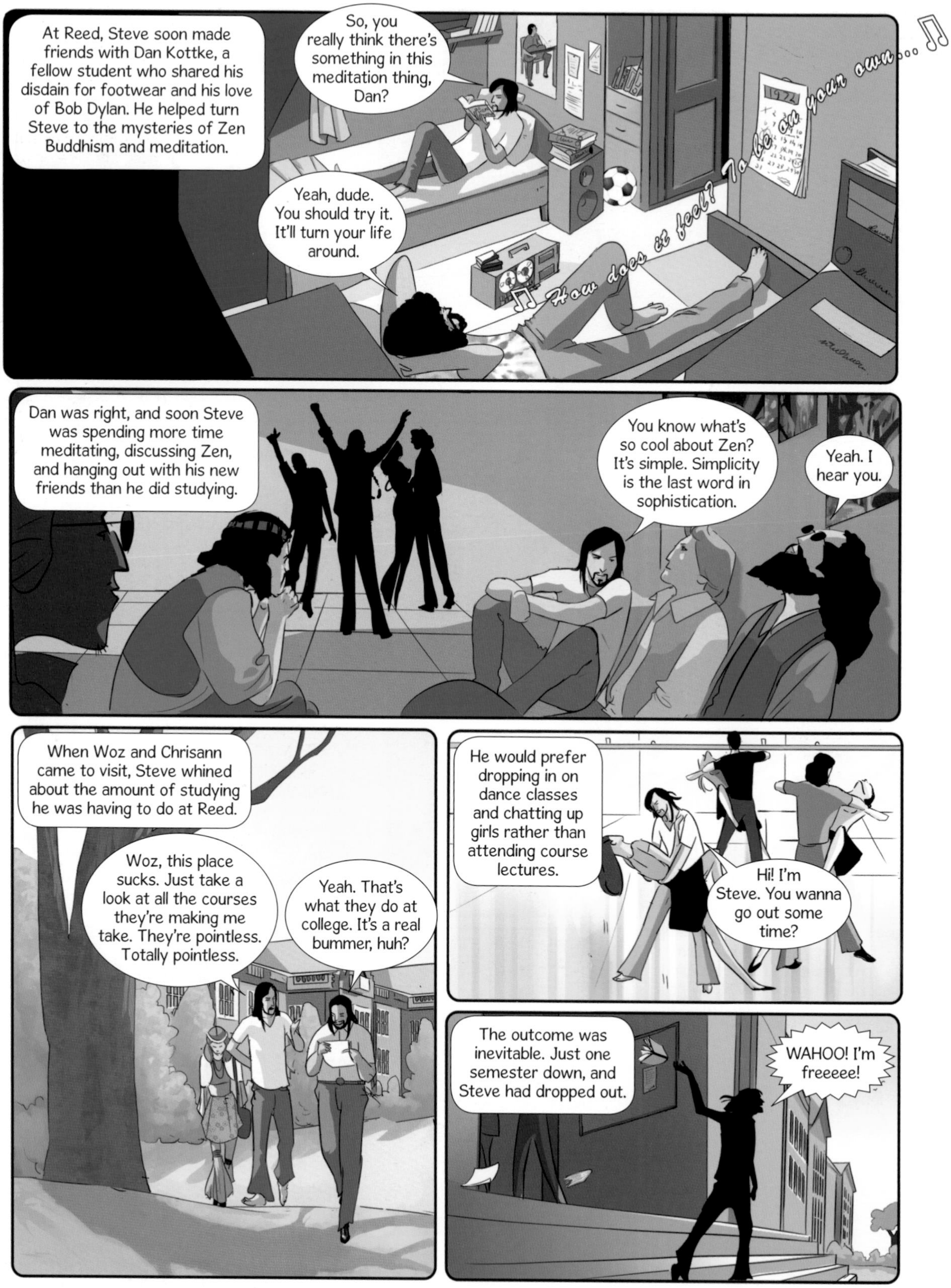
At Reed, Steve soon made friends with Dan Kottke, a fellow student who shared his disdain for footwear and his love of Bob Dylan. He helped turn Steve to the mysteries of Zen Buddhism and meditation.
So, you really think there's something in this meditation thing, Dan?
Yeah, dude. You should try it. It'll turn your life around.
How does it feel? To be on your own...
Dan was right, and soon Steve was spending more time meditating, discussing Zen, and hanging out with his new friends than he did studying.
You know what's so cool about Zen? It's simple. Simplicity is the last word in sophistication.
Yeah. I hear you.
When Woz and Chrisann came to visit, Steve whined about the amount of studying he was having to do at Reed.
Woz, this place sucks. Just take a look at all the courses they're making me take. They're pointless. Totally pointless.
Yeah. That's what they do at college. It's a real bummer, huh?
He would prefer dropping in on dance classes and chatting up girls rather than attending course lectures.
Hi! I'm Steve. You wanna go out some time?
The outcome was inevitable. Just one semester down, and Steve had dropped out.
WAHOO! I'm freeeee!

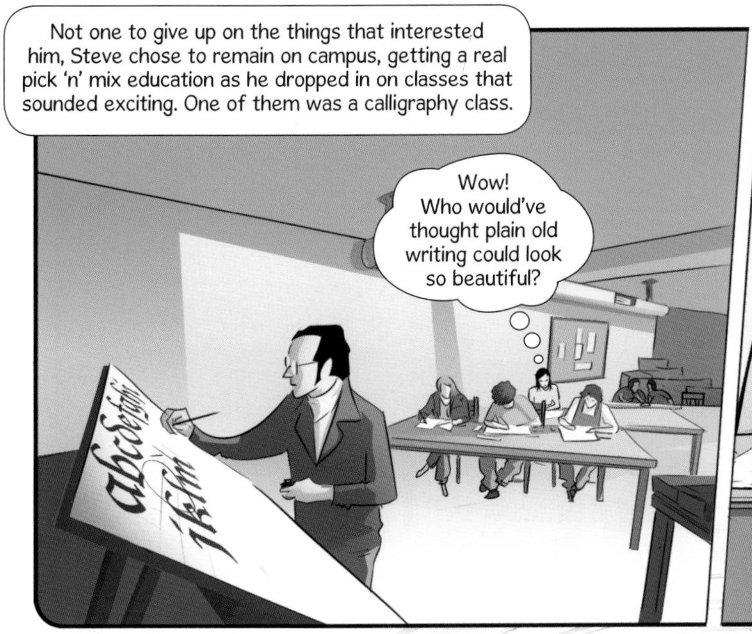
Not one to give up on the things that interested him, Steve chose to remain on campus, getting a real pick 'n' mix education as he dropped in on classes that sounded exciting. One of them was a calligraphy class.
Wow! Who would've thought plain old writing could look so beautiful?

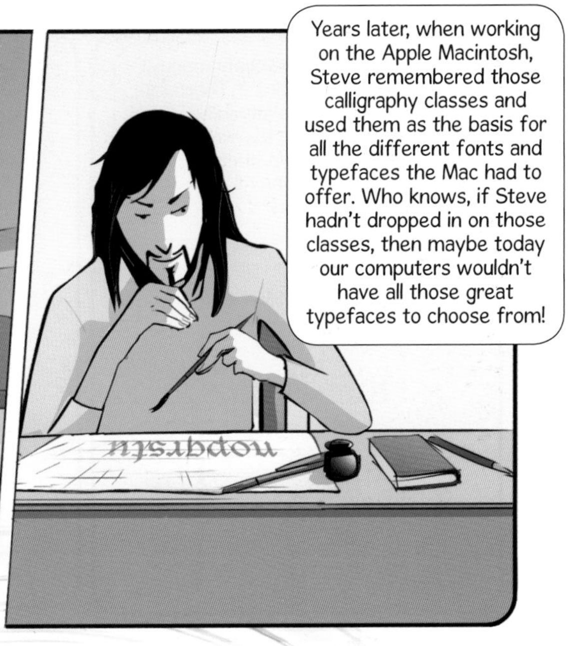
Years later, when working on the Apple Macintosh, Steve remembered those calligraphy classes and used them as the basis for all the different fonts and typefaces the Mac had to offer. Who knows, if Steve hadn't dropped in on those classes, then maybe today our computers wouldn't have all those great typefaces to choose from!

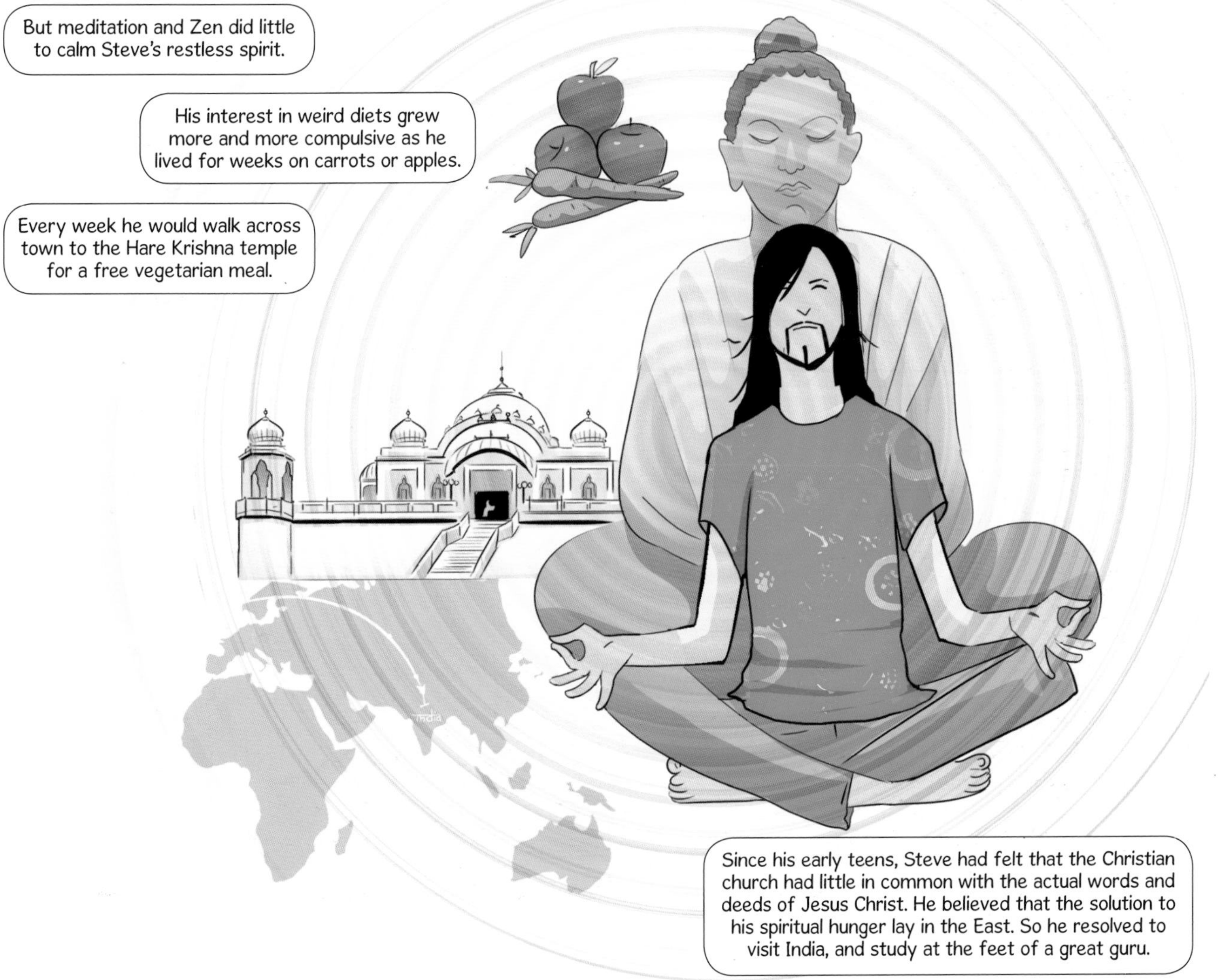
But meditation and Zen did little to calm Steve's restless spirit.
His interest in weird diets grew more and more compulsive as he lived for weeks on carrots or apples.
Every week he would walk across town to the Hare Krishna temple for a free vegetarian meal.
Since his early teens, Steve had felt that the Christian church had little in common with the actual words and deeds of Jesus Christ. He believed that the solution to his spiritual hunger lay in the East. So he resolved to visit India, and study at the feet of a great guru.

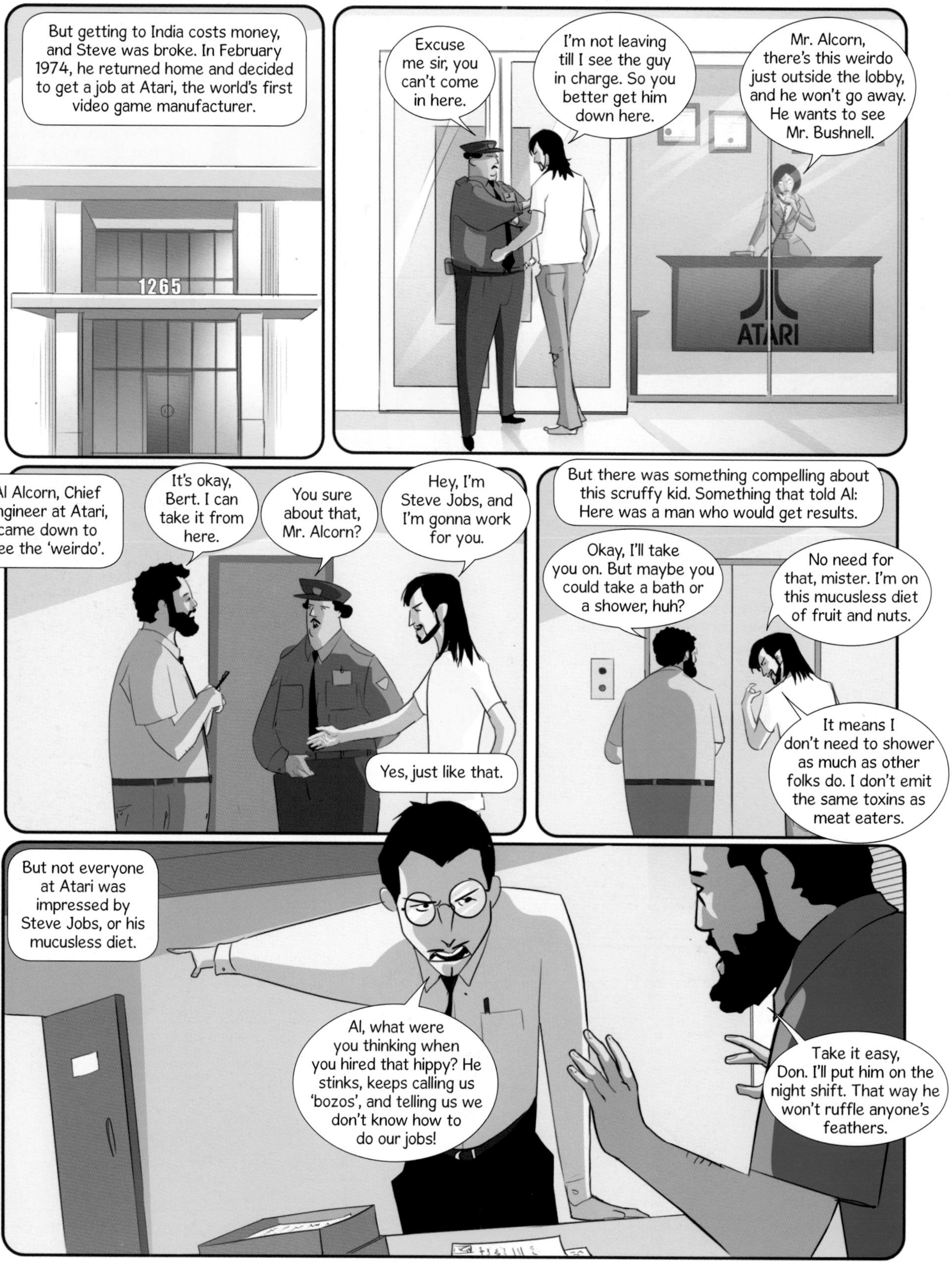

But getting to India costs money, and Steve was broke. In February 1974, he returned home and decided to get a job at Atari, the world's first video game manufacturer.
1265
Excuse me sir, you can't come in here.
I'm not leaving till I see the guy in charge. So you better get him down here.
Mr. Alcorn, there's this weirdo just outside the lobby, and he won't go away. He wants to see Mr. Bushnell.
ATARI
Al Alcorn, Chief Engineer at Atari, came down to see the 'weirdo'.
It's okay, Bert. I can take it from here.
You sure about that, Mr. Alcorn?
Hey, I'm Steve Jobs, and I'm gonna work for you.
Yes, just like that.
But there was something compelling about this scruffy kid. Something that told Al: Here was a man who would get results.
Okay, I'll take you on. But maybe you could take a bath or a shower, huh?
No need for that, mister. I'm on this mucusless diet of fruit and nuts.
It means I don't need to shower as much as other folks do. I don't emit the same toxins as meat eaters.
But not everyone at Atari was impressed by Steve Jobs, or his mucusless diet.
Al, what were you thinking when you hired that hippy? He stinks, keeps calling us 'bozos', and telling us we don't know how to do our jobs!
Take it easy, Don. I'll put him on the night shift. That way he won't ruffle anyone's feathers.

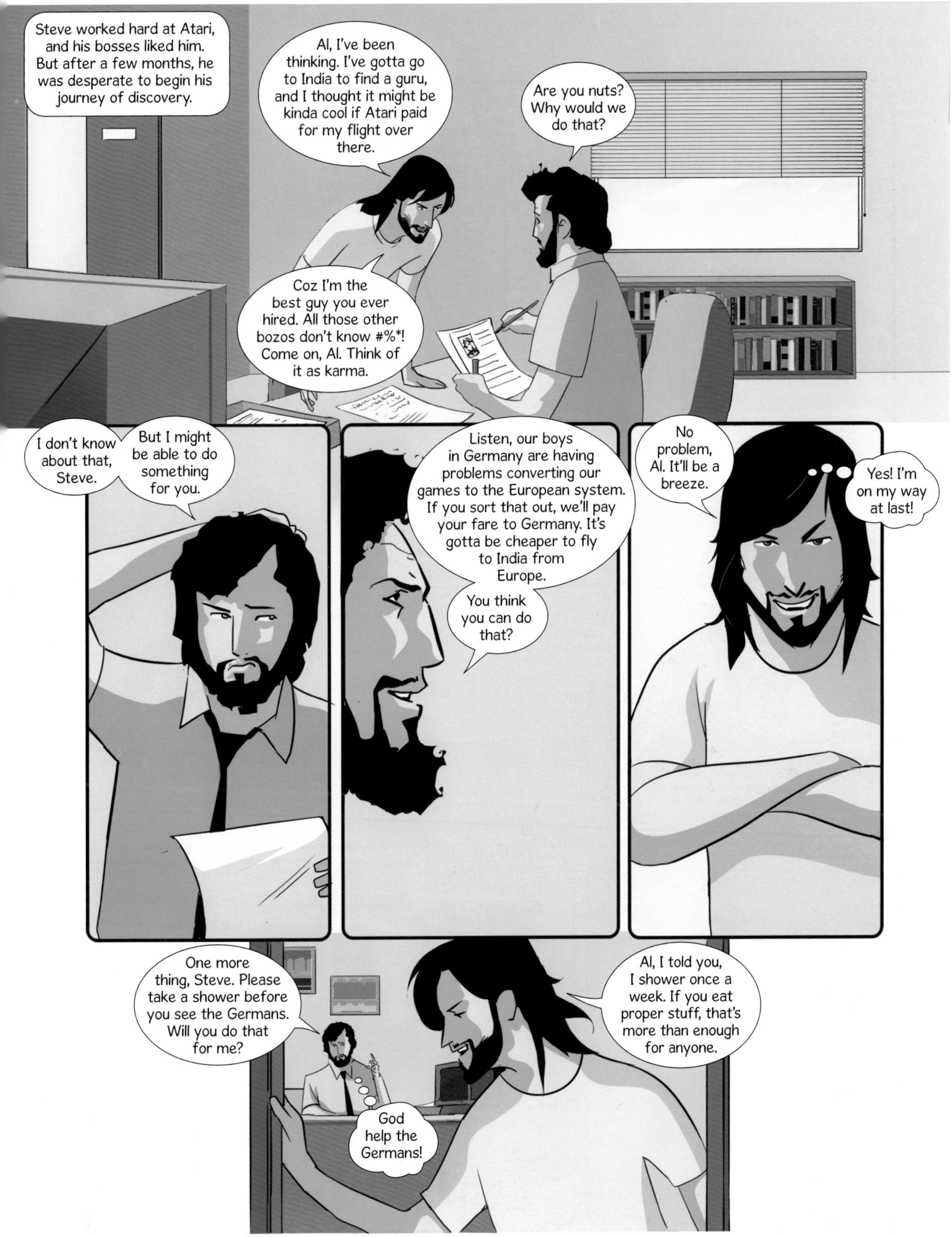
Steve worked hard at Atari, and his bosses liked him. But after a few months, he was desperate to begin his journey of discovery.
Al, I've been thinking. I've gotta go to India to find a guru, and I thought it might be kinda cool if Atari paid for my flight over there.
Are you nuts? Why would we do that?
Coz I'm the best guy you ever hired. All those other bozos don't know #%*! Come on, Al. Think of it as karma.
I don't know about that, Steve.
But I might be able to do something for you.
Listen, our boys in Germany are having problems converting our games to the European system. If you sort that out, we'll pay your fare to Germany. It's gotta be cheaper to fly to India from Europe.
You think you can do that?
No problem, Al. It'll be a breeze.
Yes! I'm on my way at last!
One more thing, Steve. Please take a shower before you see the Germans. Will you do that for me?
Al, I told you, I shower once a week. If you eat proper stuff, that's more than enough for anyone.
God help the Germans!

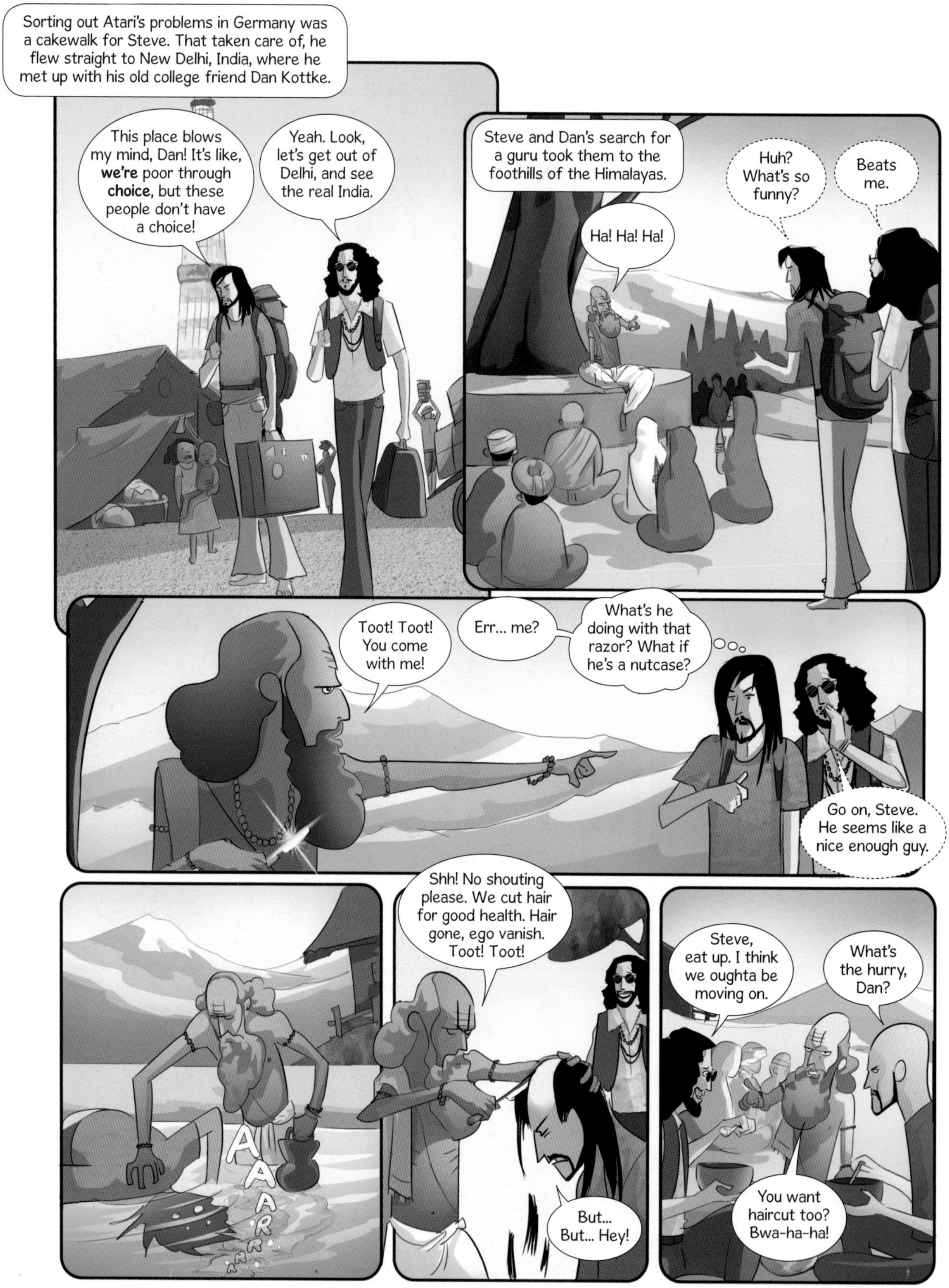
Sorting out Atari's problems in Germany was a cakewalk for Steve. That taken care of, he flew straight to New Delhi, India, where he met up with his old college friend Dan Kottke.
This place blows my mind, Dan! It's like, **we're** poor through **choice**, but these people don't have a choice!
Yeah. Look, let's get out of Delhi, and see the real India.
Steve and Dan's search for a guru took them to the foothills of the Himalayas.
Ha! Ha! Ha!
Huh? What's so funny?
Beats me.
Toot! Toot! You come with me!
Err... me?
What's he doing with that razor? What if he's a nutcase?
Go on, Steve. He seems like a nice enough guy.
AAARRR
Shh! No shouting please. We cut hair for good health. Hair gone, ego vanish. Toot! Toot!
But... But... Hey!
Steve, eat up. I think we oughta be moving on.
What's the hurry, Dan?
You want haircut too? Bwa-ha-ha!

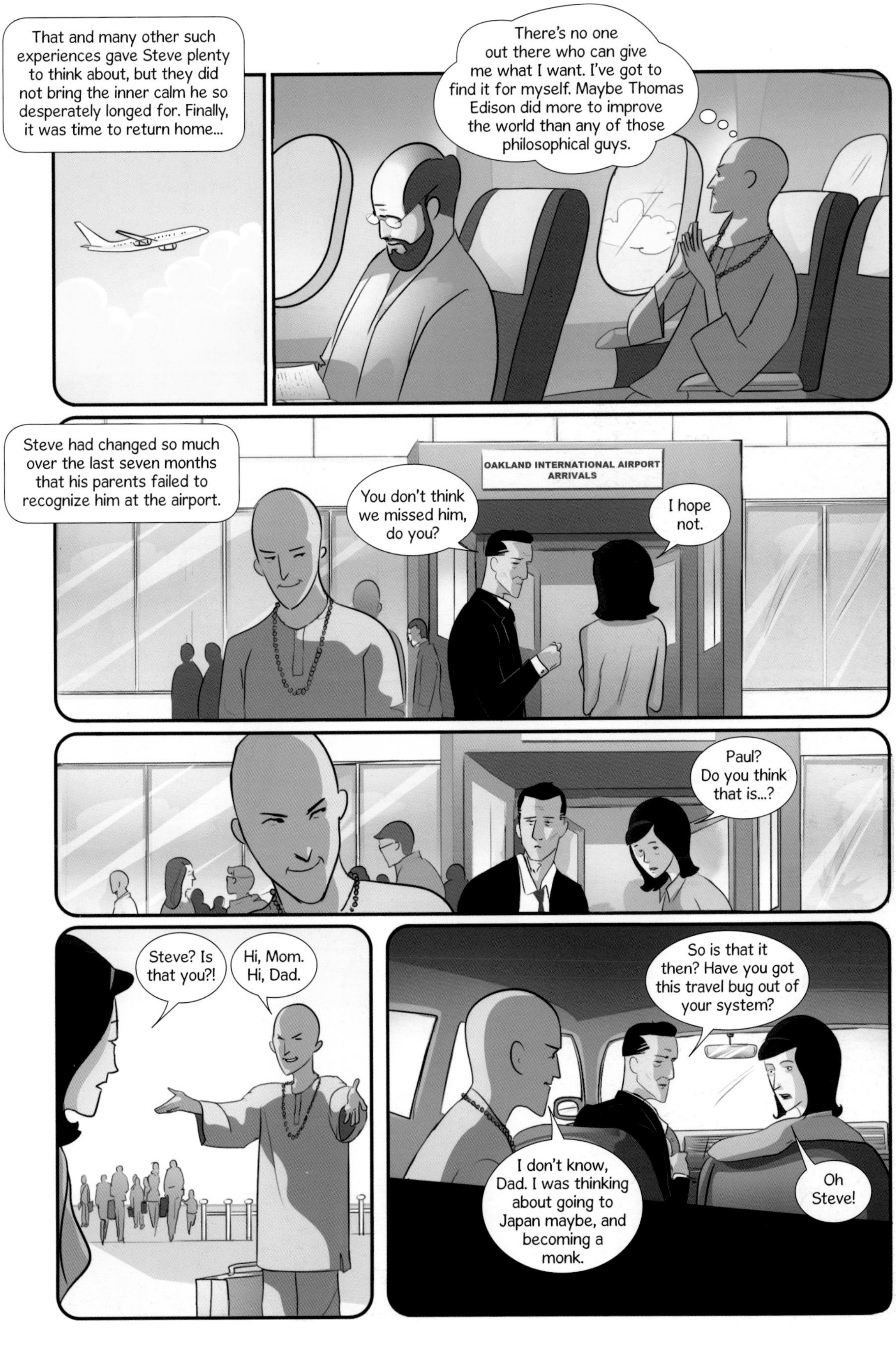
That and many other such experiences gave Steve plenty to think about, but they did not bring the inner calm he so desperately longed for. Finally, it was time to return home...
There's no one out there who can give me what I want. I've got to find it for myself. Maybe Thomas Edison did more to improve the world than any of those philosophical guys.
Steve had changed so much over the last seven months that his parents failed to recognize him at the airport.
OAKLAND INTERNATIONAL AIRPORT ARRIVALS
You don't think we missed him, do you?
I hope not.
Paul? Do you think that is...?
Steve? Is that you?!
Hi, Mom. Hi, Dad.
So is that it then? Have you got this travel bug out of your system?
I don't know, Dad. I was thinking about going to Japan maybe, and becoming a monk.
Oh Steve!

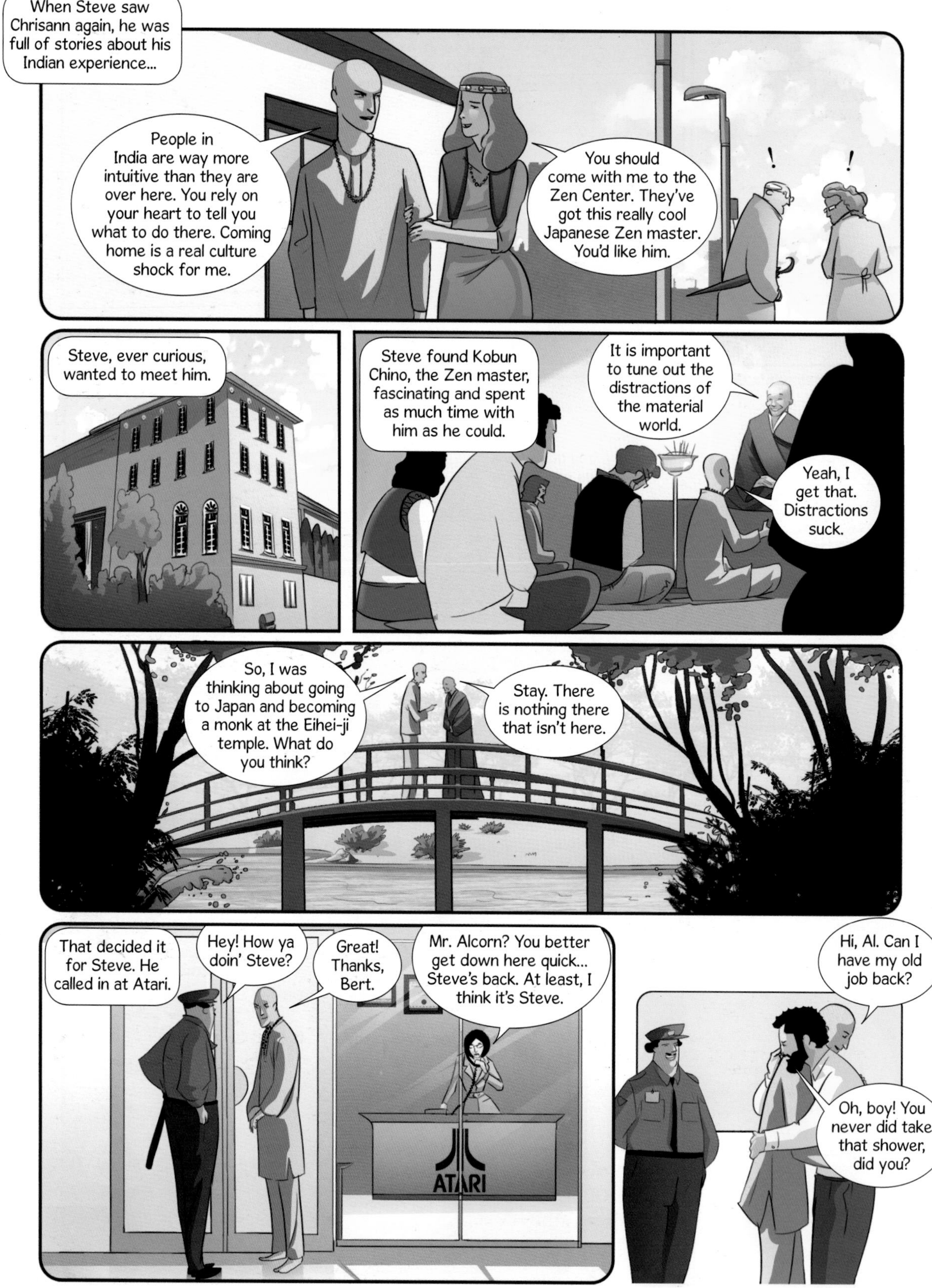
When Steve saw Chrisann again, he was full of stories about his Indian experience...
People in India are way more intuitive than they are over here. You rely on your heart to tell you what to do there. Coming home is a real culture shock for me.
You should come with me to the Zen Center. They've got this really cool Japanese Zen master. You'd like him.
!
!
Steve, ever curious, wanted to meet him.
Steve found Kobun Chino, the Zen master, fascinating and spent as much time with him as he could.
It is important to tune out the distractions of the material world.
Yeah, I get that. Distractions suck.
So, I was thinking about going to Japan and becoming a monk at the Eihei-ji temple. What do you think?
Stay. There is nothing there that isn't here.
That decided it for Steve. He called in at Atari.
Hey! How ya doin' Steve?
Great! Thanks, Bert.
Mr. Alcorn? You better get down here quick... Steve's back. At least, I think it's Steve.
ATARI
Hi, Al. Can I have my old job back?
Oh, boy! You never did take that shower, did you?

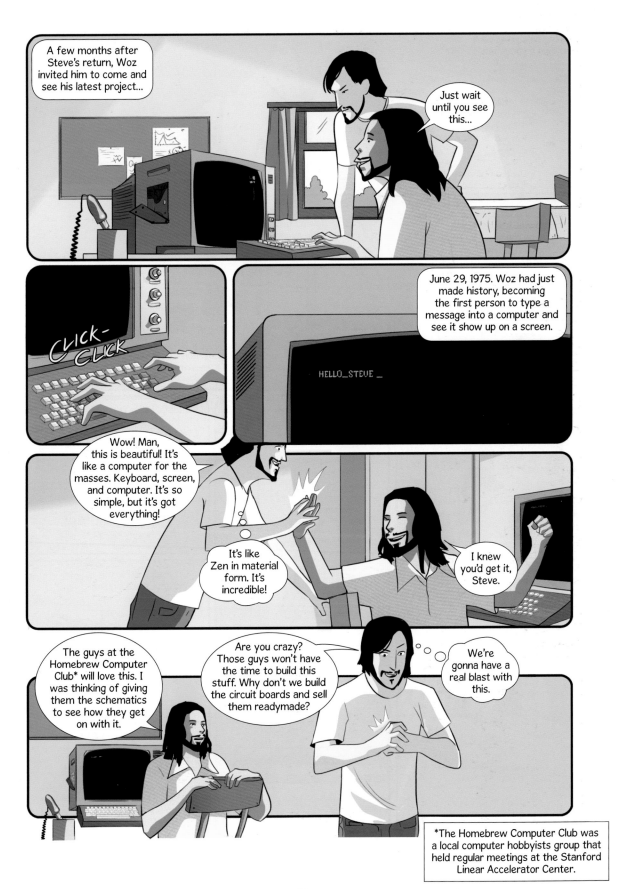

A few months after Steve's return, Woz invited him to come and see his latest project...

Just wait until you see this...

CLICK-CLICK

HELLO_STEVE _

June 29, 1975. Woz had just made history, becoming the first person to type a message into a computer and see it show up on a screen.

Wow! Man, this is beautiful! It's like a computer for the masses. Keyboard, screen, and computer. It's so simple, but it's got everything!

It's like Zen in material form. It's incredible!

I knew you'd get it, Steve.

The guys at the Homebrew Computer Club* will love this. I was thinking of giving them the schematics to see how they get on with it.

Are you crazy? Those guys won't have the time to build this stuff. Why don't we build the circuit boards and sell them readymade?

We're gonna have a real blast with this.

*The Homebrew Computer Club was a local computer hobbyists group that held regular meetings at the Stanford Linear Accelerator Center.

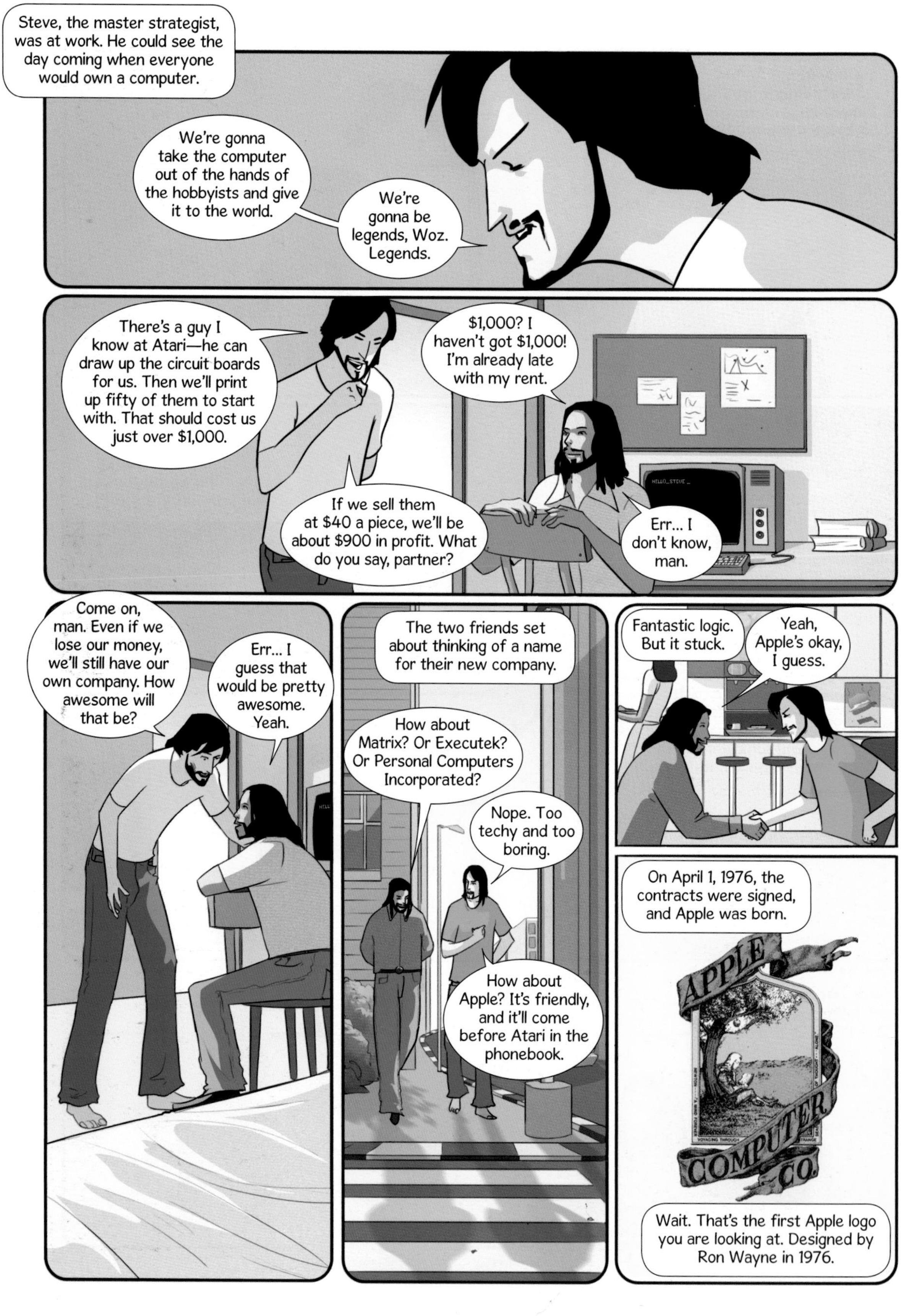

Steve, the master strategist, was at work. He could see the day coming when everyone would own a computer.
We're gonna take the computer out of the hands of the hobbyists and give it to the world.
We're gonna be legends, Woz. Legends.
There's a guy I know at Atari—he can draw up the circuit boards for us. Then we'll print up fifty of them to start with. That should cost us just over $1,000.
$1,000? I haven't got $1,000! I'm already late with my rent.
If we sell them at $40 a piece, we'll be about $900 in profit. What do you say, partner?
Err... I don't know, man.
Come on, man. Even if we lose our money, we'll still have our own company. How awesome will that be?
Err... I guess that would be pretty awesome. Yeah.
The two friends set about thinking of a name for their new company.
How about Matrix? Or Executek? Or Personal Computers Incorporated?
Nope. Too techy and too boring.
How about Apple? It's friendly, and it'll come before Atari in the phonebook.
Fantastic logic. But it stuck.
Yeah, Apple's okay, I guess.
On April 1, 1976, the contracts were signed, and Apple was born.
APPLE COMPUTER CO.
Wait. That's the first Apple logo you are looking at. Designed by Ron Wayne in 1976.

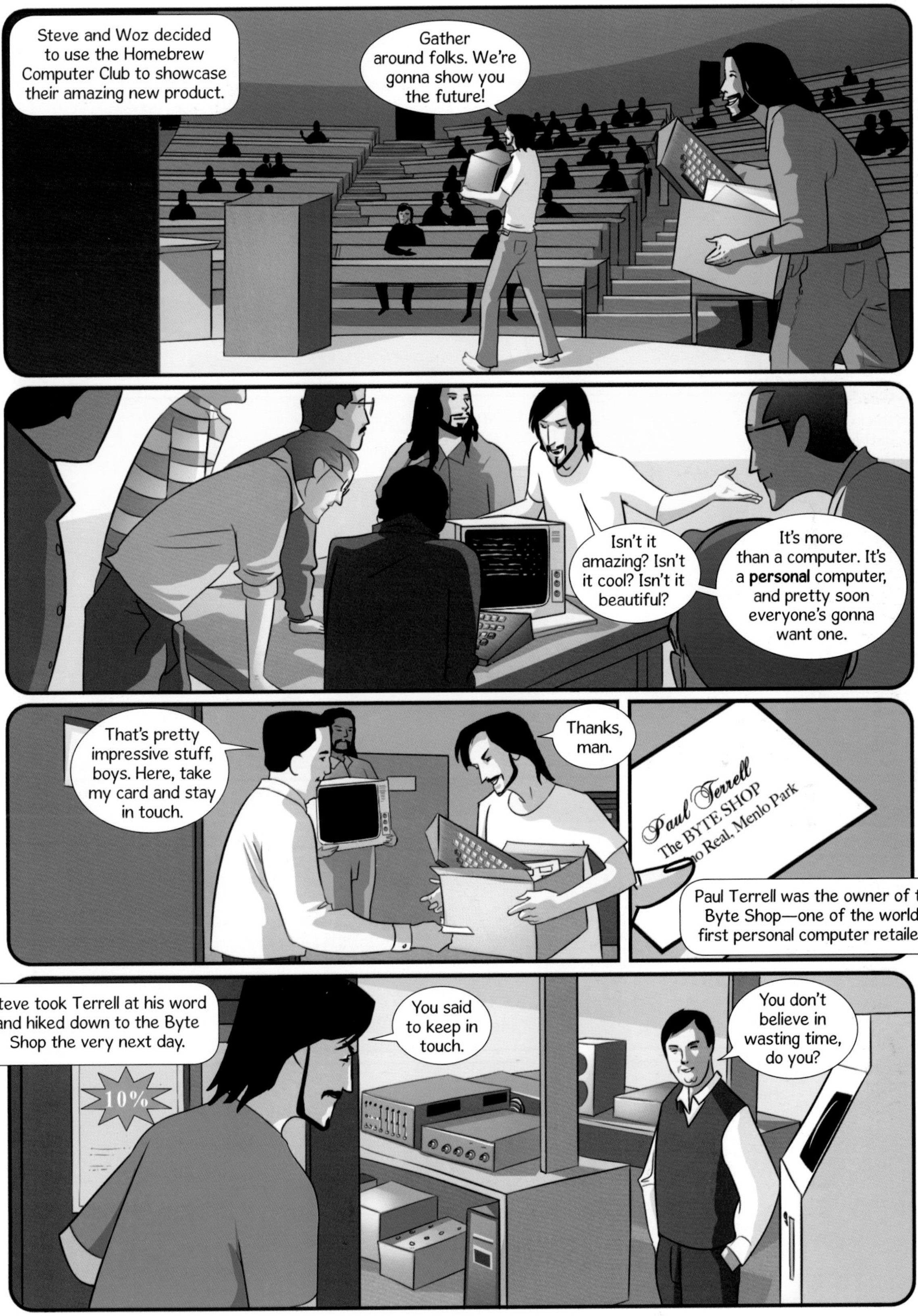
Steve and Woz decided to use the Homebrew Computer Club to showcase their amazing new product.
Gather around folks. We're gonna show you the future!
Isn't it amazing? Isn't it cool? Isn't it beautiful?
It's more than a computer. It's a **personal** computer, and pretty soon everyone's gonna want one.
That's pretty impressive stuff, boys. Here, take my card and stay in touch.
Thanks, man.
Paul Terrell
The BYTE SHOP
Real, Menlo Park
Paul Terrell was the owner of the Byte Shop—one of the world's first personal computer retailers.
Steve took Terrell at his word and hiked down to the Byte Shop the very next day.
10%
You said to keep in touch.
You don't believe in wasting time, do you?

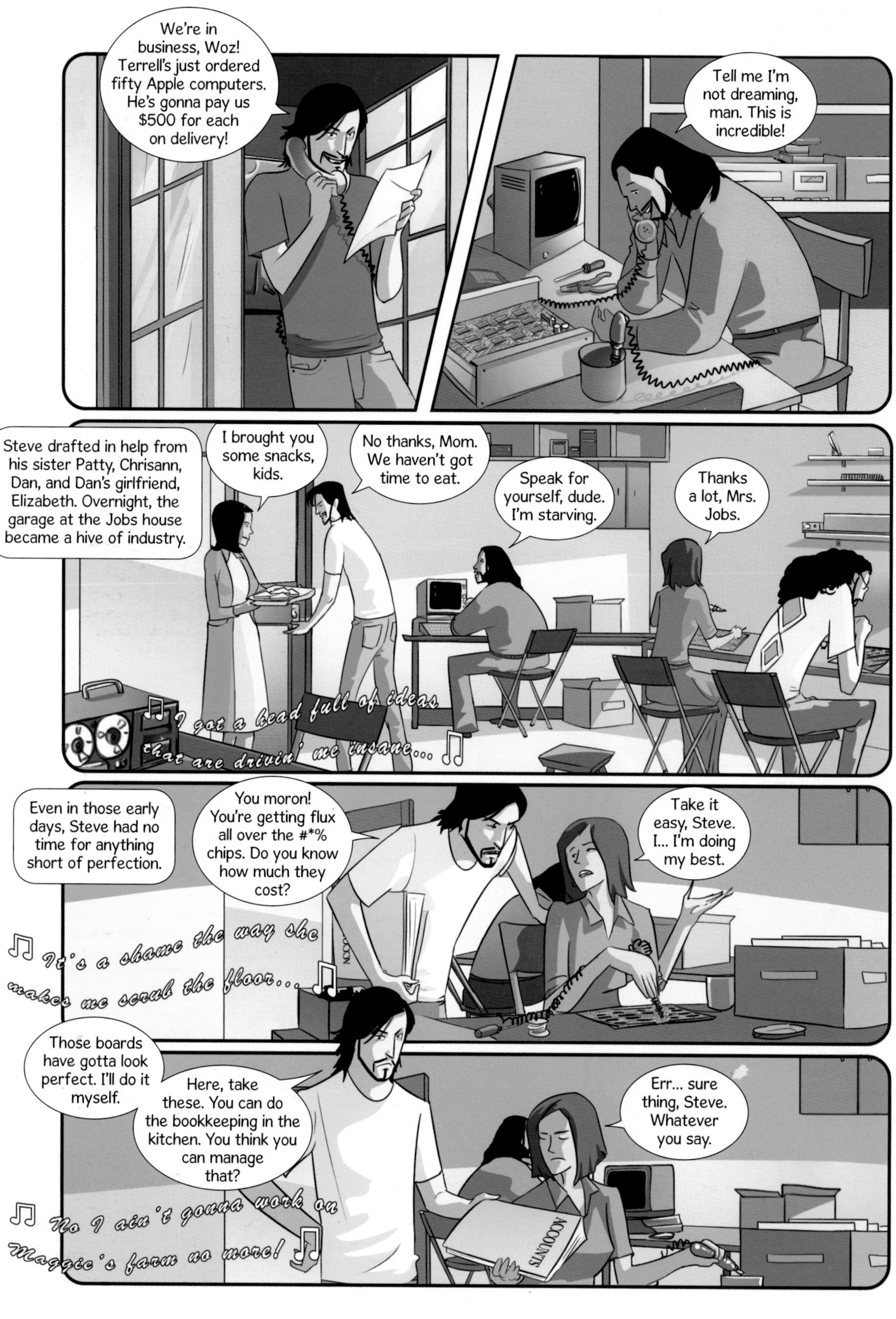

We're in business, Woz! Terrell's just ordered fifty Apple computers. He's gonna pay us $500 for each on delivery!
Tell me I'm not dreaming, man. This is incredible!
Steve drafted in help from his sister Patty, Chrisann, Dan, and Dan's girlfriend, Elizabeth. Overnight, the garage at the Jobs house became a hive of industry.
I brought you some snacks, kids.
No thanks, Mom. We haven't got time to eat.
Speak for yourself, dude. I'm starving.
Thanks a lot, Mrs. Jobs.
♫ I got a head full of ideas that are drivin' me insane... ♫
Even in those early days, Steve had no time for anything short of perfection.
You moron! You're getting flux all over the #*% chips. Do you know how much they cost?
Take it easy, Steve. I... I'm doing my best.
♫ It's a shame the way she makes me scrub the floor... ♫
Those boards have gotta look perfect. I'll do it myself.
Here, take these. You can do the bookkeeping in the kitchen. You think you can manage that?
Err... sure thing, Steve. Whatever you say.
♫ No I ain't gonna work on Maggie's farm no more! ♫
ACCOUNTS

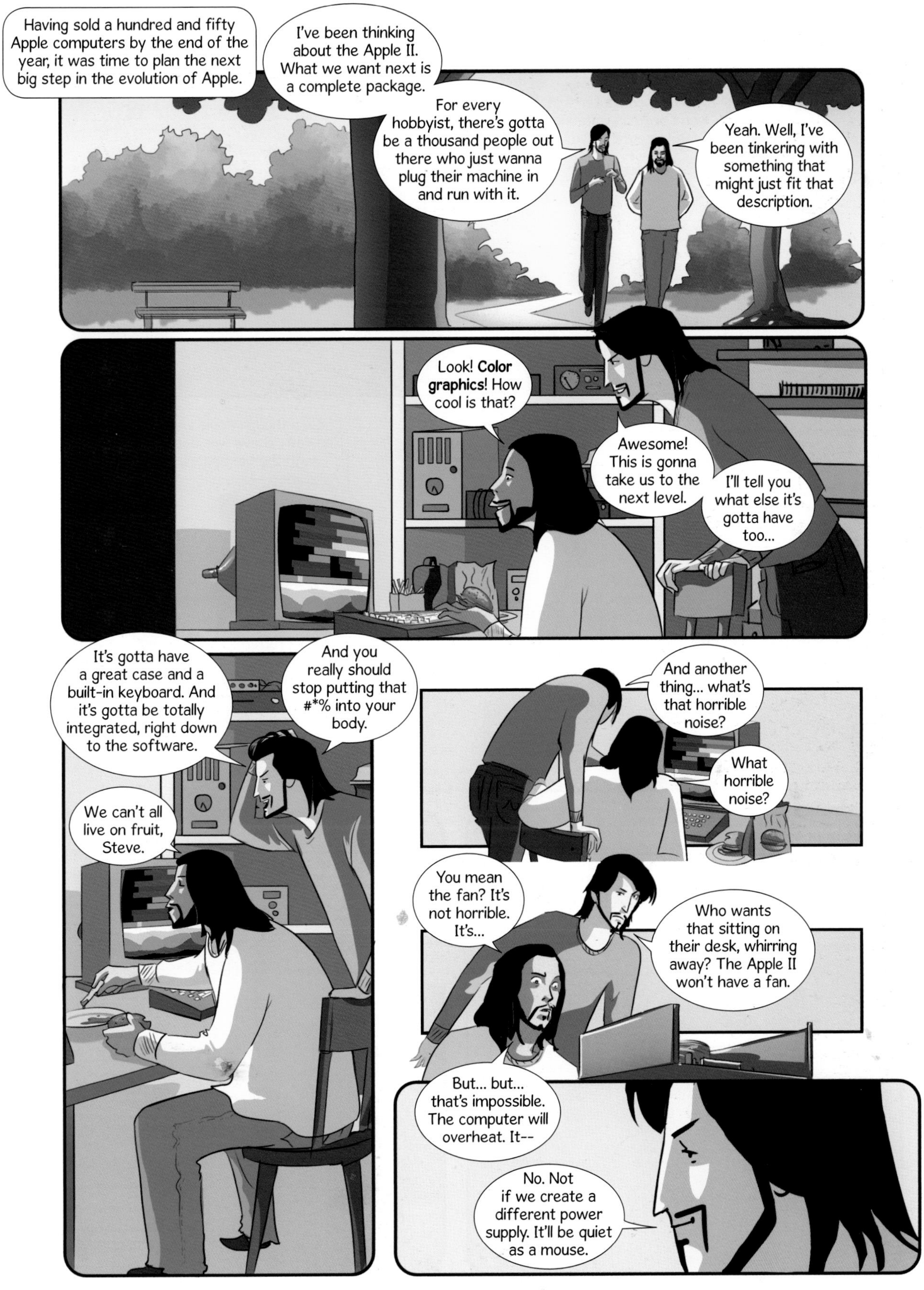
Having sold a hundred and fifty Apple computers by the end of the year, it was time to plan the next big step in the evolution of Apple.
I've been thinking about the Apple II. What we want next is a complete package.
For every hobbyist, there's gotta be a thousand people out there who just wanna plug their machine in and run with it.
Yeah. Well, I've been tinkering with something that might just fit that description.
Look! **Color graphics**! How cool is that?
Awesome! This is gonna take us to the next level.
I'll tell you what else it's gotta have too...
It's gotta have a great case and a built-in keyboard. And it's gotta be totally integrated, right down to the software.
And you really should stop putting that #*% into your body.
We can't all live on fruit, Steve.
And another thing... what's that horrible noise?
What horrible noise?
You mean the fan? It's not horrible. It's...
Who wants that sitting on their desk, whirring away? The Apple II won't have a fan.
But... but... that's impossible. The computer will overheat. It--
No. Not if we create a different power supply. It'll be quiet as a mouse.

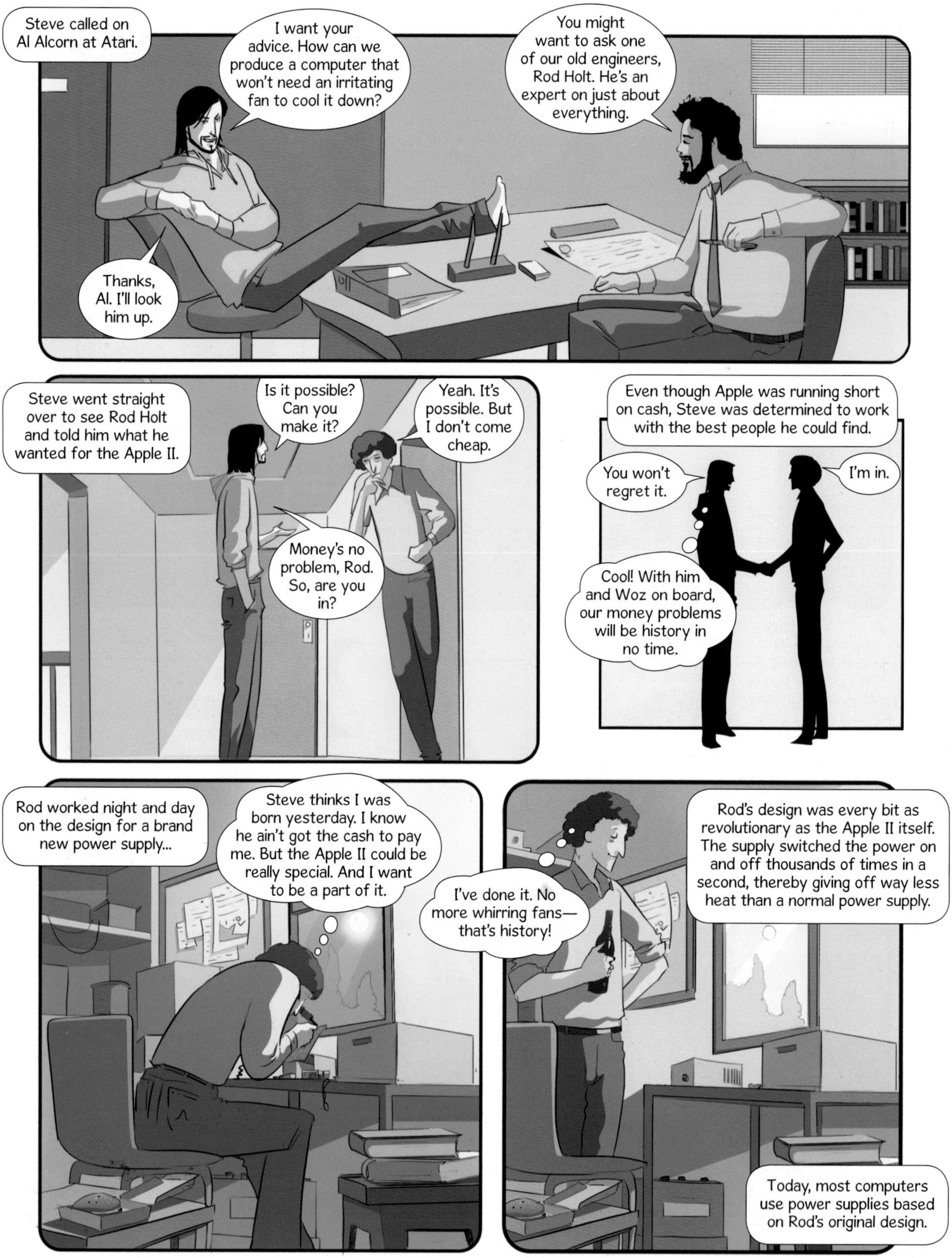

Steve called on Al Alcorn at Atari.
I want your advice. How can we produce a computer that won't need an irritating fan to cool it down?
You might want to ask one of our old engineers, Rod Holt. He's an expert on just about everything.
Thanks, Al. I'll look him up.
Steve went straight over to see Rod Holt and told him what he wanted for the Apple II.
Is it possible? Can you make it?
Yeah. It's possible. But I don't come cheap.
Money's no problem, Rod. So, are you in?
Even though Apple was running short on cash, Steve was determined to work with the best people he could find.
You won't regret it.
I'm in.
Cool! With him and Woz on board, our money problems will be history in no time.
Rod worked night and day on the design for a brand new power supply...
Steve thinks I was born yesterday. I know he ain't got the cash to pay me. But the Apple II could be really special. And I want to be a part of it.
I've done it. No more whirring fans—that's history!
Rod's design was every bit as revolutionary as the Apple II itself. The supply switched the power on and off thousands of times in a second, thereby giving off way less heat than a normal power supply.
Today, most computers use power supplies based on Rod's original design.

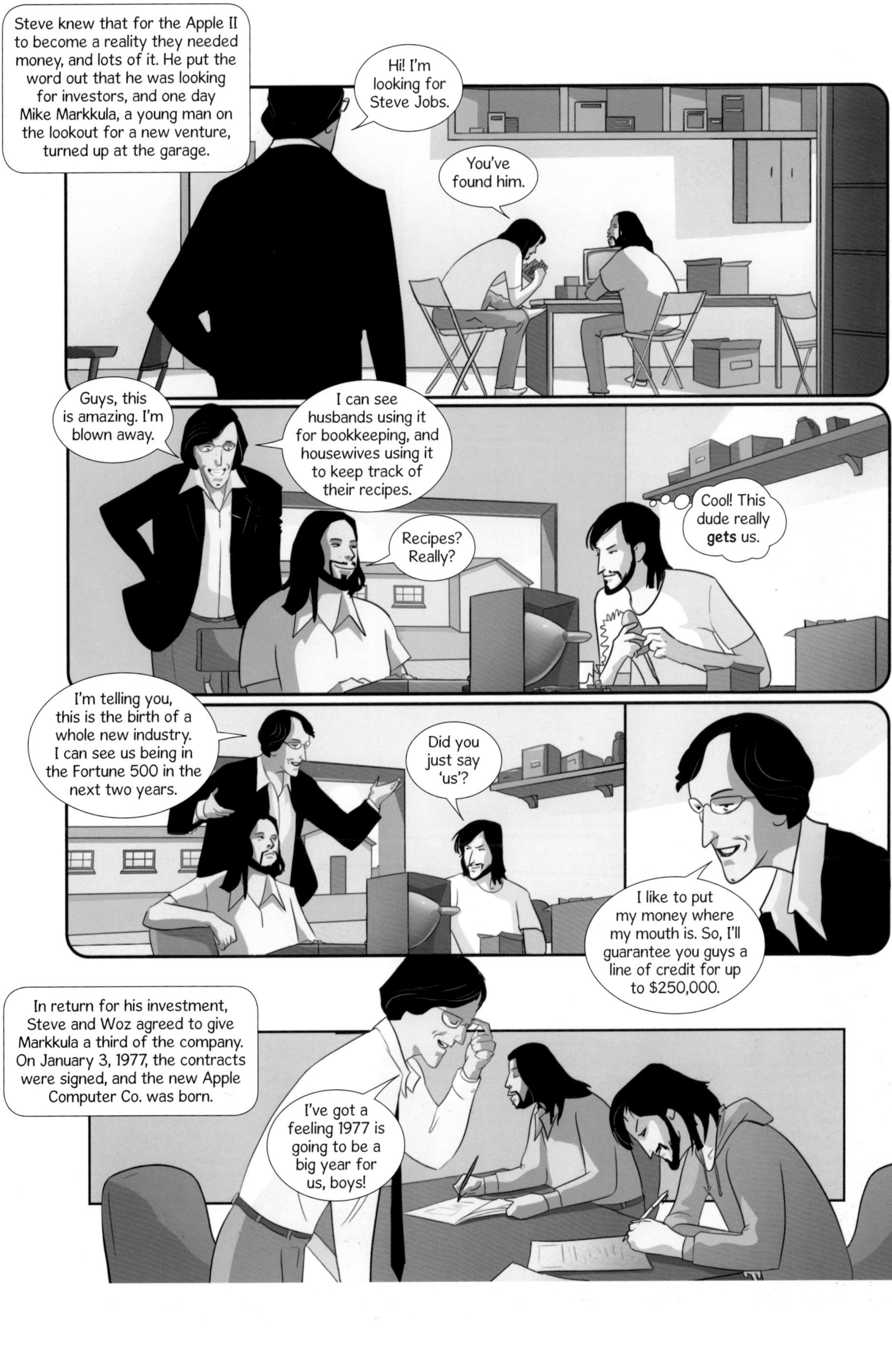

Steve knew that for the Apple II to become a reality they needed money, and lots of it. He put the word out that he was looking for investors, and one day Mike Markkula, a young man on the lookout for a new venture, turned up at the garage.
Hi! I'm looking for Steve Jobs.
You've found him.
Guys, this is amazing. I'm blown away.
I can see husbands using it for bookkeeping, and housewives using it to keep track of their recipes.
Recipes? Really?
Cool! This dude really **gets** us.
I'm telling you, this is the birth of a whole new industry. I can see us being in the Fortune 500 in the next two years.
Did you just say 'us'?
I like to put my money where my mouth is. So, I'll guarantee you guys a line of credit for up to $250,000.
In return for his investment, Steve and Woz agreed to give Markkula a third of the company. On January 3, 1977, the contracts were signed, and the new Apple Computer Co. was born.
I've got a feeling 1977 is going to be a big year for us, boys!

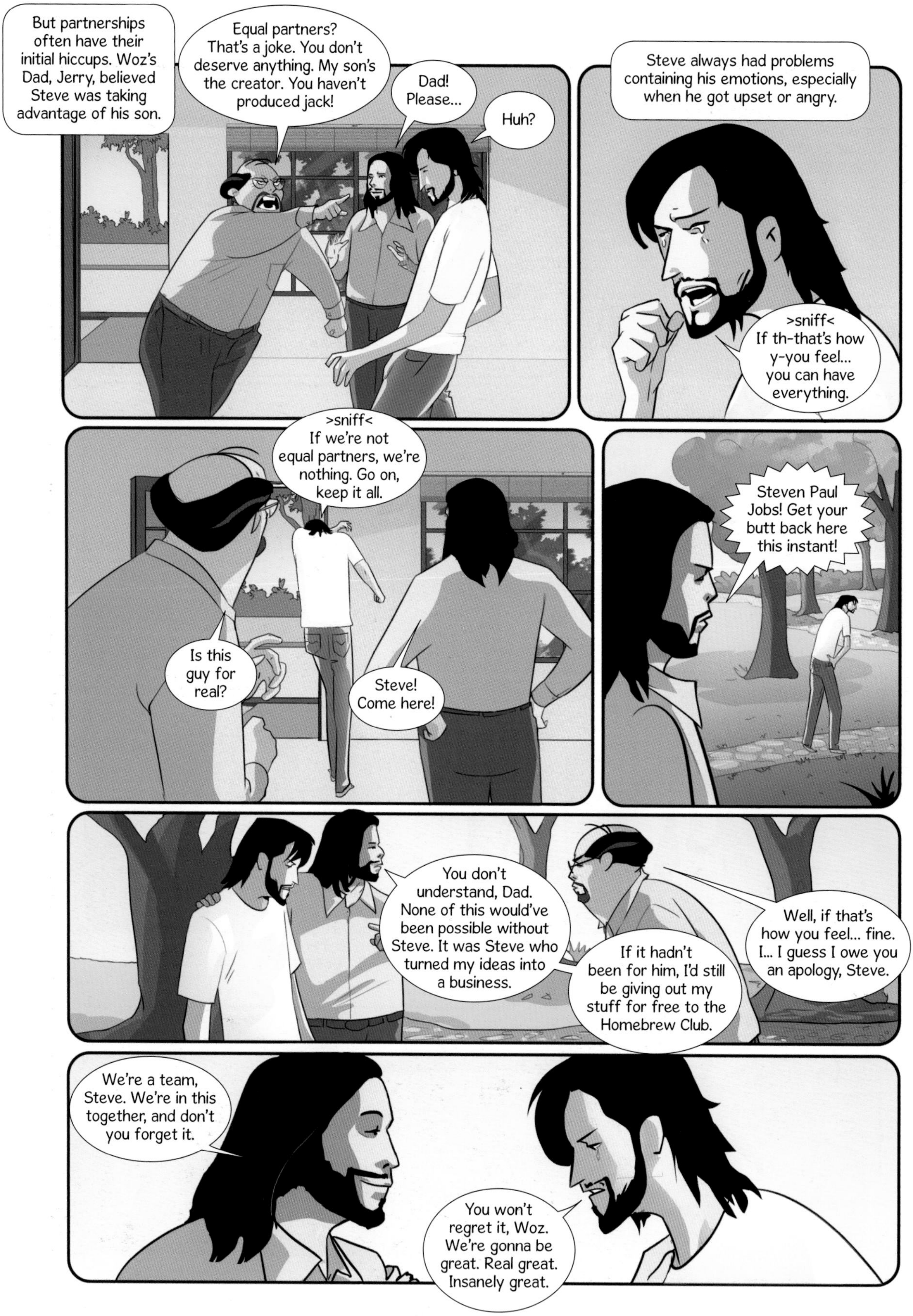
But partnerships often have their initial hiccups. Woz's Dad, Jerry, believed Steve was taking advantage of his son.
Equal partners? That's a joke. You don't deserve anything. My son's the creator. You haven't produced jack!
Dad! Please...
Huh?
Steve always had problems containing his emotions, especially when he got upset or angry.
>sniff< If th-that's how y-you feel... you can have everything.
>sniff< If we're not equal partners, we're nothing. Go on, keep it all.
Is this guy for real?
Steve! Come here!
Steven Paul Jobs! Get your butt back here this instant!
You don't understand, Dad. None of this would've been possible without Steve. It was Steve who turned my ideas into a business.
If it hadn't been for him, I'd still be giving out my stuff for free to the Homebrew Club.
Well, if that's how you feel... fine. I... I guess I owe you an apology, Steve.
We're a team, Steve. We're in this together, and don't you forget it.
You won't regret it, Woz. We're gonna be great. Real great. Insanely great.

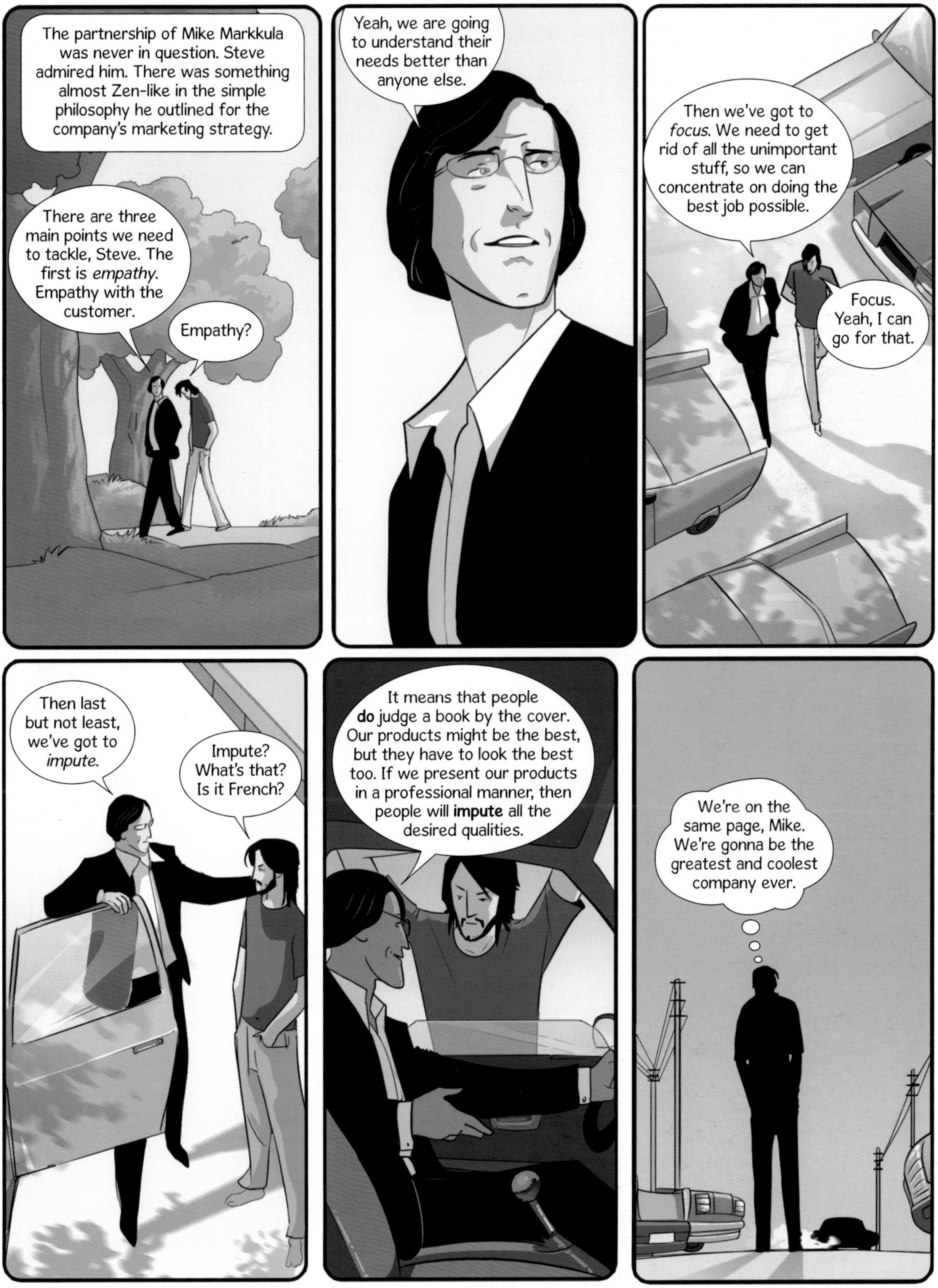
The partnership of Mike Markkula was never in question. Steve admired him. There was something almost Zen-like in the simple philosophy he outlined for the company's marketing strategy.
There are three main points we need to tackle, Steve. The first is *empathy*. Empathy with the customer.
Empathy?
Yeah, we are going to understand their needs better than anyone else.
Then we've got to *focus*. We need to get rid of all the unimportant stuff, so we can concentrate on doing the best job possible.
Focus. Yeah, I can go for that.
Then last but not least, we've got to *impute*.
Impute? What's that? Is it French?
It means that people **do** judge a book by the cover. Our products might be the best, but they have to look the best too. If we present our products in a professional manner, then people will **impute** all the desired qualities.
We're on the same page, Mike. We're gonna be the greatest and coolest company ever.

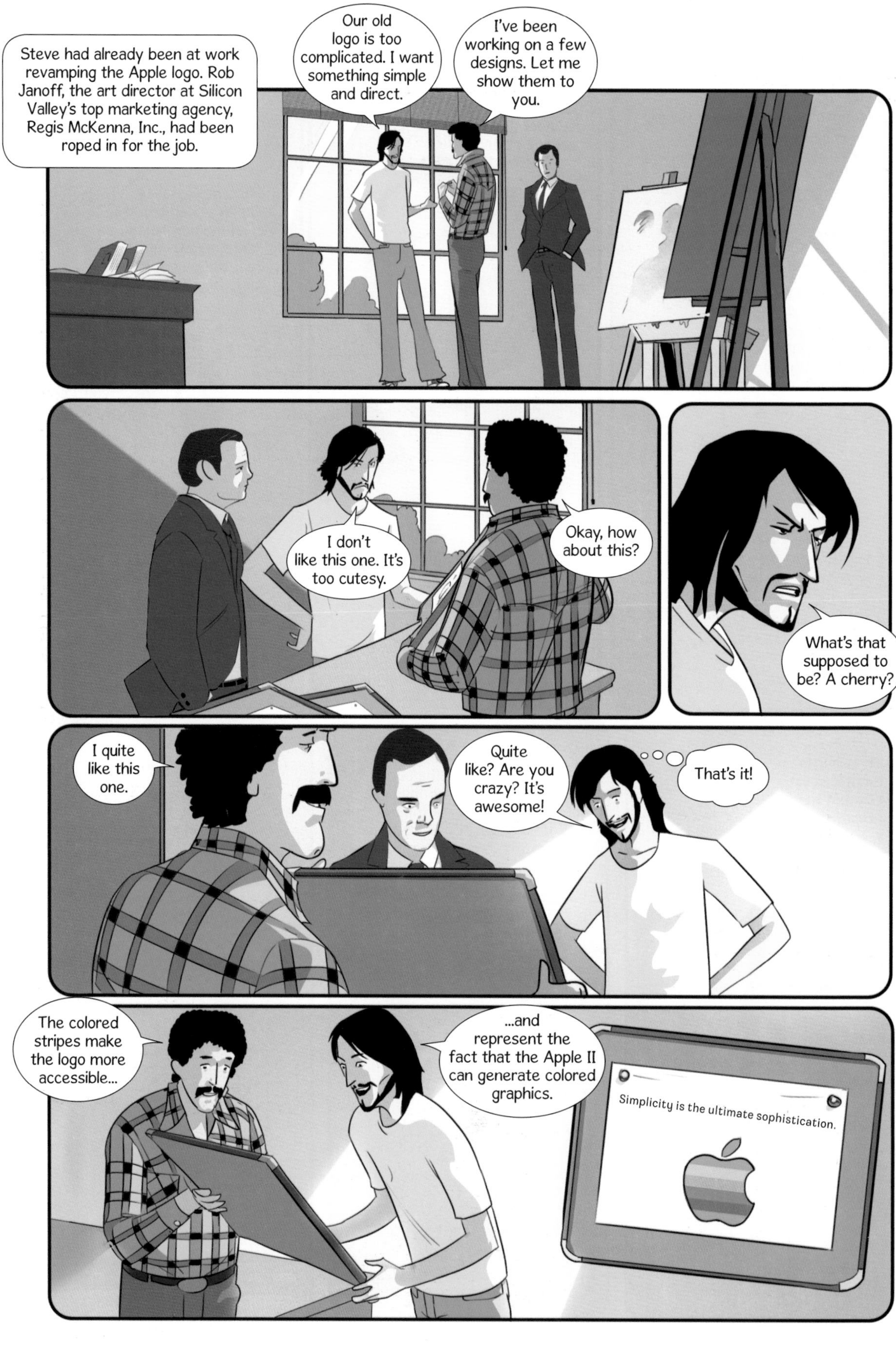
Steve had already been at work revamping the Apple logo. Rob Janoff, the art director at Silicon Valley's top marketing agency, Regis McKenna, Inc., had been roped in for the job.
Our old logo is too complicated. I want something simple and direct.
I've been working on a few designs. Let me show them to you.
I don't like this one. It's too cutesy.
Okay, how about this?
What's that supposed to be? A cherry?
I quite like this one.
Quite like? Are you crazy? It's awesome!
That's it!
The colored stripes make the logo more accessible...
...and represent the fact that the Apple II can generate colored graphics.
Simplicity is the ultimate sophistication.

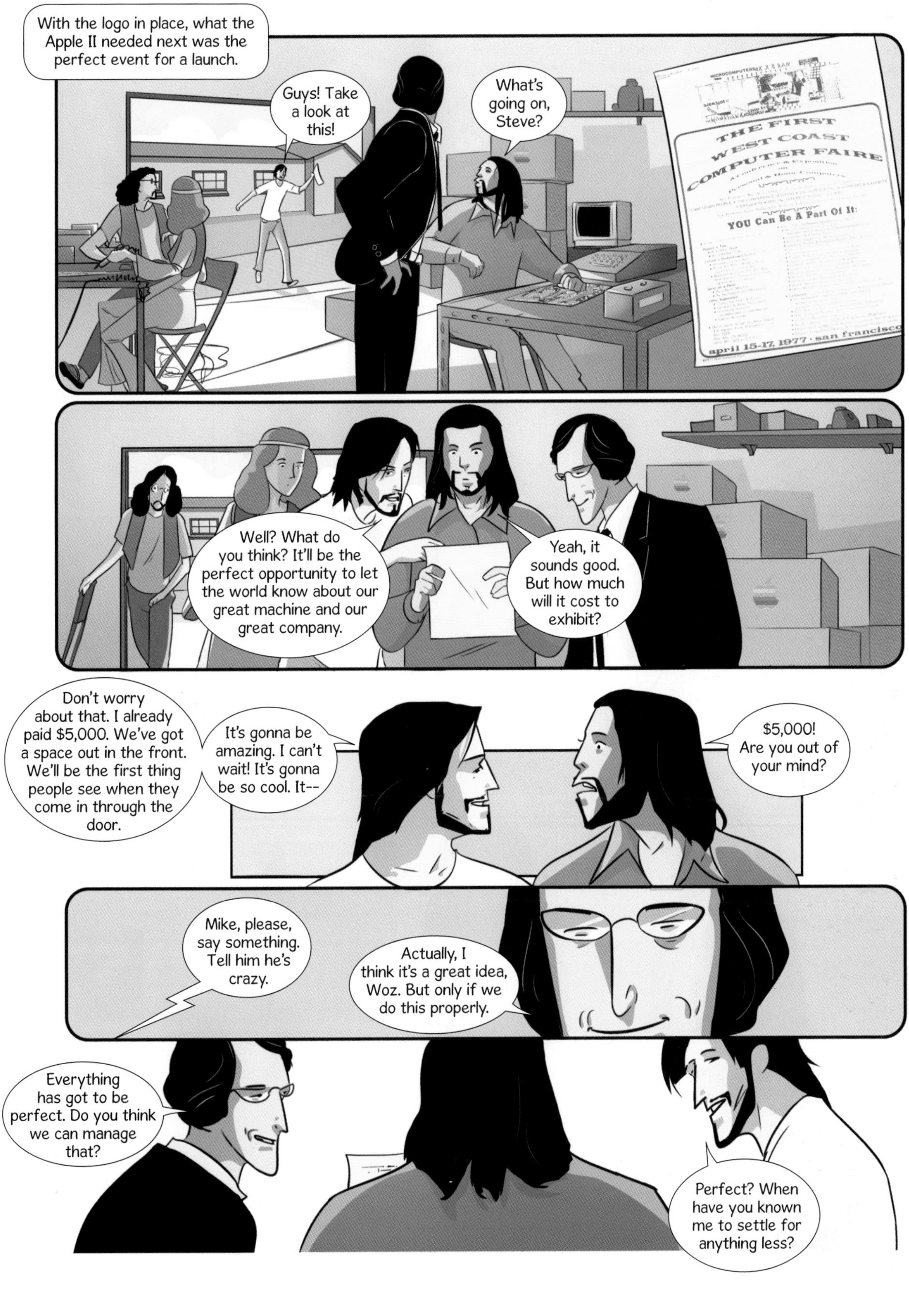
With the logo in place, what the Apple II needed next was the perfect event for a launch.
Guys! Take a look at this!
What's going on, Steve?
THE FIRST WEST COAST COMPUTER FAIRE
YOU Can Be A Part Of It:
april 15-17, 1977 · san francisco
Well? What do you think? It'll be the perfect opportunity to let the world know about our great machine and our great company.
Yeah, it sounds good. But how much will it cost to exhibit?
Don't worry about that. I already paid $5,000. We've got a space out in the front. We'll be the first thing people see when they come in through the door.
It's gonna be amazing. I can't wait! It's gonna be so cool. It--
$5,000! Are you out of your mind?
Mike, please, say something. Tell him he's crazy.
Actually, I think it's a great idea, Woz. But only if we do this properly.
Everything has got to be perfect. Do you think we can manage that?
Perfect? When have you known me to settle for anything less?

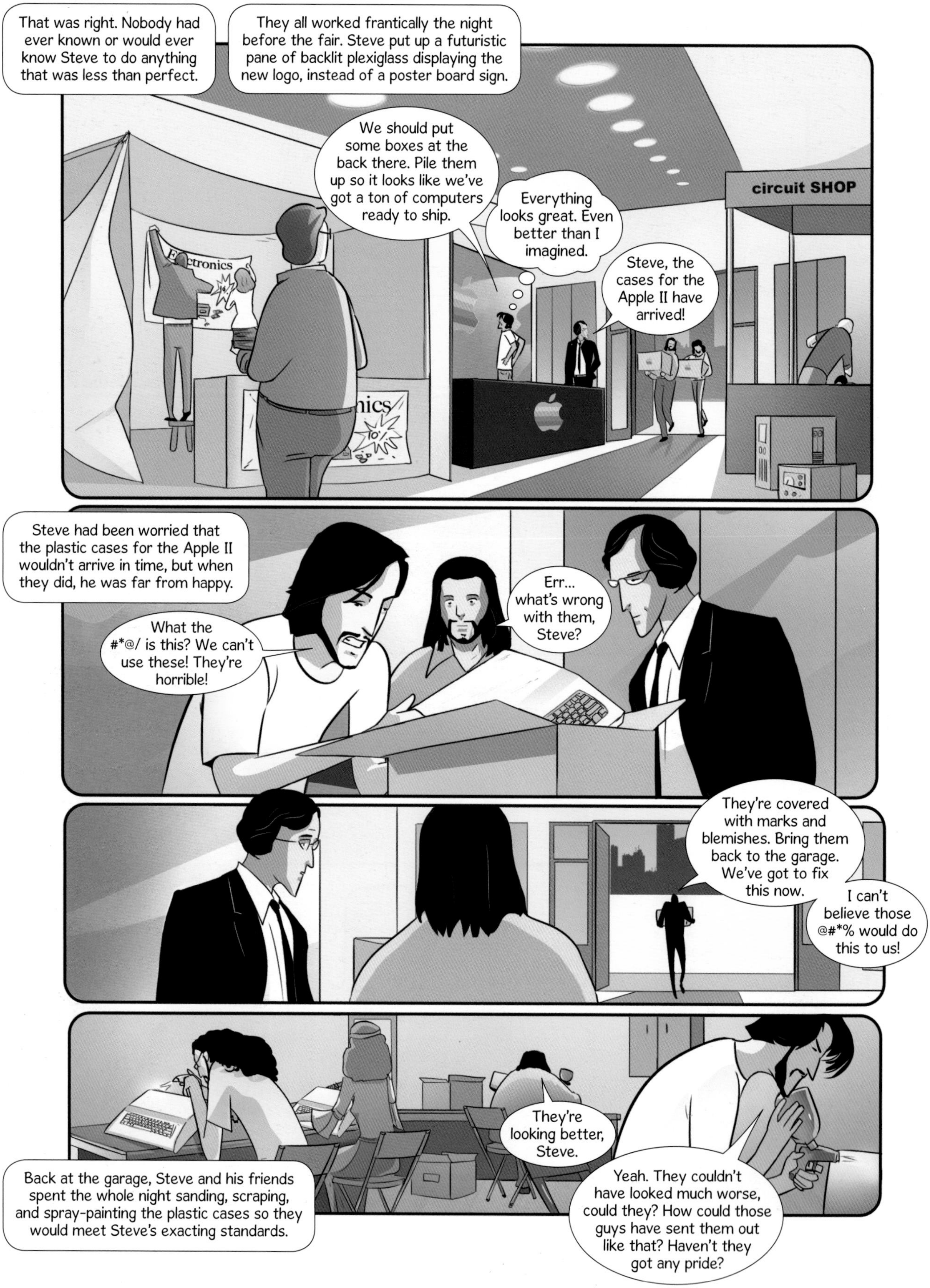
That was right. Nobody had ever known or would ever know Steve to do anything that was less than perfect.
They all worked frantically the night before the fair. Steve put up a futuristic pane of backlit plexiglass displaying the new logo, instead of a poster board sign.
We should put some boxes at the back there. Pile them up so it looks like we've got a ton of computers ready to ship.
Everything looks great. Even better than I imagined.
Steve, the cases for the Apple II have arrived!
circuit SHOP
Steve had been worried that the plastic cases for the Apple II wouldn't arrive in time, but when they did, he was far from happy.
What the #*@/ is this? We can't use these! They're horrible!
Err... what's wrong with them, Steve?
They're covered with marks and blemishes. Bring them back to the garage. We've got to fix this now.
I can't believe those @#*% would do this to us!
They're looking better, Steve.
Back at the garage, Steve and his friends spent the whole night sanding, scraping, and spray-painting the plastic cases so they would meet Steve's exacting standards.
Yeah. They couldn't have looked much worse, could they? How could those guys have sent them out like that? Haven't they got any pride?

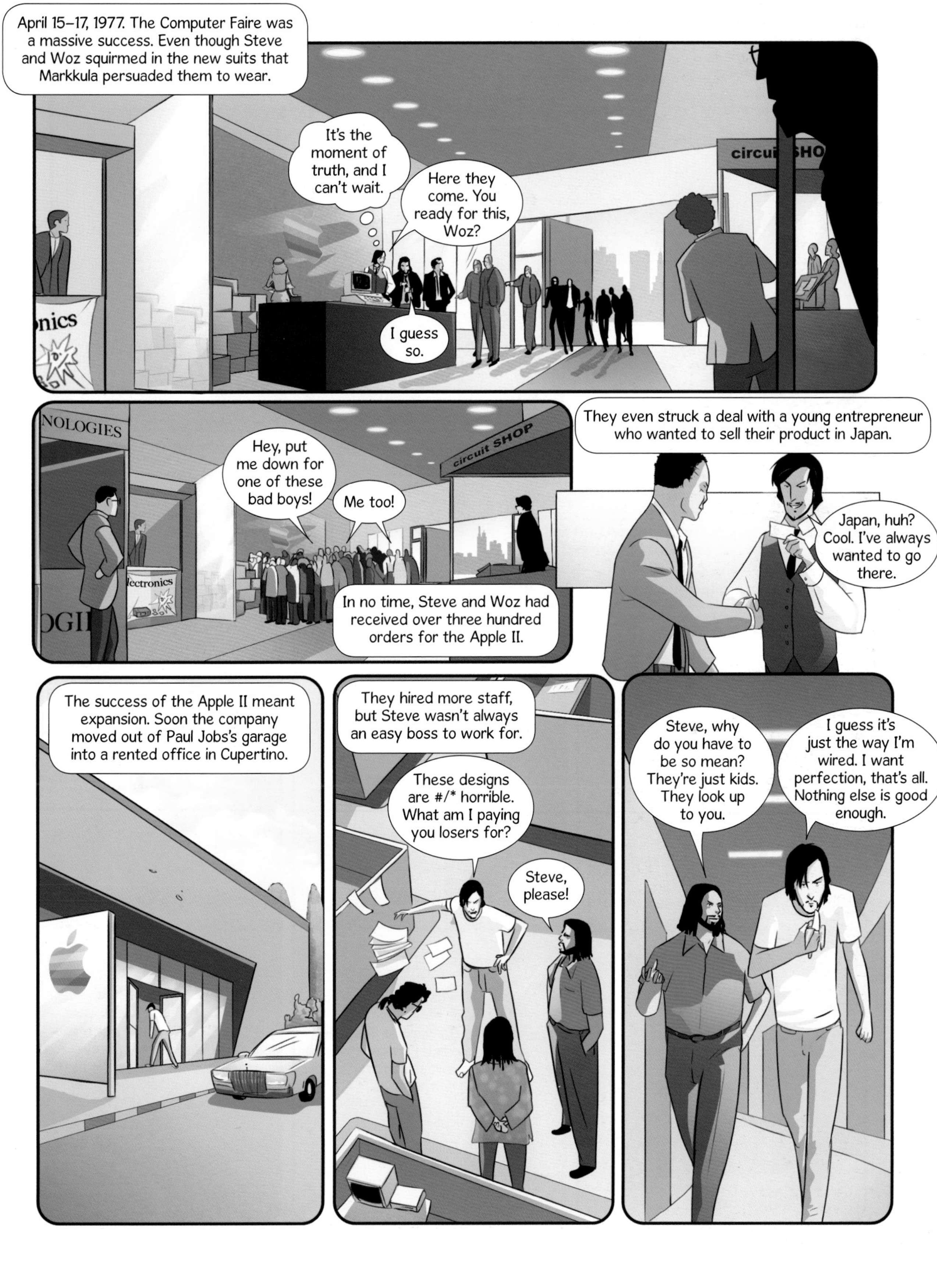
April 15–17, 1977. The Computer Faire was a massive success. Even though Steve and Woz squirmed in the new suits that Markkula persuaded them to wear.
It's the moment of truth, and I can't wait.
Here they come. You ready for this, Woz?
I guess so.
circuit SHOP
nics
NOLOGIES
circuit SHOP
Hey, put me down for one of these bad boys!
Me too!
lectronics
OGI
In no time, Steve and Woz had received over three hundred orders for the Apple II.
They even struck a deal with a young entrepreneur who wanted to sell their product in Japan.
Japan, huh? Cool. I've always wanted to go there.
The success of the Apple II meant expansion. Soon the company moved out of Paul Jobs's garage into a rented office in Cupertino.
They hired more staff, but Steve wasn't always an easy boss to work for.
These designs are #/* horrible. What am I paying you losers for?
Steve, please!
Steve, why do you have to be so mean? They're just kids. They look up to you.
I guess it's just the way I'm wired. I want perfection, that's all. Nothing else is good enough.

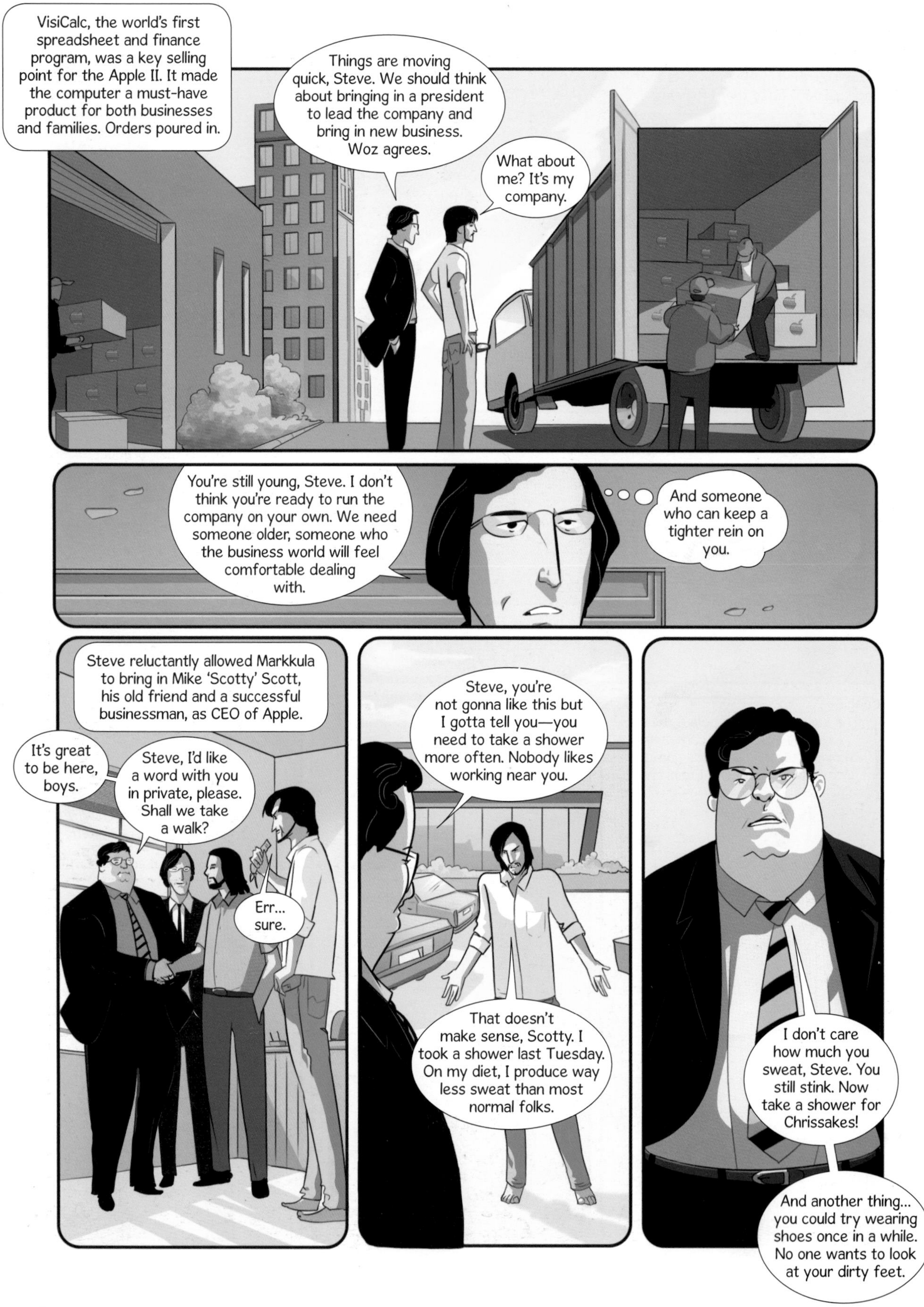
VisiCalc, the world's first spreadsheet and finance program, was a key selling point for the Apple II. It made the computer a must-have product for both businesses and families. Orders poured in.
Things are moving quick, Steve. We should think about bringing in a president to lead the company and bring in new business. Woz agrees.
What about me? It's my company.
You're still young, Steve. I don't think you're ready to run the company on your own. We need someone older, someone who the business world will feel comfortable dealing with.
And someone who can keep a tighter rein on you.
Steve reluctantly allowed Markkula to bring in Mike 'Scotty' Scott, his old friend and a successful businessman, as CEO of Apple.
It's great to be here, boys.
Steve, I'd like a word with you in private, please. Shall we take a walk?
Err... sure.
Steve, you're not gonna like this but I gotta tell you—you need to take a shower more often. Nobody likes working near you.
That doesn't make sense, Scotty. I took a shower last Tuesday. On my diet, I produce way less sweat than most normal folks.
I don't care how much you sweat, Steve. You still stink. Now take a shower for Chrissakes!
And another thing... you could try wearing shoes once in a while. No one wants to look at your dirty feet.

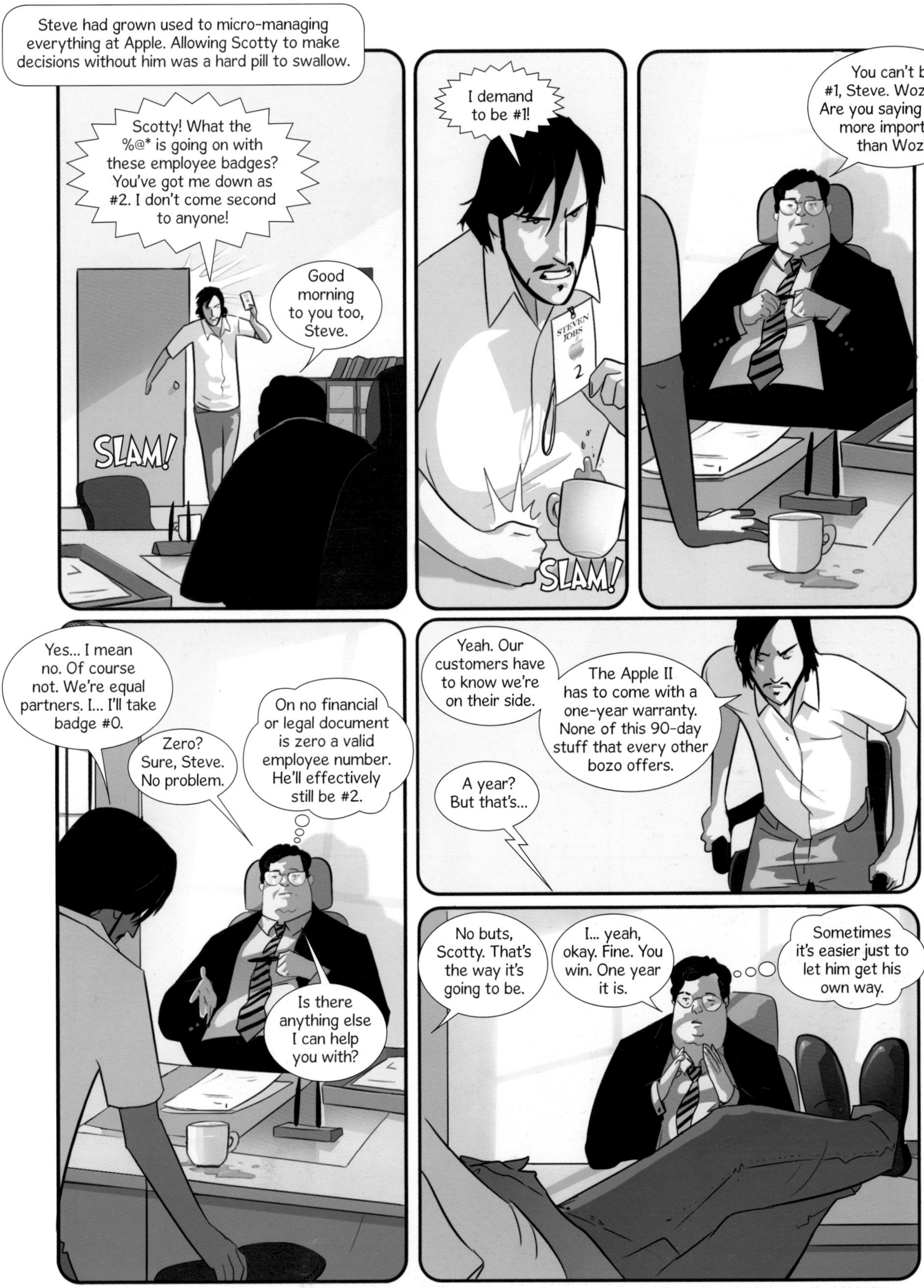

Steve had grown used to micro-managing everything at Apple. Allowing Scotty to make decisions without him was a hard pill to swallow.
Scotty! What the %@* is going on with these employee badges? You've got me down as #2. I don't come second to anyone!
Good morning to you too, Steve.
SLAM!
I demand to be #1!
STEVEN JOBS 2
SLAM!
You can't be #1, Steve. Woz is #1. Are you saying you're more important than Woz?
Yes... I mean no. Of course not. We're equal partners. I... I'll take badge #0.
Zero? Sure, Steve. No problem.
On no financial or legal document is zero a valid employee number. He'll effectively still be #2.
Is there anything else I can help you with?
Yeah. Our customers have to know we're on their side.
The Apple II has to come with a one-year warranty. None of this 90-day stuff that every other bozo offers.
A year? But that's...
No buts, Scotty. That's the way it's going to be.
I... yeah, okay. Fine. You win. One year it is.
Sometimes it's easier just to let him get his own way.

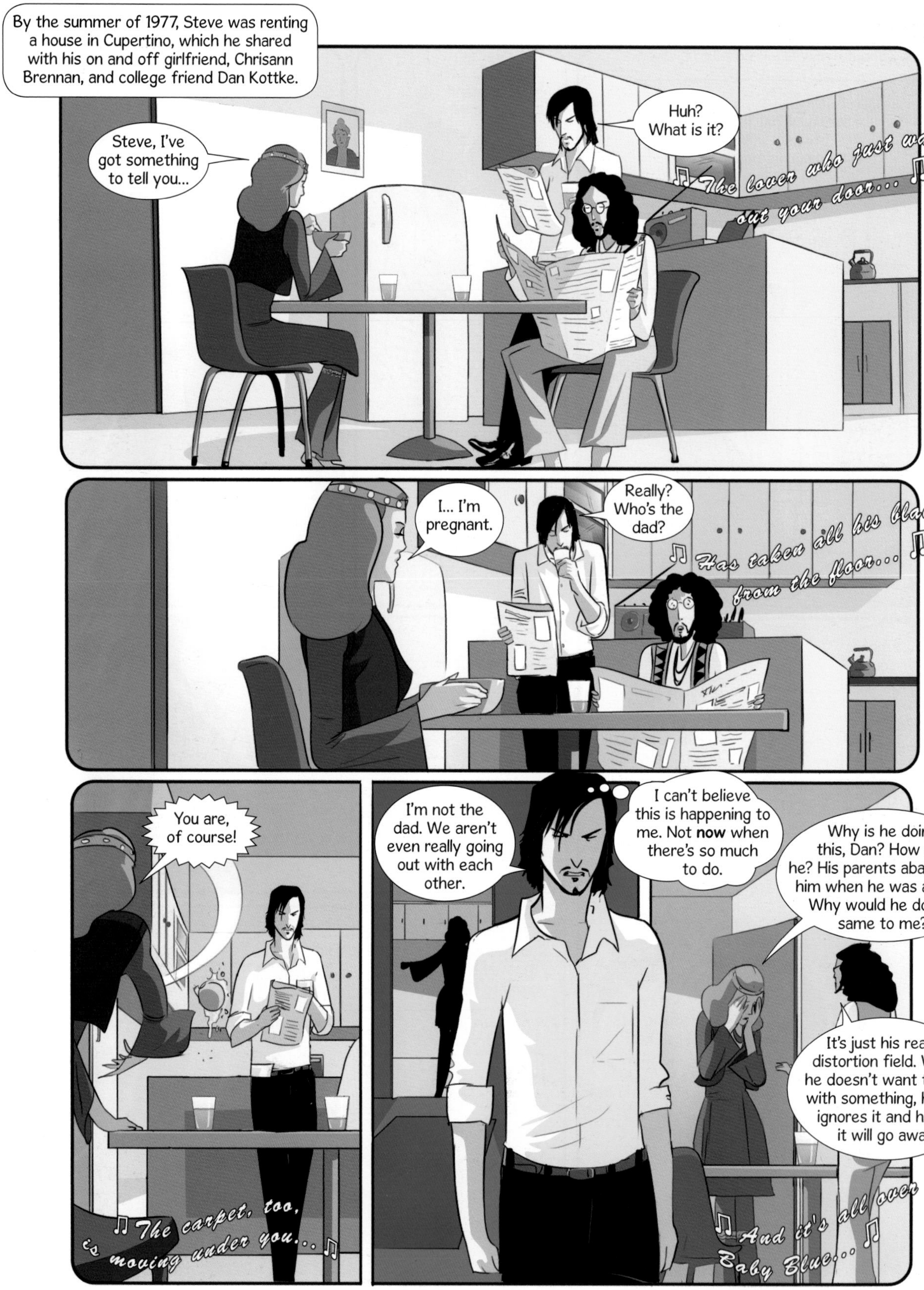

By the summer of 1977, Steve was renting a house in Cupertino, which he shared with his on and off girlfriend, Chrisann Brennan, and college friend Dan Kottke.
Steve, I've got something to tell you...
Huh? What is it?
♫ The lover who just walked out your door... ♫
I... I'm pregnant.
Really? Who's the dad?
♫ Has taken all his blankets from the floor... ♫
You are, of course!
♫ The carpet, too, is moving under you... ♫
I'm not the dad. We aren't even really going out with each other.
I can't believe this is happening to me. Not **now** when there's so much to do.
Why is he doing this, Dan? How can he? His parents abandoned him when he was a baby. Why would he do the same to me?
It's just his reality distortion field. When he doesn't want to deal with something, he just ignores it and hopes it will go away.
♫ And it's all over now, Baby Blue... ♫

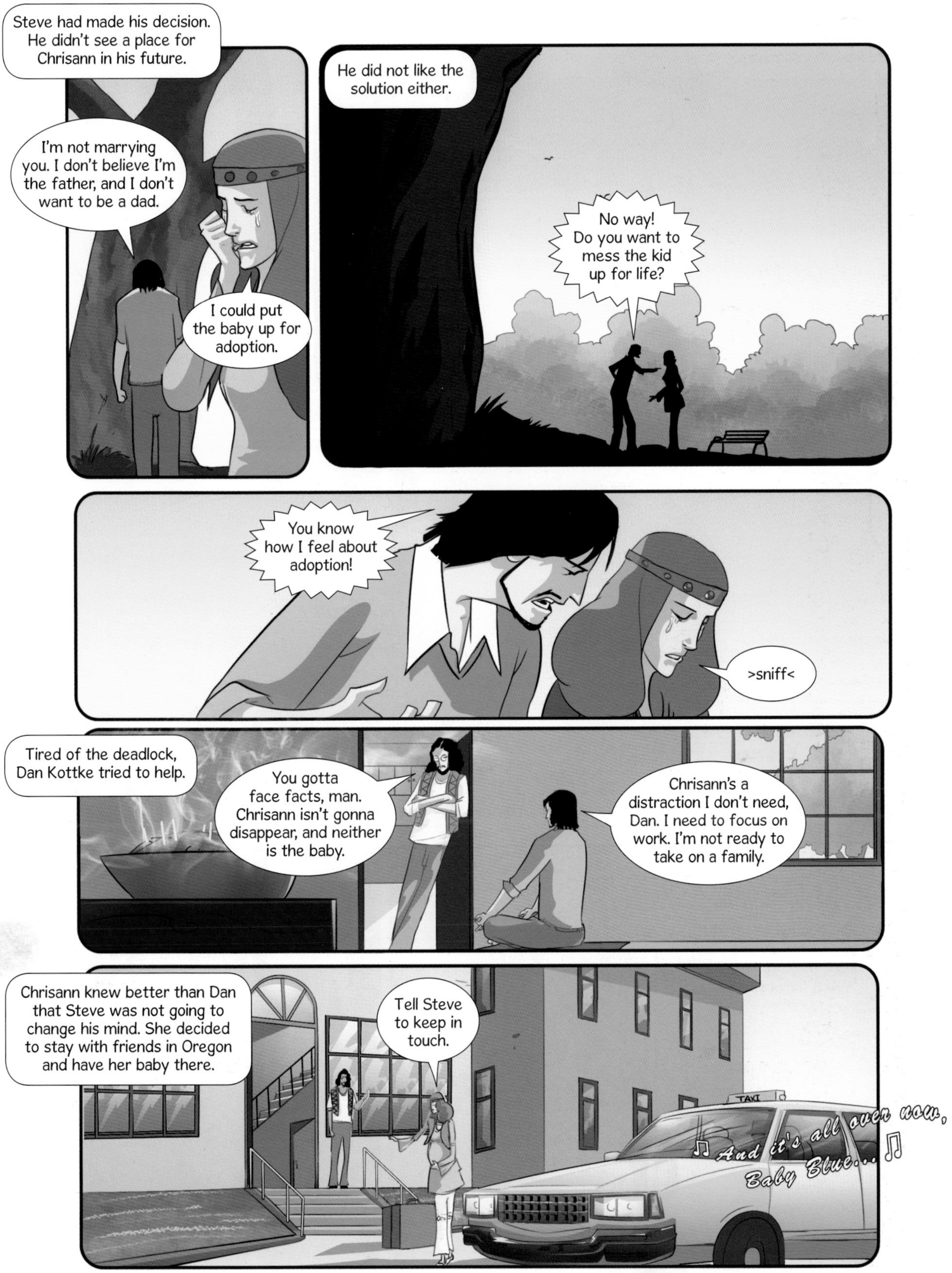

Steve had made his decision. He didn't see a place for Chrisann in his future.
I'm not marrying you. I don't believe I'm the father, and I don't want to be a dad.
I could put the baby up for adoption.
He did not like the solution either.
No way! Do you want to mess the kid up for life?
You know how I feel about adoption!
>sniff<
Tired of the deadlock, Dan Kottke tried to help.
You gotta face facts, man. Chrisann isn't gonna disappear, and neither is the baby.
Chrisann's a distraction I don't need, Dan. I need to focus on work. I'm not ready to take on a family.
Chrisann knew better than Dan that Steve was not going to change his mind. She decided to stay with friends in Oregon and have her baby there.
Tell Steve to keep in touch.
TAXI
♫ And it's all over now, Baby Blue... ♫

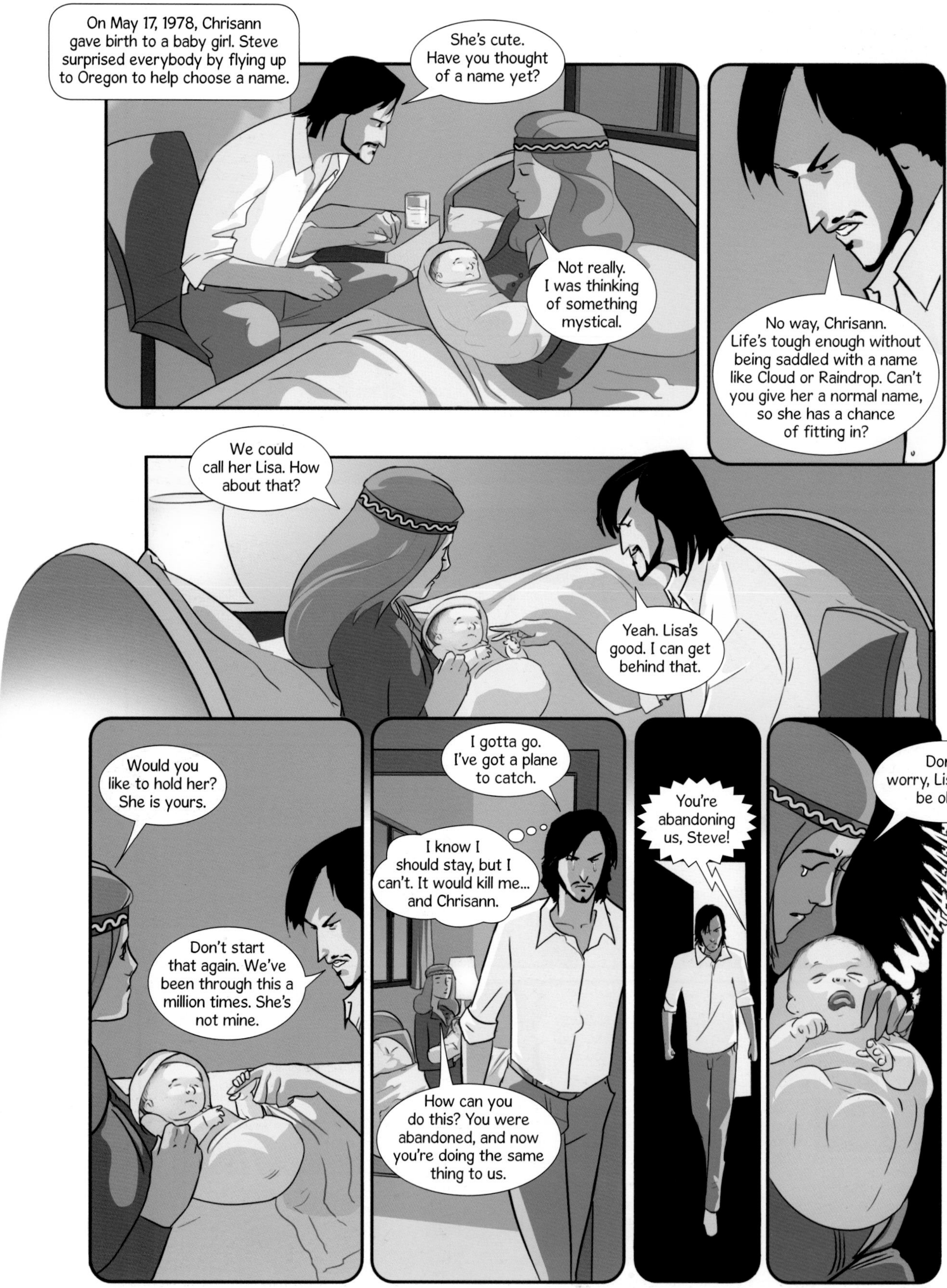
On May 17, 1978, Chrisann gave birth to a baby girl. Steve surprised everybody by flying up to Oregon to help choose a name.
She's cute. Have you thought of a name yet?
Not really. I was thinking of something mystical.
No way, Chrisann. Life's tough enough without being saddled with a name like Cloud or Raindrop. Can't you give her a normal name, so she has a chance of fitting in?
We could call her Lisa. How about that?
Yeah. Lisa's good. I can get behind that.
Would you like to hold her? She is yours.
Don't start that again. We've been through this a million times. She's not mine.
I gotta go. I've got a plane to catch.
I know I should stay, but I can't. It would kill me... and Chrisann.
How can you do this? You were abandoned, and now you're doing the same thing to us.
You're abandoning us, Steve!
Don't worry, Lisa. We'll be okay.
WAAAAAAA

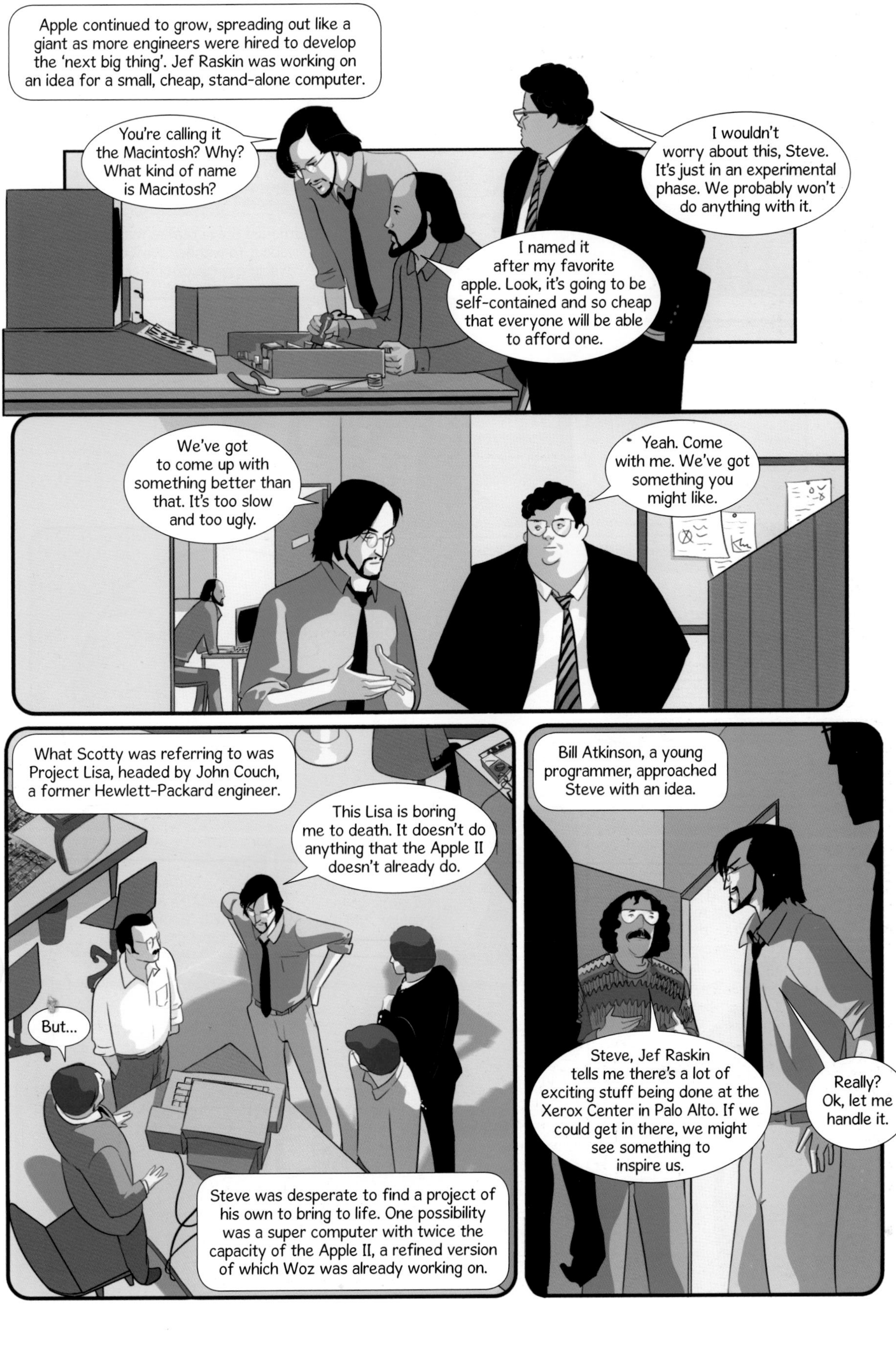
Apple continued to grow, spreading out like a giant as more engineers were hired to develop the 'next big thing'. Jef Raskin was working on an idea for a small, cheap, stand-alone computer.
You're calling it the Macintosh? Why? What kind of name is Macintosh?
I wouldn't worry about this, Steve. It's just in an experimental phase. We probably won't do anything with it.
I named it after my favorite apple. Look, it's going to be self-contained and so cheap that everyone will be able to afford one.
We've got to come up with something better than that. It's too slow and too ugly.
Yeah. Come with me. We've got something you might like.
What Scotty was referring to was Project Lisa, headed by John Couch, a former Hewlett-Packard engineer.
This Lisa is boring me to death. It doesn't do anything that the Apple II doesn't already do.
But...
Steve was desperate to find a project of his own to bring to life. One possibility was a super computer with twice the capacity of the Apple II, a refined version of which Woz was already working on.
Bill Atkinson, a young programmer, approached Steve with an idea.
Steve, Jef Raskin tells me there's a lot of exciting stuff being done at the Xerox Center in Palo Alto. If we could get in there, we might see something to inspire us.
Really? Ok, let me handle it.

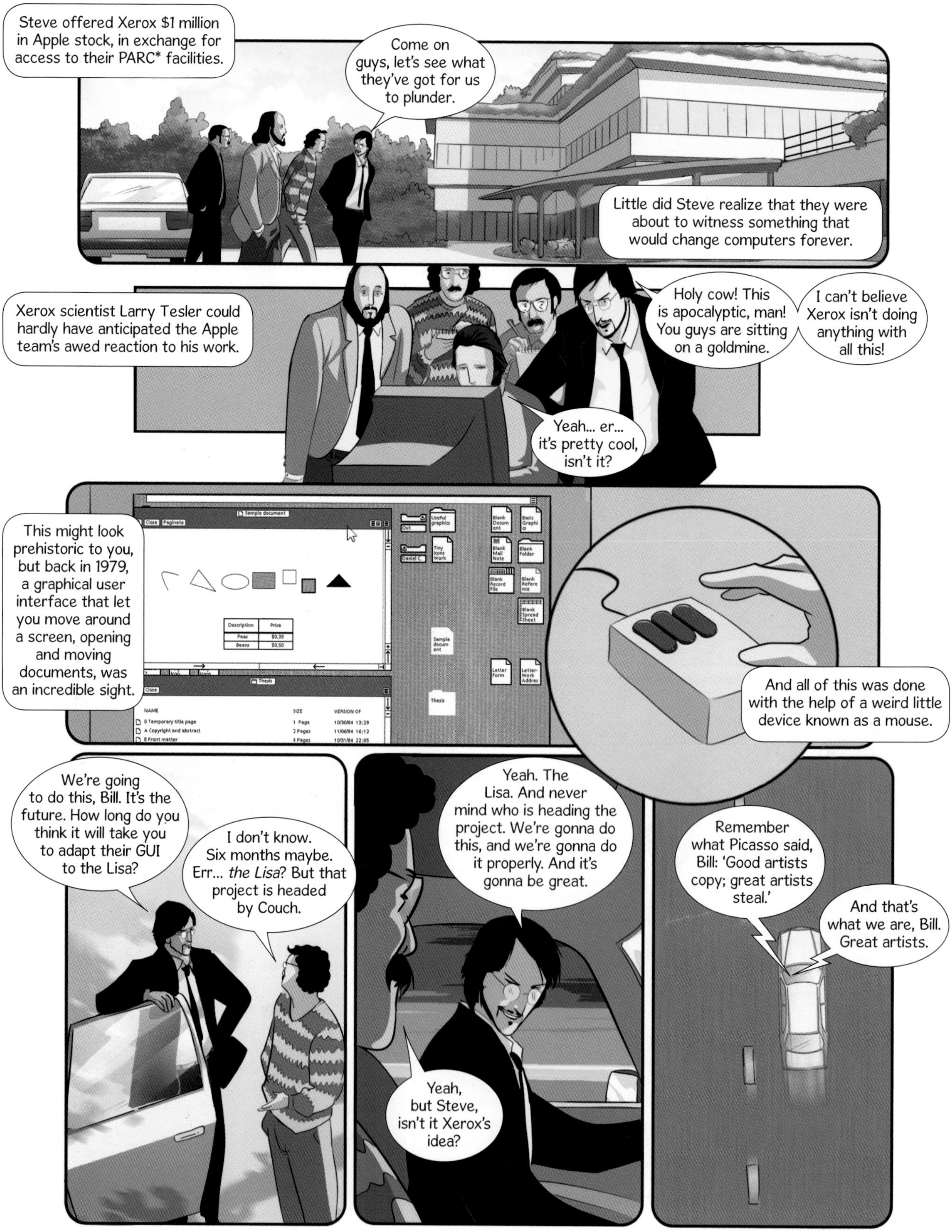
Steve offered Xerox $1 million in Apple stock, in exchange for access to their PARC* facilities.
Come on guys, let's see what they've got for us to plunder.
Little did Steve realize that they were about to witness something that would change computers forever.
Xerox scientist Larry Tesler could hardly have anticipated the Apple team's awed reaction to his work.
Holy cow! This is apocalyptic, man! You guys are sitting on a goldmine.
I can't believe Xerox isn't doing anything with all this!
Yeah... er... it's pretty cool, isn't it?
This might look prehistoric to you, but back in 1979, a graphical user interface that let you move around a screen, opening and moving documents, was an incredible sight.
And all of this was done with the help of a weird little device known as a mouse.
We're going to do this, Bill. It's the future. How long do you think it will take you to adapt their GUI to the Lisa?
I don't know. Six months maybe. Err... *the Lisa*? But that project is headed by Couch.
Yeah. The Lisa. And never mind who is heading the project. We're gonna do this, and we're gonna do it properly. And it's gonna be great.
Yeah, but Steve, isn't it Xerox's idea?
Remember what Picasso said, Bill: 'Good artists copy; great artists steal.'
And that's what we are, Bill. Great artists.

*Palo Alto Research Center

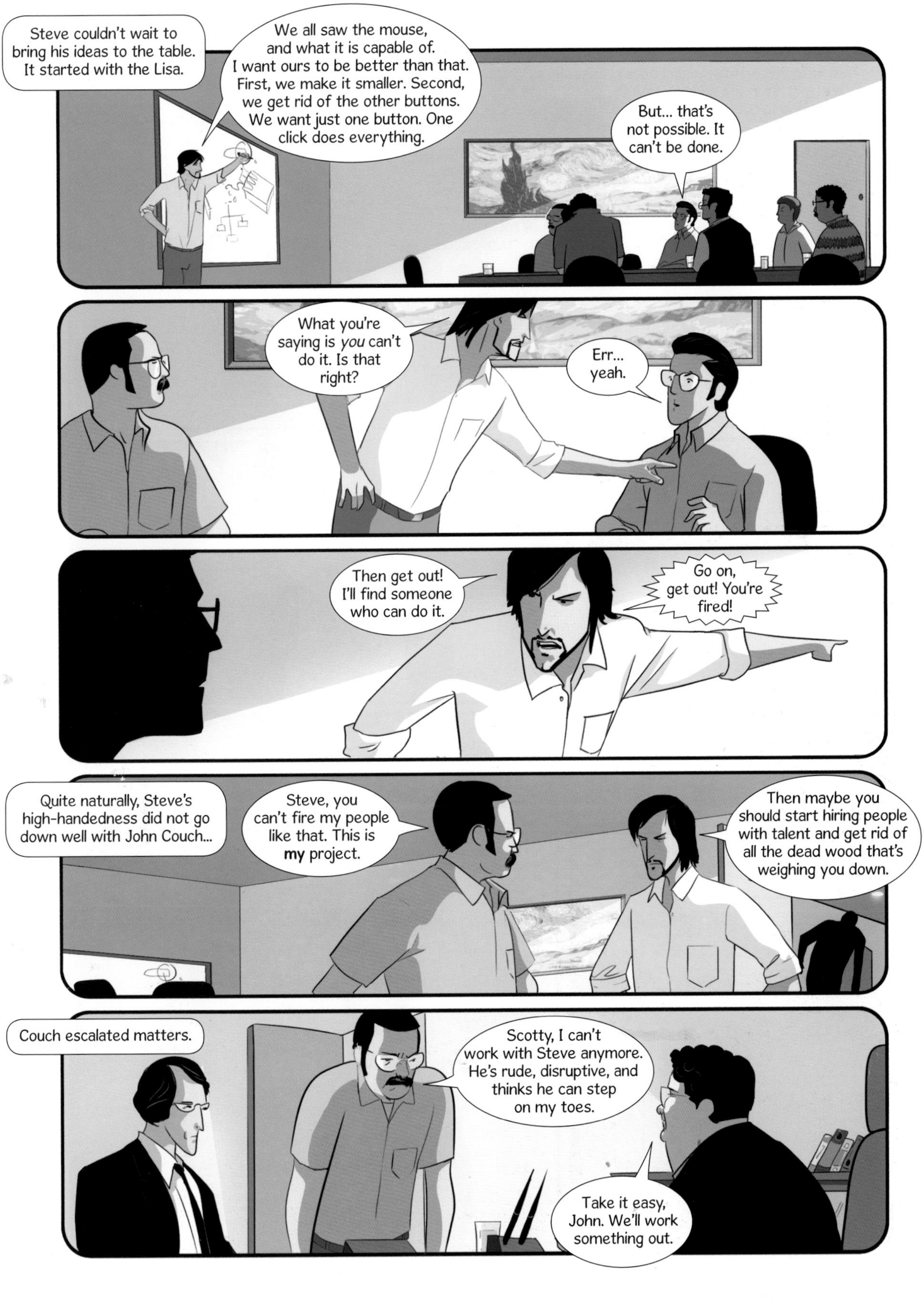
Steve couldn't wait to bring his ideas to the table. It started with the Lisa.
We all saw the mouse, and what it is capable of. I want ours to be better than that. First, we make it smaller. Second, we get rid of the other buttons. We want just one button. One click does everything.
But... that's not possible. It can't be done.
What you're saying is *you* can't do it. Is that right?
Err... yeah.
Then get out! I'll find someone who can do it.
Go on, get out! You're fired!
Quite naturally, Steve's high-handedness did not go down well with John Couch...
Steve, you can't fire my people like that. This is **my** project.
Then maybe you should start hiring people with talent and get rid of all the dead wood that's weighing you down.
Couch escalated matters.
Scotty, I can't work with Steve anymore. He's rude, disruptive, and thinks he can step on my toes.
Take it easy, John. We'll work something out.

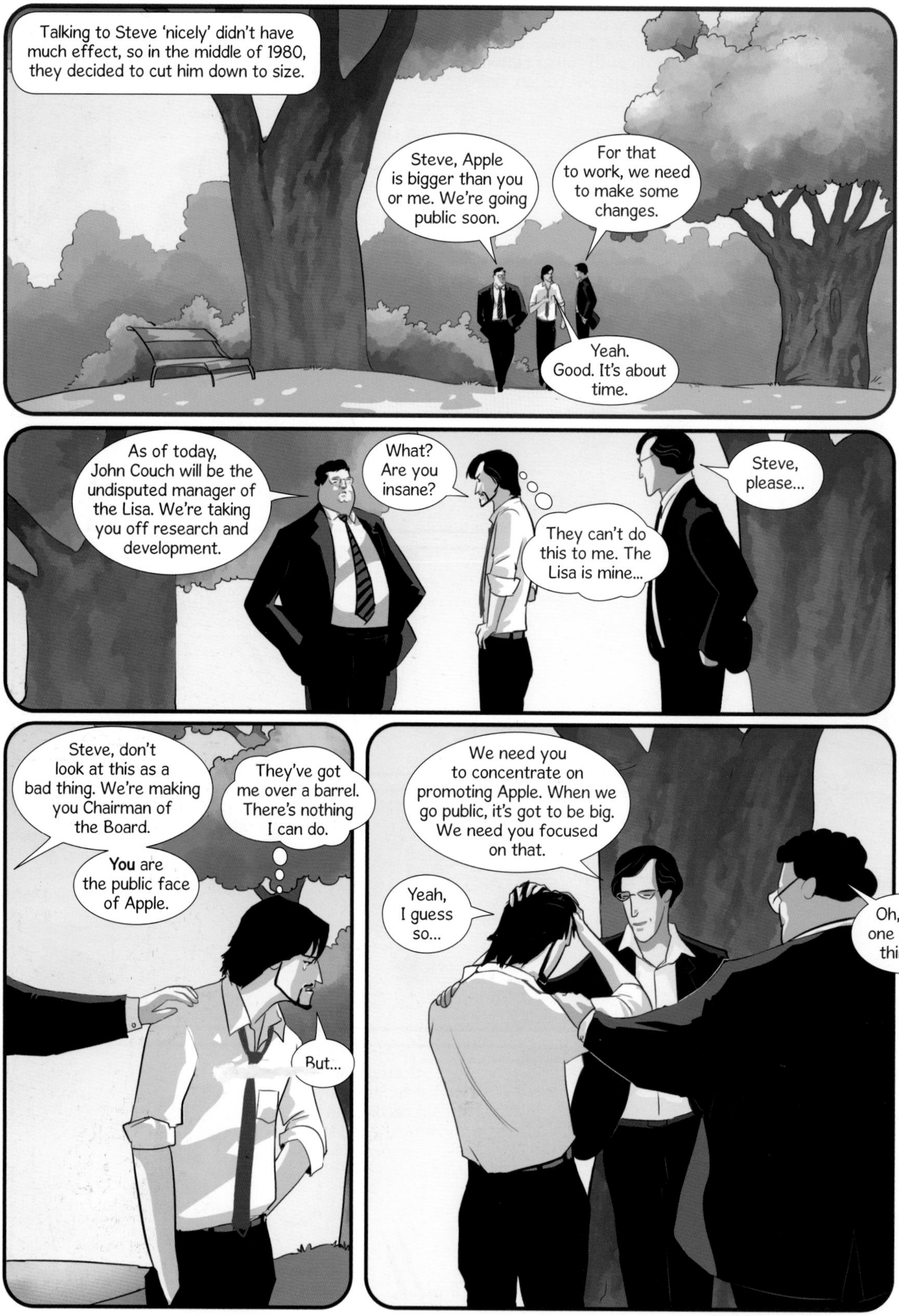
Talking to Steve 'nicely' didn't have much effect, so in the middle of 1980, they decided to cut him down to size.
Steve, Apple is bigger than you or me. We're going public soon.
For that to work, we need to make some changes.
Yeah. Good. It's about time.
As of today, John Couch will be the undisputed manager of the Lisa. We're taking you off research and development.
What? Are you insane?
They can't do this to me. The Lisa is mine...
Steve, please...
Steve, don't look at this as a bad thing. We're making you Chairman of the Board.
You are the public face of Apple.
They've got me over a barrel. There's nothing I can do.
But...
We need you to concentrate on promoting Apple. When we go public, it's got to be big. We need you focused on that.
Yeah, I guess so...
Oh, and one other thing...

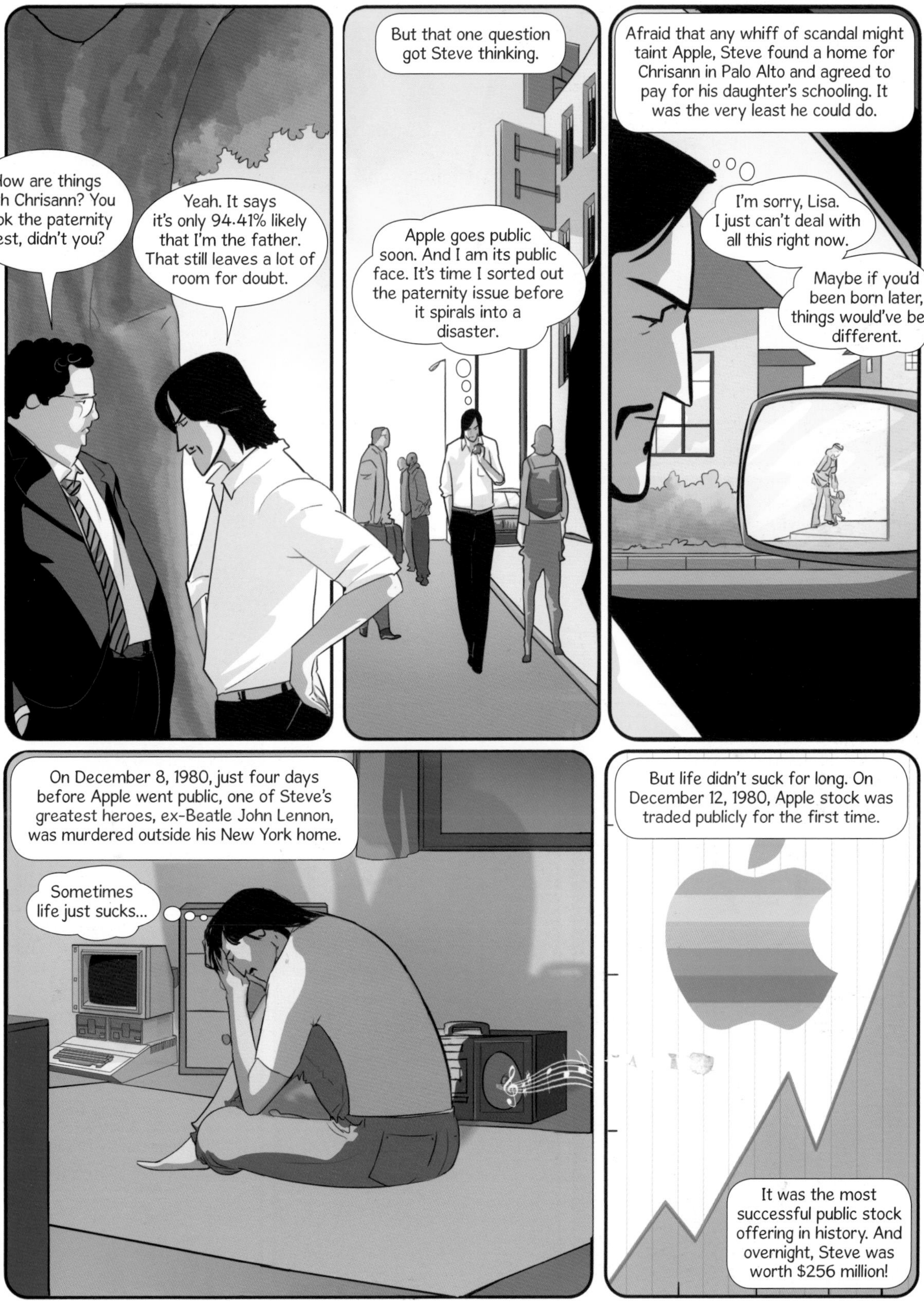
How are things with Chrisann? You took the paternity test, didn't you?
Yeah. It says it's only 94.41% likely that I'm the father. That still leaves a lot of room for doubt.
But that one question got Steve thinking.
Apple goes public soon. And I am its public face. It's time I sorted out the paternity issue before it spirals into a disaster.
Afraid that any whiff of scandal might taint Apple, Steve found a home for Chrisann in Palo Alto and agreed to pay for his daughter's schooling. It was the very least he could do.
I'm sorry, Lisa. I just can't deal with all this right now.
Maybe if you'd been born later, things would've been different.
On December 8, 1980, just four days before Apple went public, one of Steve's greatest heroes, ex-Beatle John Lennon, was murdered outside his New York home.
Sometimes life just sucks...
But life didn't suck for long. On December 12, 1980, Apple stock was traded publicly for the first time.
It was the most successful public stock offering in history. And overnight, Steve was worth $256 million!

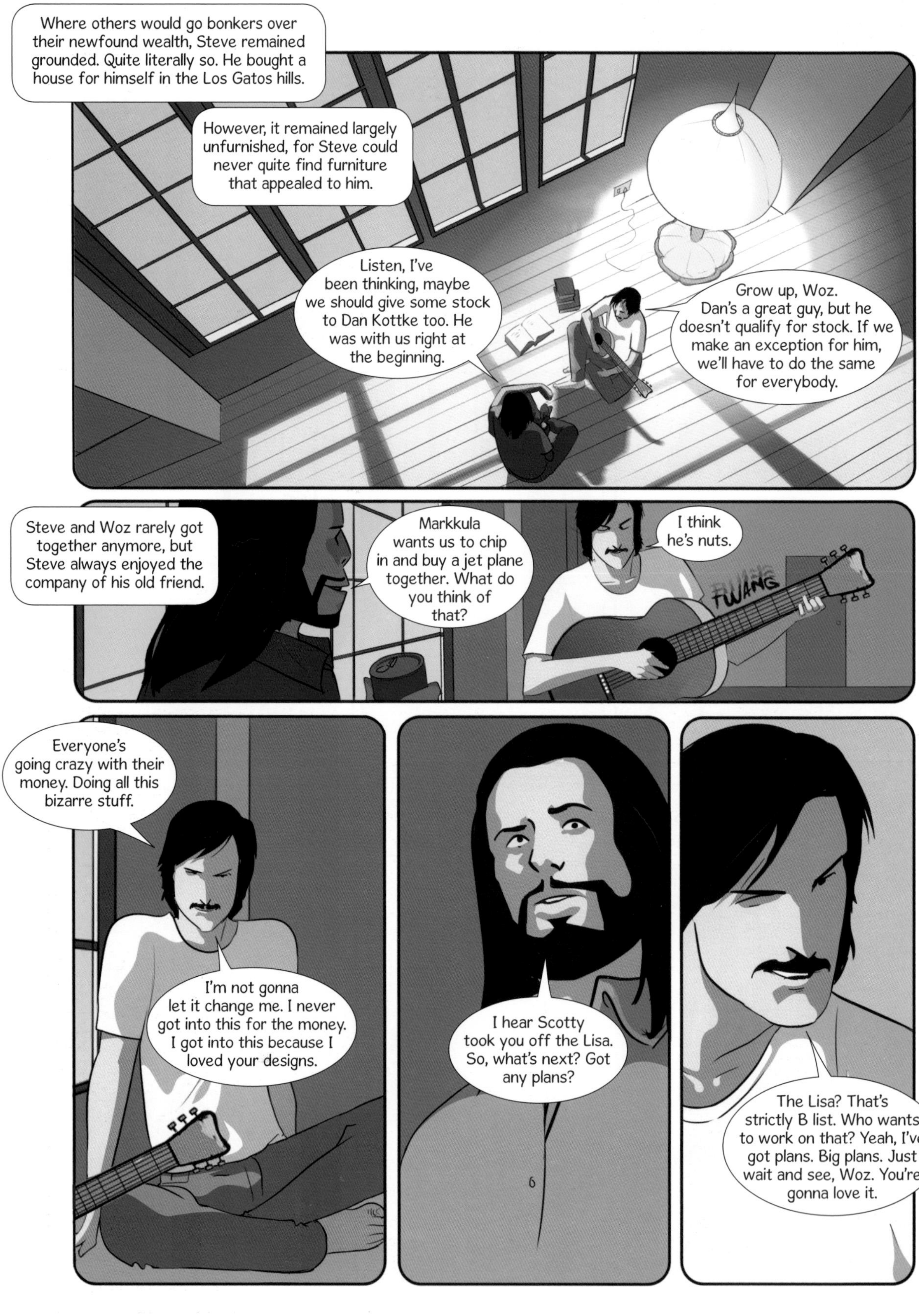
Where others would go bonkers over their newfound wealth, Steve remained grounded. Quite literally so. He bought a house for himself in the Los Gatos hills.
However, it remained largely unfurnished, for Steve could never quite find furniture that appealed to him.
Listen, I've been thinking, maybe we should give some stock to Dan Kottke too. He was with us right at the beginning.
Grow up, Woz. Dan's a great guy, but he doesn't qualify for stock. If we make an exception for him, we'll have to do the same for everybody.
Steve and Woz rarely got together anymore, but Steve always enjoyed the company of his old friend.
Markkula wants us to chip in and buy a jet plane together. What do you think of that?
I think he's nuts.
TWANG
Everyone's going crazy with their money. Doing all this bizarre stuff.
I'm not gonna let it change me. I never got into this for the money. I got into this because I loved your designs.
I hear Scotty took you off the Lisa. So, what's next? Got any plans?
The Lisa? That's strictly B list. Who wants to work on that? Yeah, I've got plans. Big plans. Just wait and see, Woz. You're gonna love it.

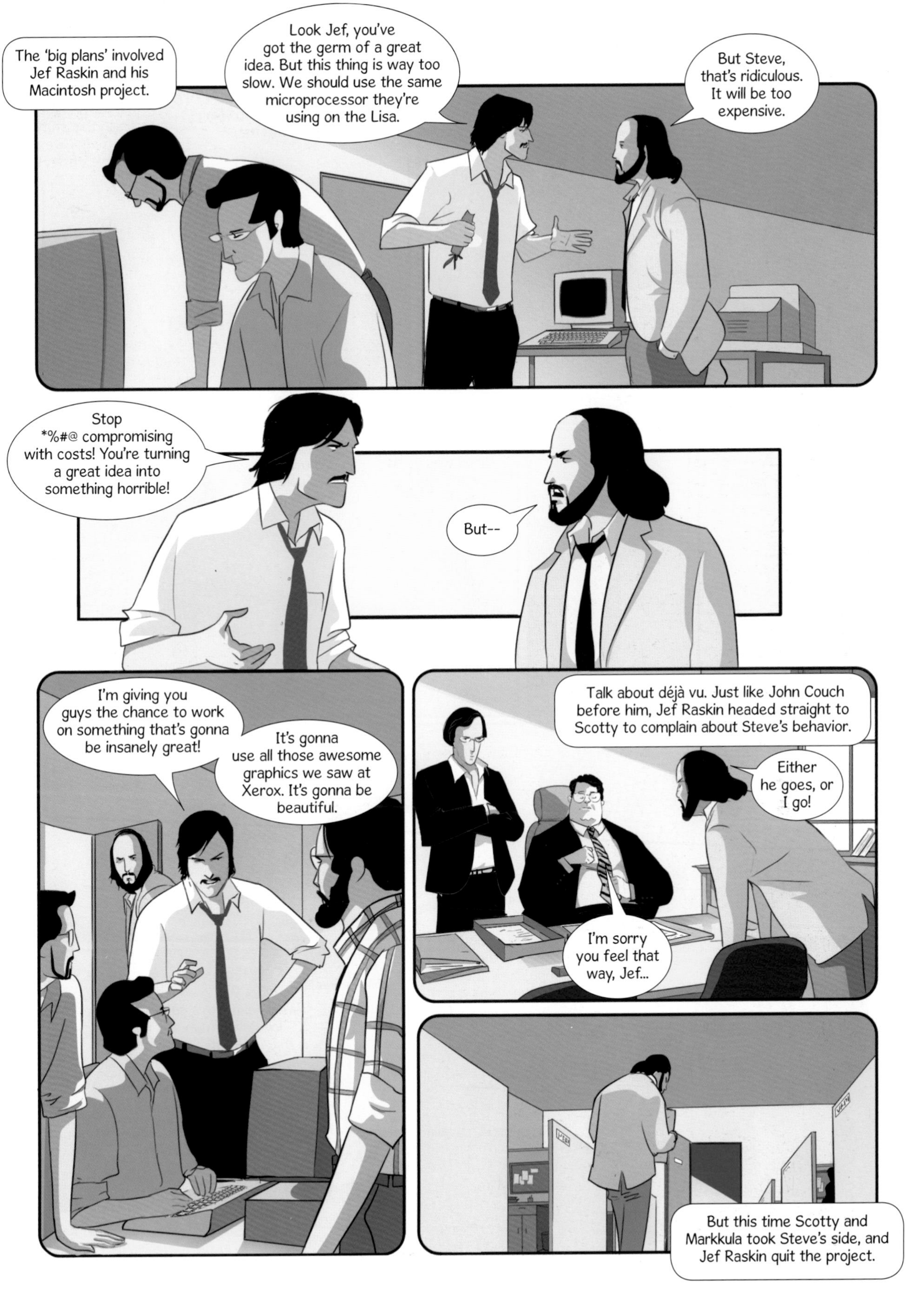

The 'big plans' involved Jef Raskin and his Macintosh project.
Look Jef, you've got the germ of a great idea. But this thing is way too slow. We should use the same microprocessor they're using on the Lisa.
But Steve, that's ridiculous. It will be too expensive.
Stop *%#@ compromising with costs! You're turning a great idea into something horrible!
But--
I'm giving you guys the chance to work on something that's gonna be insanely great!
It's gonna use all those awesome graphics we saw at Xerox. It's gonna be beautiful.
Talk about déjà vu. Just like John Couch before him, Jef Raskin headed straight to Scotty to complain about Steve's behavior.
Either he goes, or I go!
I'm sorry you feel that way, Jef...
But this time Scotty and Markkula took Steve's side, and Jef Raskin quit the project.

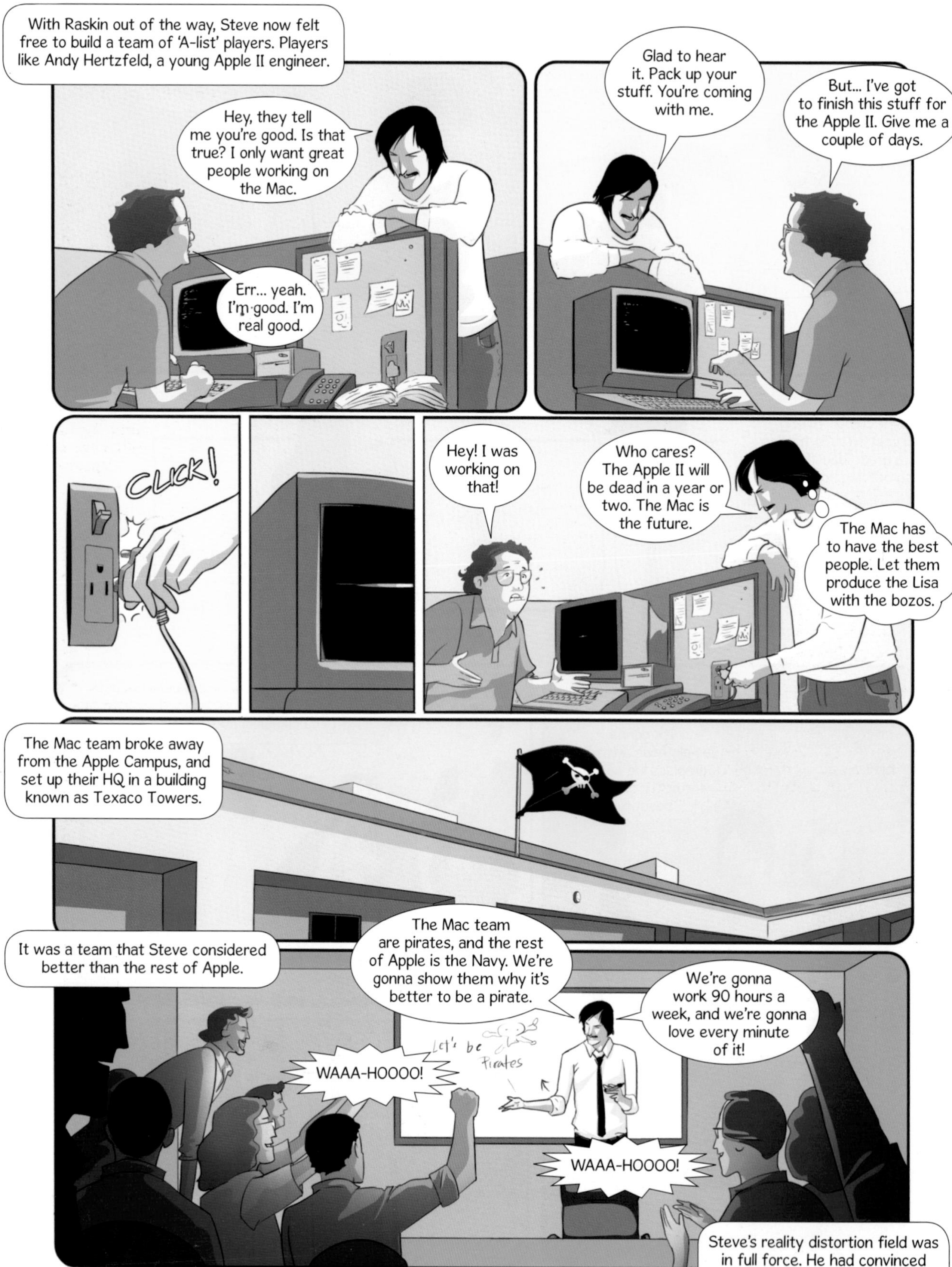

With Raskin out of the way, Steve now felt free to build a team of 'A-list' players. Players like Andy Hertzfeld, a young Apple II engineer.
Hey, they tell me you're good. Is that true? I only want great people working on the Mac.
Err... yeah. I'm good. I'm real good.
Glad to hear it. Pack up your stuff. You're coming with me.
But... I've got to finish this stuff for the Apple II. Give me a couple of days.
CLICK!
Hey! I was working on that!
Who cares? The Apple II will be dead in a year or two. The Mac is the future.
The Mac has to have the best people. Let them produce the Lisa with the bozos.
The Mac team broke away from the Apple Campus, and set up their HQ in a building known as Texaco Towers.
It was a team that Steve considered better than the rest of Apple.
The Mac team are pirates, and the rest of Apple is the Navy. We're gonna show them why it's better to be a pirate.
We're gonna work 90 hours a week, and we're gonna love every minute of it!
Let's be Pirates
WAAA-HOOOO!
WAAA-HOOOO!
Steve's reality distortion field was in full force. He had convinced the entire team that they really were capable of greatness.

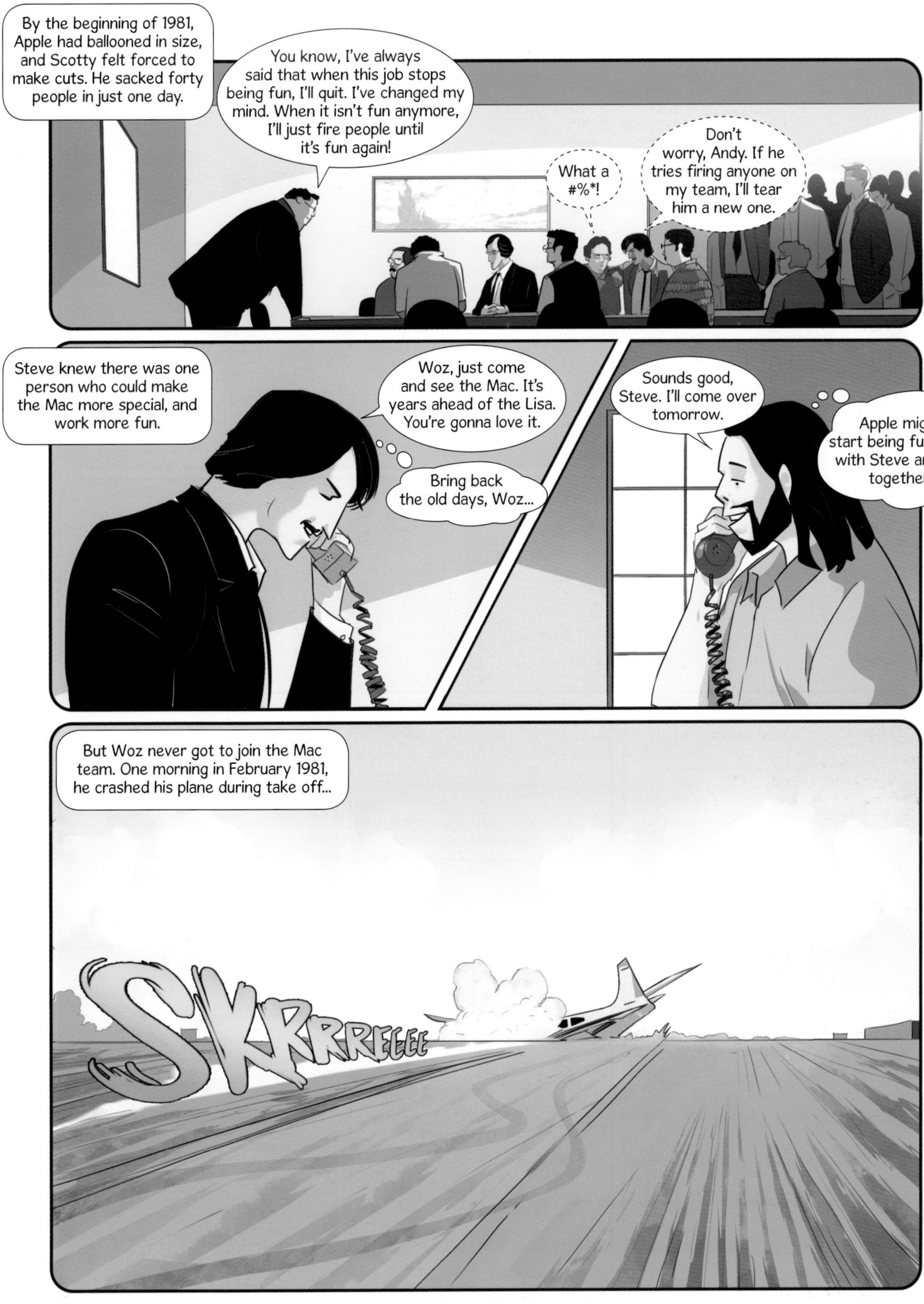
By the beginning of 1981, Apple had ballooned in size, and Scotty felt forced to make cuts. He sacked forty people in just one day.
You know, I've always said that when this job stops being fun, I'll quit. I've changed my mind. When it isn't fun anymore, I'll just fire people until it's fun again!
What a #%*!
Don't worry, Andy. If he tries firing anyone on my team, I'll tear him a new one.
Steve knew there was one person who could make the Mac more special, and work more fun.
Woz, just come and see the Mac. It's years ahead of the Lisa. You're gonna love it.
Bring back the old days, Woz...
Sounds good, Steve. I'll come over tomorrow.
Apple might start being fun again with Steve and me together.
But Woz never got to join the Mac team. One morning in February 1981, he crashed his plane during take off...
SKRRREEEE

As Woz drifted in and out of consciousness, Steve had his distraught parents brought to the hospital.

Don't die on me, Woz. The world needs you.

My poor, sweet boy!

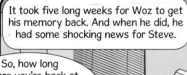

He's out of danger, but he's got amnesia. He wanted to know what he was doing in the hospital.

Don't worry. He'll get his memory back. He's alive, that's what counts.

He's going to be fine. He's got to be fine.

It took five long weeks for Woz to get his memory back. And when he did, he had some shocking news for Steve.

So, how long before you're back at work? We could sure use you on the Mac. It'll be just like the old days.

I... I'm not coming back, Steve. All of this has helped me put things in perspective.

I'm taking a break from Apple. I'm going back to college. It's about time I got my degree.

Wow! I never saw that coming. Good luck, man!

Listen, I'm late for a progress meeting. Stay in touch, yeah?

Yeah. You too.

Steve handled the disappointment well.

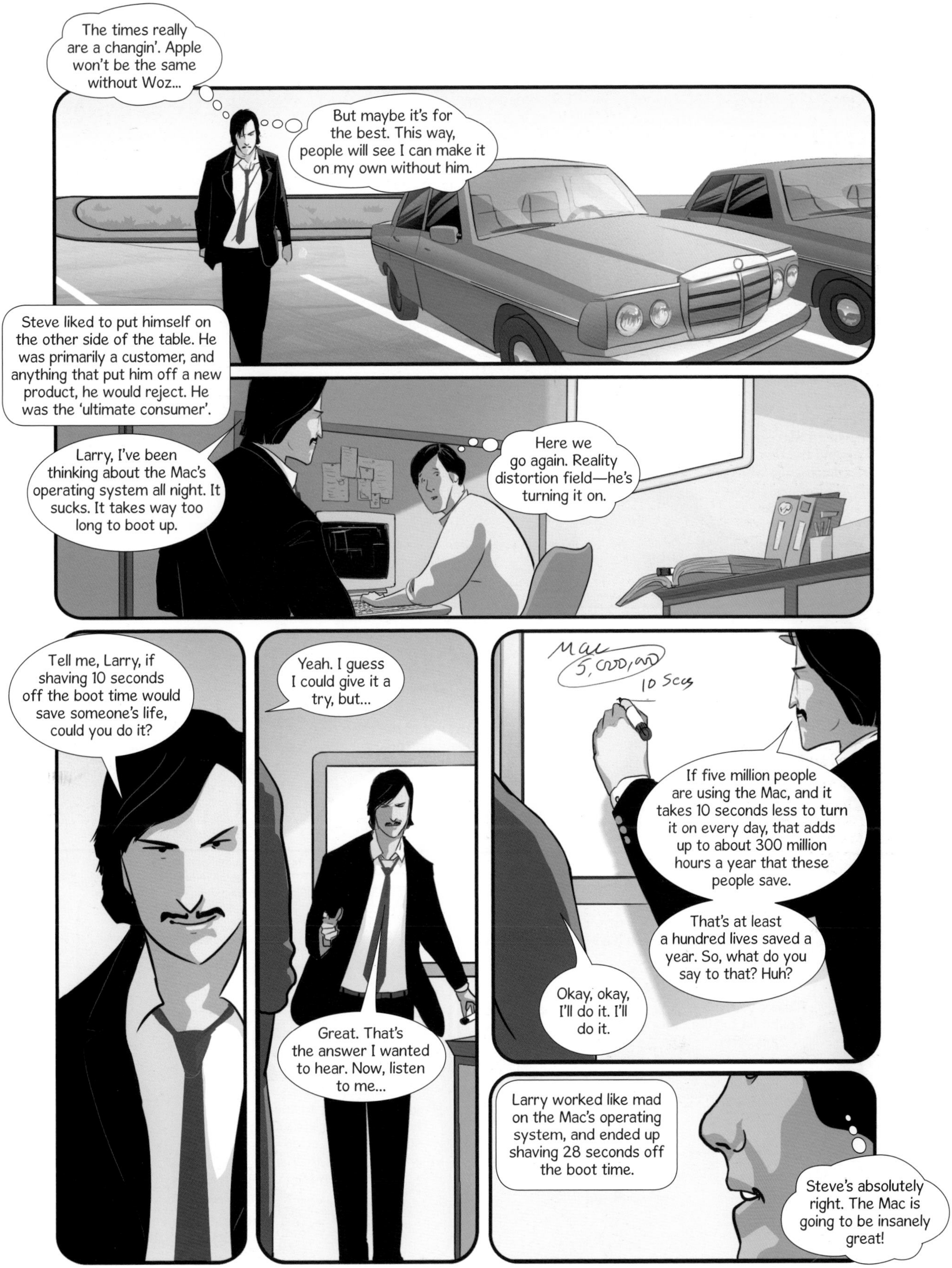

The times really are a changin'. Apple won't be the same without Woz...
But maybe it's for the best. This way, people will see I can make it on my own without him.
Steve liked to put himself on the other side of the table. He was primarily a customer, and anything that put him off a new product, he would reject. He was the 'ultimate consumer'.
Larry, I've been thinking about the Mac's operating system all night. It sucks. It takes way too long to boot up.
Here we go again. Reality distortion field—he's turning it on.
Tell me, Larry, if shaving 10 seconds off the boot time would save someone's life, could you do it?
Yeah. I guess I could give it a try, but...
Great. That's the answer I wanted to hear. Now, listen to me...
Mac
5,000,000
10 Secs
If five million people are using the Mac, and it takes 10 seconds less to turn it on every day, that adds up to about 300 million hours a year that these people save.
That's at least a hundred lives saved a year. So, what do you say to that? Huh?
Okay, okay, I'll do it. I'll do it.
Larry worked like mad on the Mac's operating system, and ended up shaving 28 seconds off the boot time.
Steve's absolutely right. The Mac is going to be insanely great!

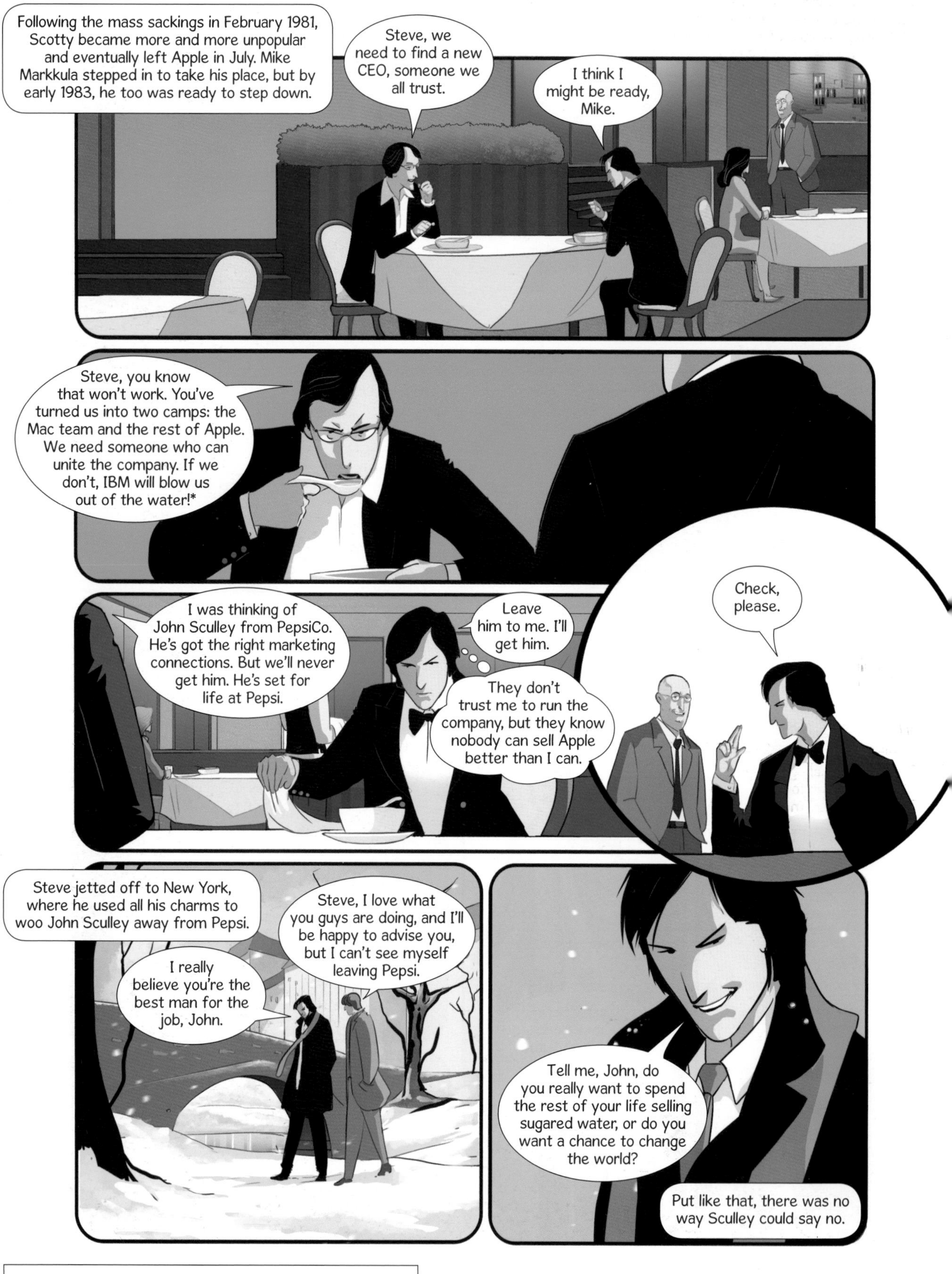
Following the mass sackings in February 1981, Scotty became more and more unpopular and eventually left Apple in July. Mike Markkula stepped in to take his place, but by early 1983, he too was ready to step down.
Steve, we need to find a new CEO, someone we all trust.
I think I might be ready, Mike.
Steve, you know that won't work. You've turned us into two camps: the Mac team and the rest of Apple. We need someone who can unite the company. If we don't, IBM will blow us out of the water!*
I was thinking of John Sculley from PepsiCo. He's got the right marketing connections. But we'll never get him. He's set for life at Pepsi.
Leave him to me. I'll get him.
They don't trust me to run the company, but they know nobody can sell Apple better than I can.
Check, please.
Steve jetted off to New York, where he used all his charms to woo John Sculley away from Pepsi.
I really believe you're the best man for the job, John.
Steve, I love what you guys are doing, and I'll be happy to advise you, but I can't see myself leaving Pepsi.
Tell me, John, do you really want to spend the rest of your life selling sugared water, or do you want a chance to change the world?
Put like that, there was no way Sculley could say no.

*IBM had released their own personal computer in the summer of 1981 and were proving to be fierce competitors.

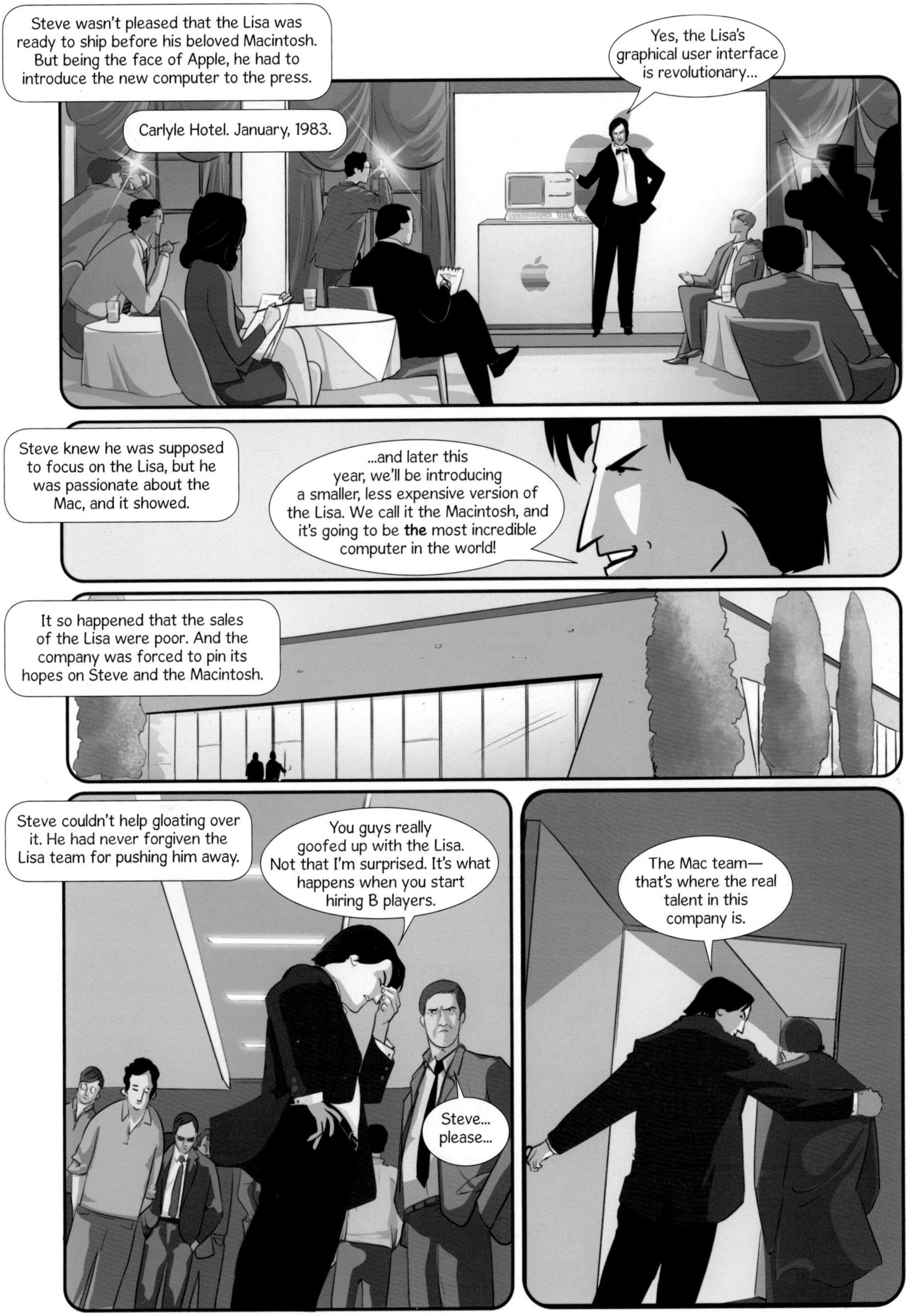
Steve wasn't pleased that the Lisa was ready to ship before his beloved Macintosh. But being the face of Apple, he had to introduce the new computer to the press.
Carlyle Hotel. January, 1983.
Yes, the Lisa's graphical user interface is revolutionary...
Steve knew he was supposed to focus on the Lisa, but he was passionate about the Mac, and it showed.
...and later this year, we'll be introducing a smaller, less expensive version of the Lisa. We call it the Macintosh, and it's going to be **the** most incredible computer in the world!
It so happened that the sales of the Lisa were poor. And the company was forced to pin its hopes on Steve and the Macintosh.
Steve couldn't help gloating over it. He had never forgiven the Lisa team for pushing him away.
You guys really goofed up with the Lisa. Not that I'm surprised. It's what happens when you start hiring B players.
Steve... please...
The Mac team—that's where the real talent in this company is.

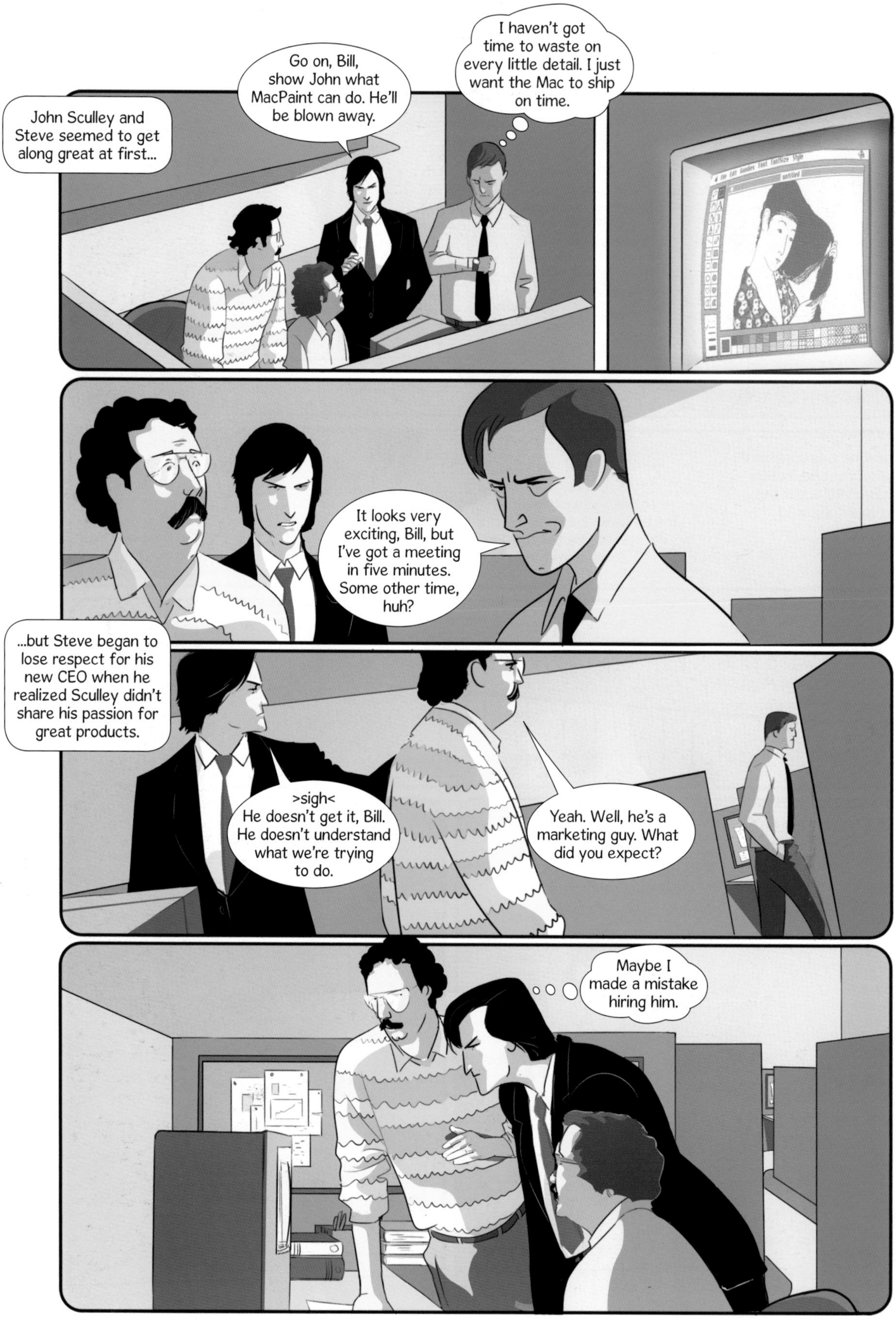
John Sculley and Steve seemed to get along great at first...
Go on, Bill, show John what MacPaint can do. He'll be blown away.
I haven't got time to waste on every little detail. I just want the Mac to ship on time.
It looks very exciting, Bill, but I've got a meeting in five minutes. Some other time, huh?
...but Steve began to lose respect for his new CEO when he realized Sculley didn't share his passion for great products.
>sigh< He doesn't get it, Bill. He doesn't understand what we're trying to do.
Yeah. Well, he's a marketing guy. What did you expect?
Maybe I made a mistake hiring him.

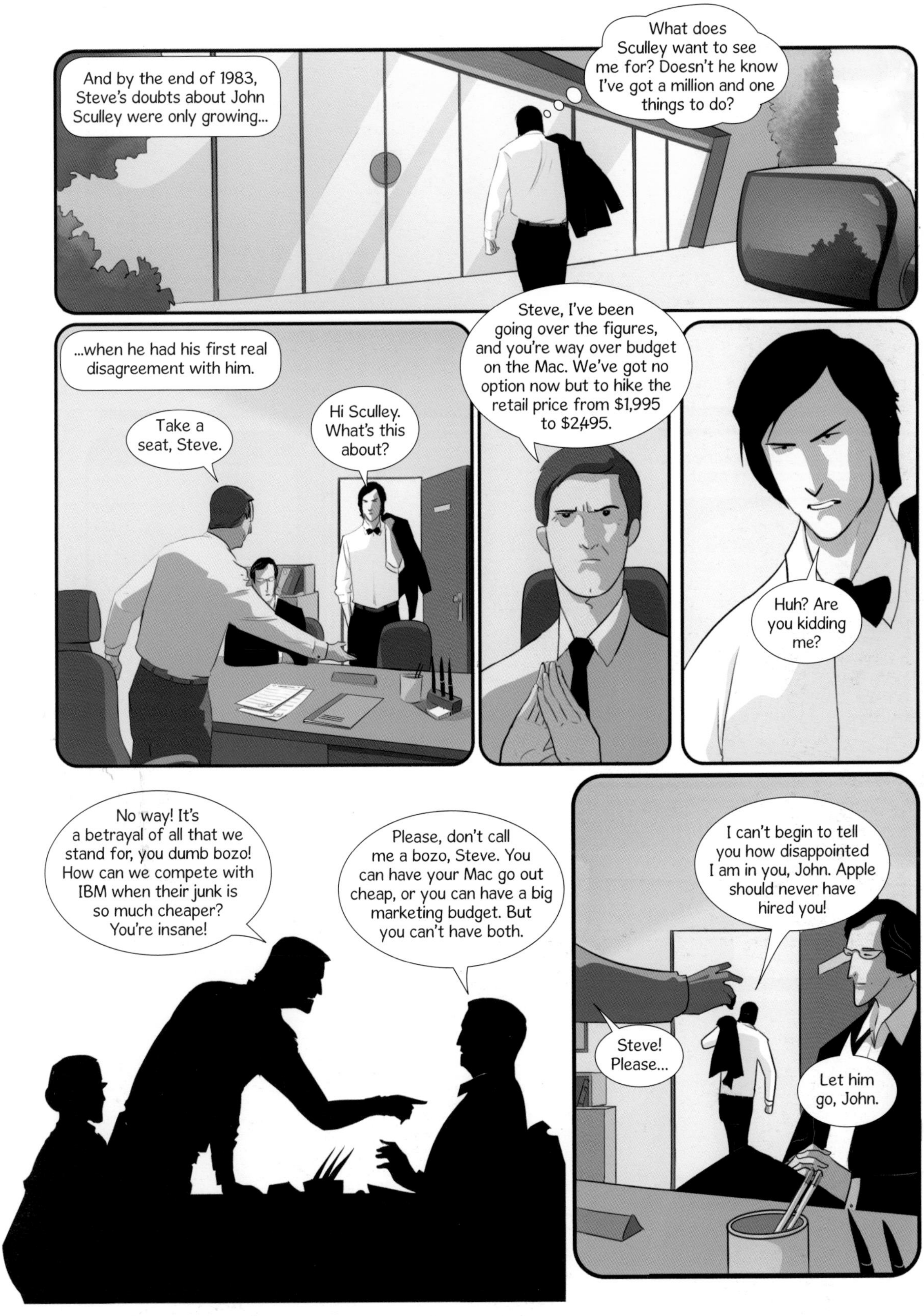
And by the end of 1983, Steve's doubts about John Sculley were only growing...
What does Sculley want to see me for? Doesn't he know I've got a million and one things to do?
...when he had his first real disagreement with him.
Take a seat, Steve.
Hi Sculley. What's this about?
Steve, I've been going over the figures, and you're way over budget on the Mac. We've got no option now but to hike the retail price from $1,995 to $2,495.
Huh? Are you kidding me?
No way! It's a betrayal of all that we stand for, you dumb bozo! How can we compete with IBM when their junk is so much cheaper? You're insane!
Please, don't call me a bozo, Steve. You can have your Mac go out cheap, or you can have a big marketing budget. But you can't have both.
I can't begin to tell you how disappointed I am in you, John. Apple should never have hired you!
Steve! Please...
Let him go, John.

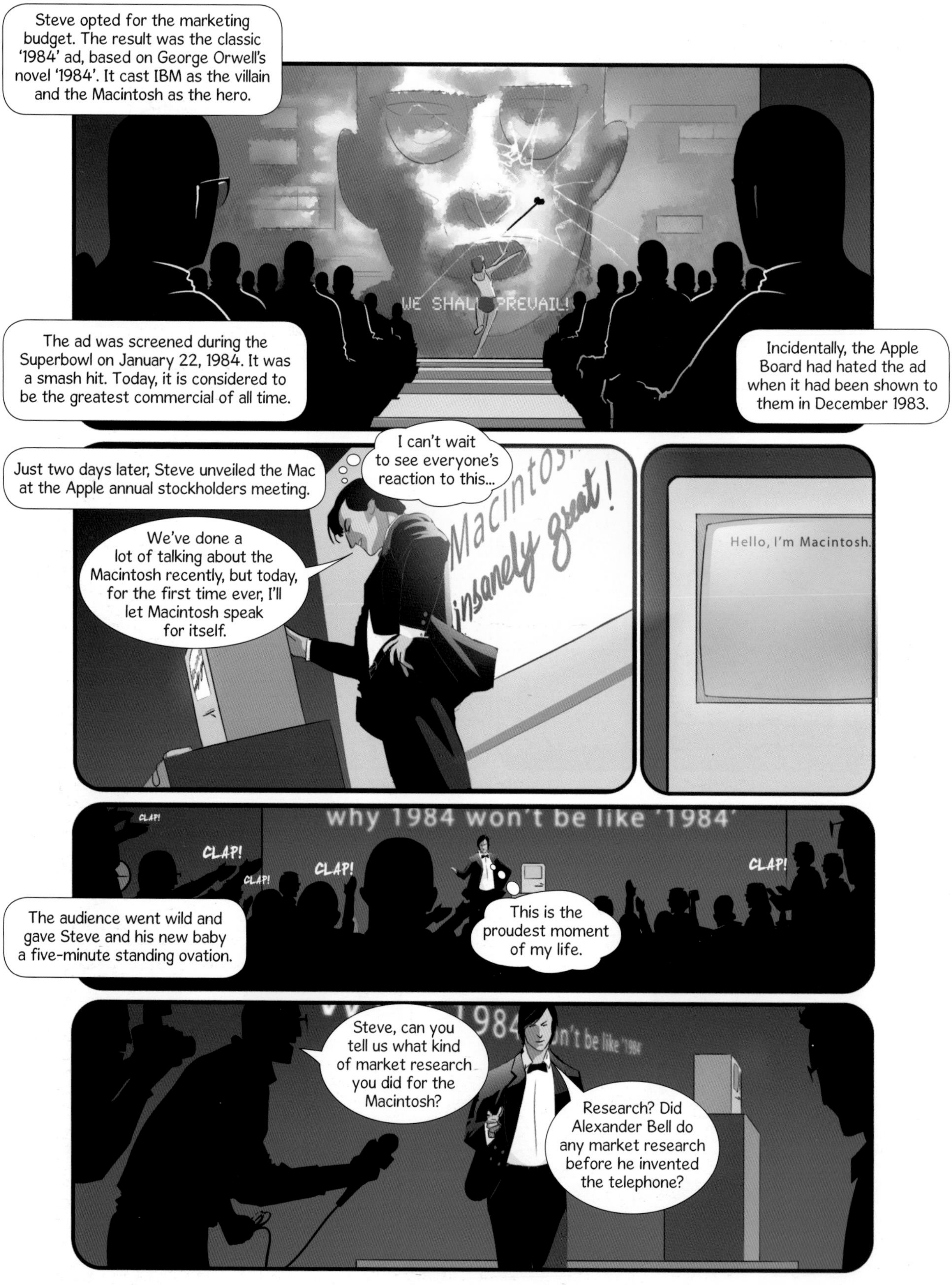
Steve opted for the marketing budget. The result was the classic '1984' ad, based on George Orwell's novel '1984'. It cast IBM as the villain and the Macintosh as the hero.
WE SHAL PREVAIL!
The ad was screened during the Superbowl on January 22, 1984. It was a smash hit. Today, it is considered to be the greatest commercial of all time.
Incidentally, the Apple Board had hated the ad when it had been shown to them in December 1983.
Just two days later, Steve unveiled the Mac at the Apple annual stockholders meeting.
I can't wait to see everyone's reaction to this...
Macintos
insanely great!
We've done a lot of talking about the Macintosh recently, but today, for the first time ever, I'll let Macintosh speak for itself.
Hello, I'm Macintosh.
why 1984 won't be like '1984'
CLAP!
CLAP!
CLAP!
CLAP!
CLAP!
The audience went wild and gave Steve and his new baby a five-minute standing ovation.
This is the proudest moment of my life.
Steve, can you tell us what kind of market research you did for the Macintosh?
Research? Did Alexander Bell do any market research before he invented the telephone?

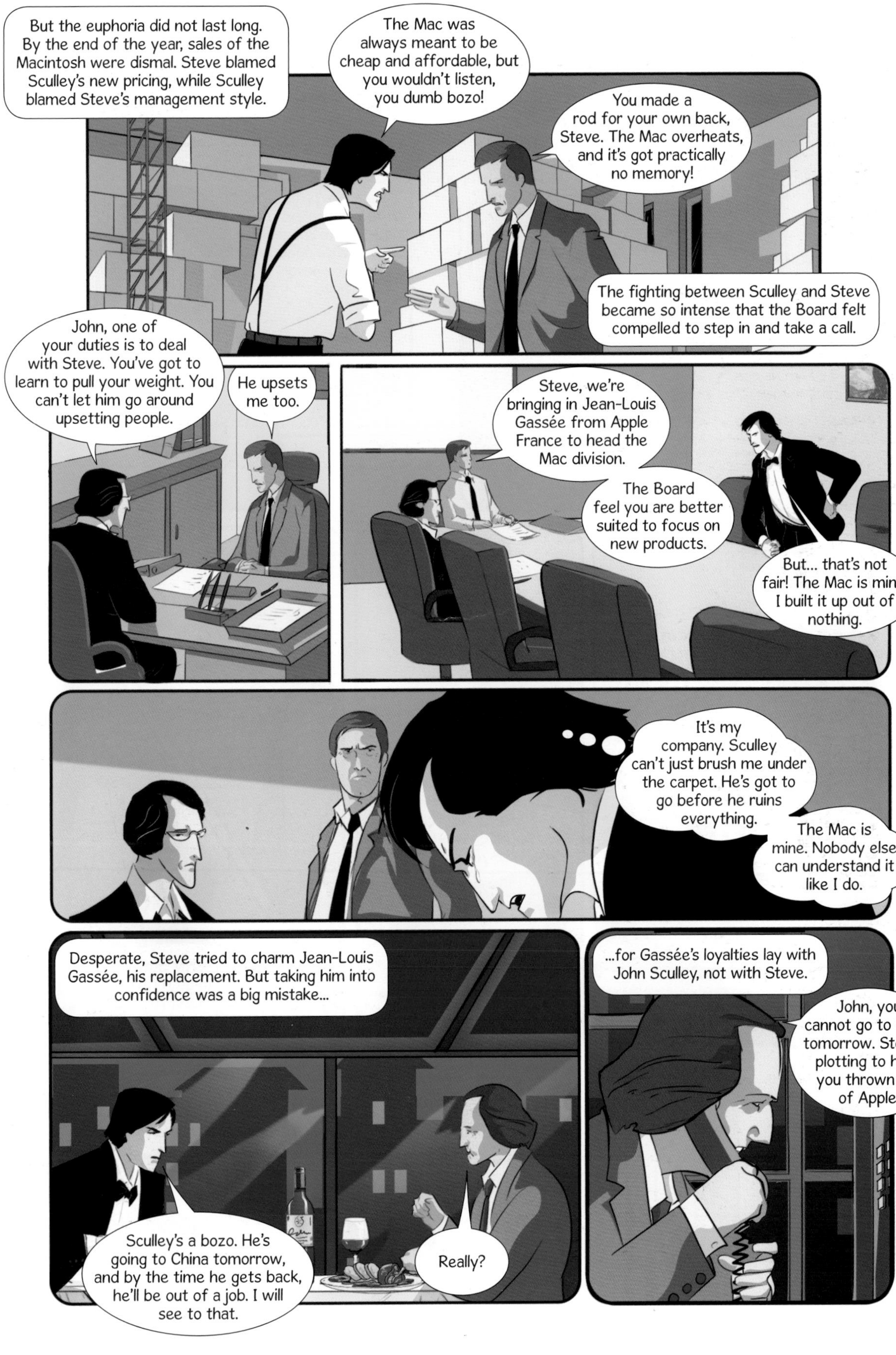
But the euphoria did not last long. By the end of the year, sales of the Macintosh were dismal. Steve blamed Sculley's new pricing, while Sculley blamed Steve's management style.
The Mac was always meant to be cheap and affordable, but you wouldn't listen, you dumb bozo!
You made a rod for your own back, Steve. The Mac overheats, and it's got practically no memory!
The fighting between Sculley and Steve became so intense that the Board felt compelled to step in and take a call.
John, one of your duties is to deal with Steve. You've got to learn to pull your weight. You can't let him go around upsetting people.
He upsets me too.
Steve, we're bringing in Jean-Louis Gassée from Apple France to head the Mac division.
The Board feel you are better suited to focus on new products.
But... that's not fair! The Mac is mine! I built it up out of nothing.
It's my company. Sculley can't just brush me under the carpet. He's got to go before he ruins everything.
The Mac is mine. Nobody else can understand it like I do.
Desperate, Steve tried to charm Jean-Louis Gassée, his replacement. But taking him into confidence was a big mistake...
Sculley's a bozo. He's going to China tomorrow, and by the time he gets back, he'll be out of a job. I will see to that.
Really?
...for Gassée's loyalties lay with John Sculley, not with Steve.
John, you cannot go to China tomorrow. Steve is plotting to have you thrown out of Apple.

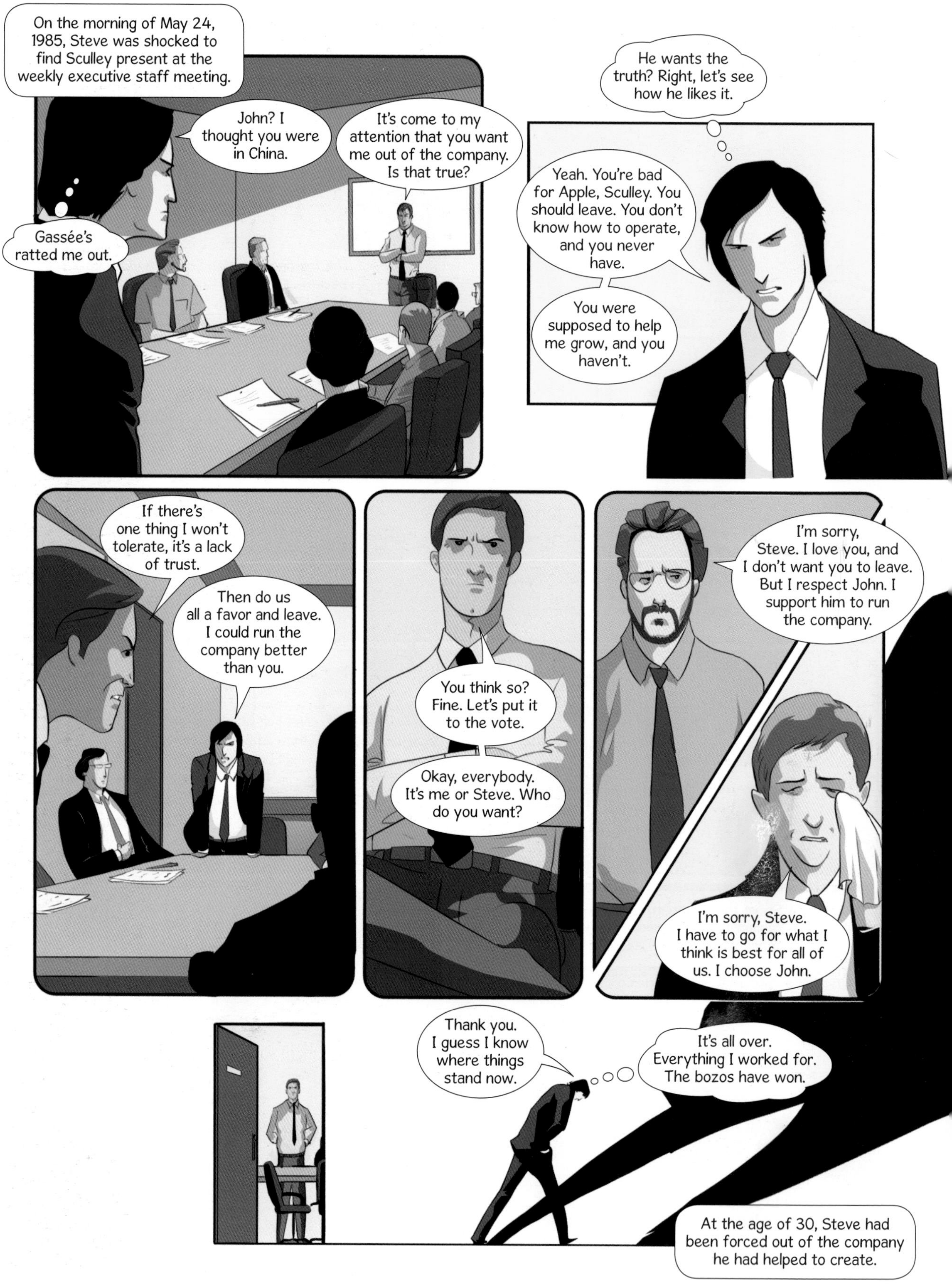

On the morning of May 24, 1985, Steve was shocked to find Sculley present at the weekly executive staff meeting.
John? I thought you were in China.
Gassée's ratted me out.
It's come to my attention that you want me out of the company. Is that true?
He wants the truth? Right, let's see how he likes it.
Yeah. You're bad for Apple, Sculley. You should leave. You don't know how to operate, and you never have.
You were supposed to help me grow, and you haven't.
If there's one thing I won't tolerate, it's a lack of trust.
Then do us all a favor and leave. I could run the company better than you.
You think so? Fine. Let's put it to the vote.
Okay, everybody. It's me or Steve. Who do you want?
I'm sorry, Steve. I love you, and I don't want you to leave. But I respect John. I support him to run the company.
I'm sorry, Steve. I have to go for what I think is best for all of us. I choose John.
Thank you. I guess I know where things stand now.
It's all over. Everything I worked for. The bozos have won.
At the age of 30, Steve had been forced out of the company he had helped to create.

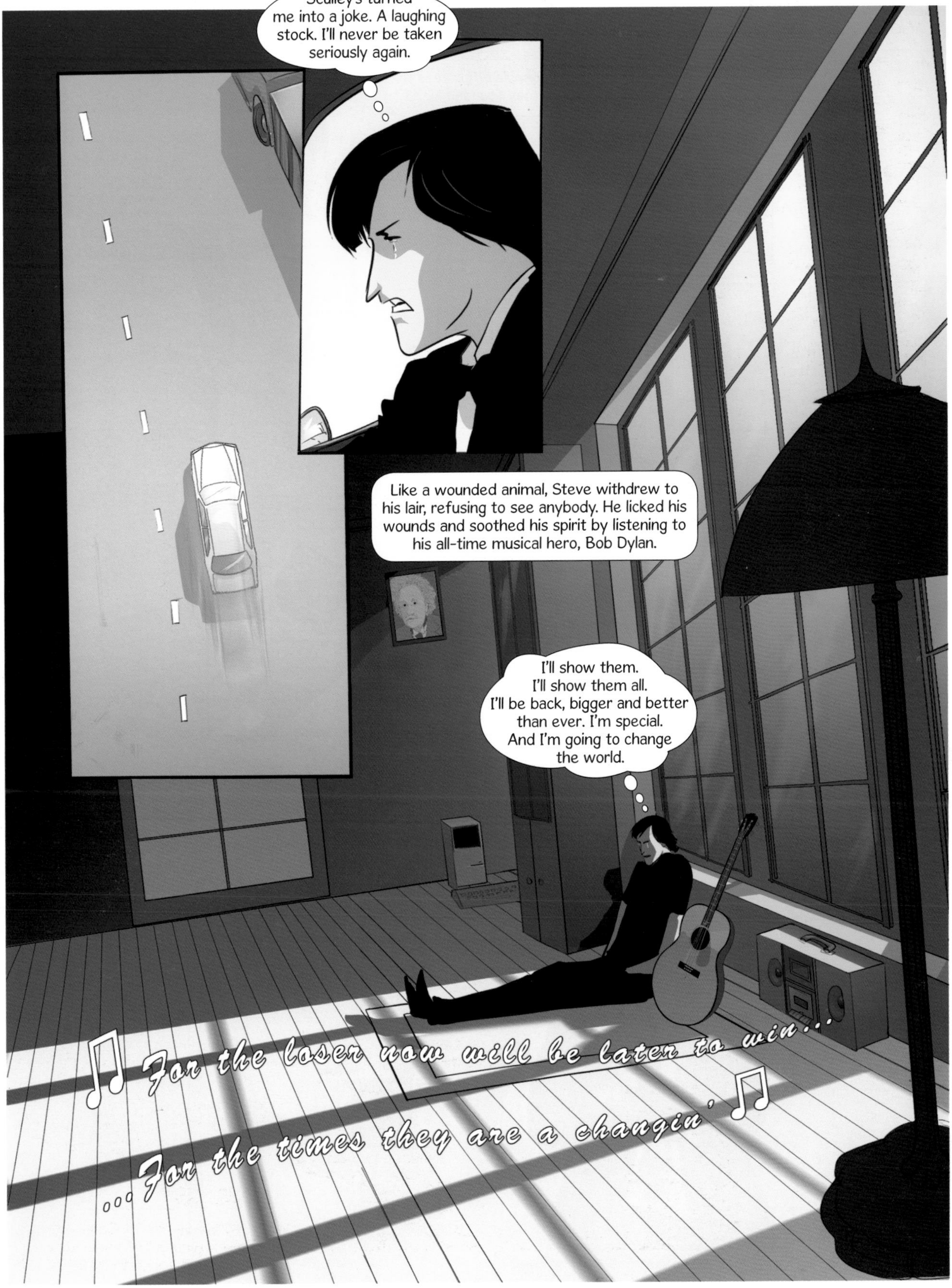

Sculley's turned me into a joke. A laughing stock. I'll never be taken seriously again.
Like a wounded animal, Steve withdrew to his lair, refusing to see anybody. He licked his wounds and soothed his spirit by listening to his all-time musical hero, Bob Dylan.
I'll show them. I'll show them all. I'll be back, bigger and better than ever. I'm special. And I'm going to change the world.
For the loser now will be later to win...
...For the times they are a changin'

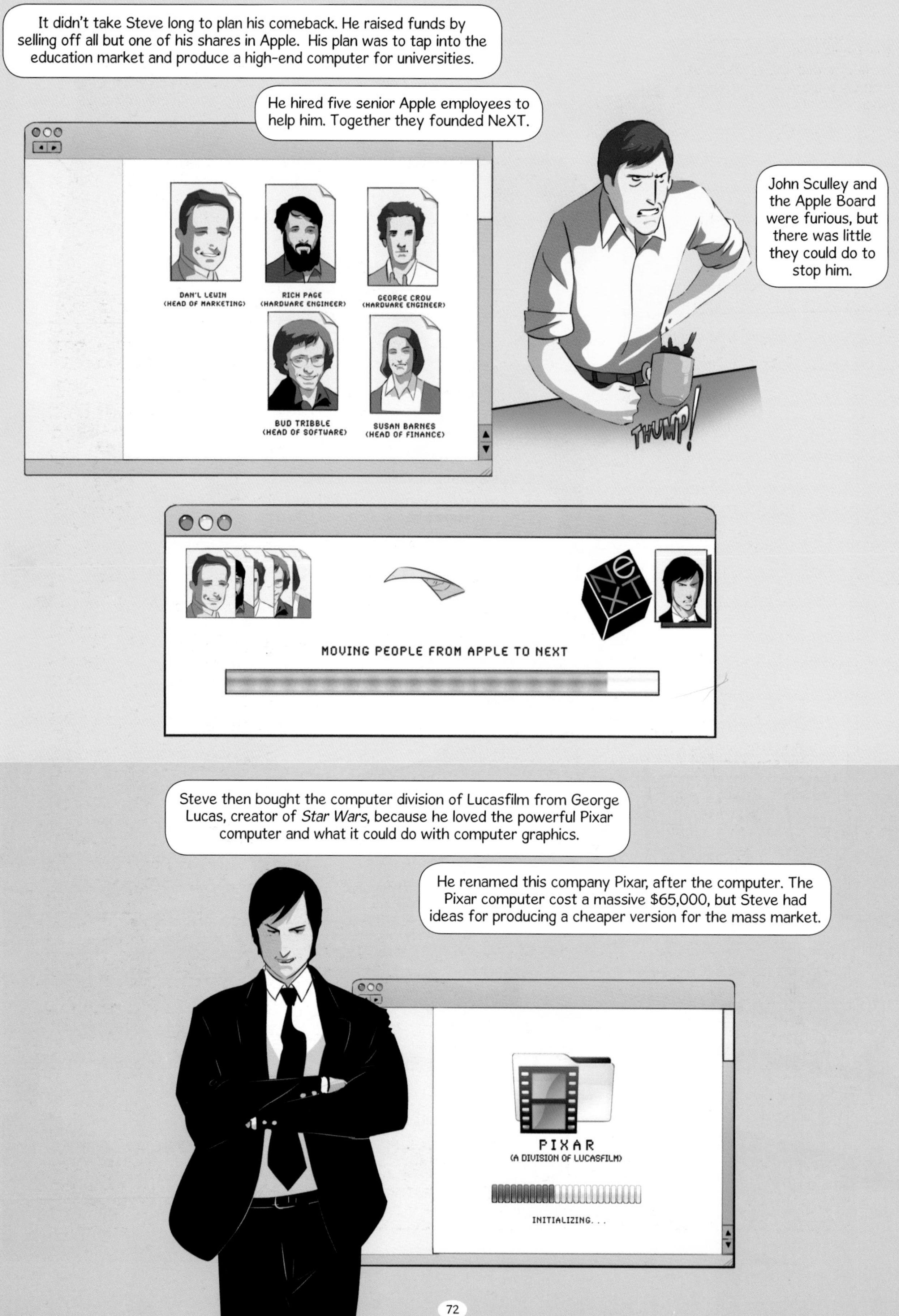

It didn't take Steve long to plan his comeback. He raised funds by selling off all but one of his shares in Apple. His plan was to tap into the education market and produce a high-end computer for universities.
He hired five senior Apple employees to help him. Together they founded NeXT.
DAN'L LEWIN (HEAD OF MARKETING)
RICH PAGE (HARDWARE ENGINEER)
GEORGE CROW (HARDWARE ENGINEER)
BUD TRIBBLE (HEAD OF SOFTWARE)
SUSAN BARNES (HEAD OF FINANCE)
John Sculley and the Apple Board were furious, but there was little they could do to stop him.
THUMP!
MOVING PEOPLE FROM APPLE TO NEXT
Steve then bought the computer division of Lucasfilm from George Lucas, creator of *Star Wars*, because he loved the powerful Pixar computer and what it could do with computer graphics.
He renamed this company Pixar, after the computer. The Pixar computer cost a massive $65,000, but Steve had ideas for producing a cheaper version for the mass market.
PIXAR
(A DIVISION OF LUCASFILM)
INITIALIZING. . .

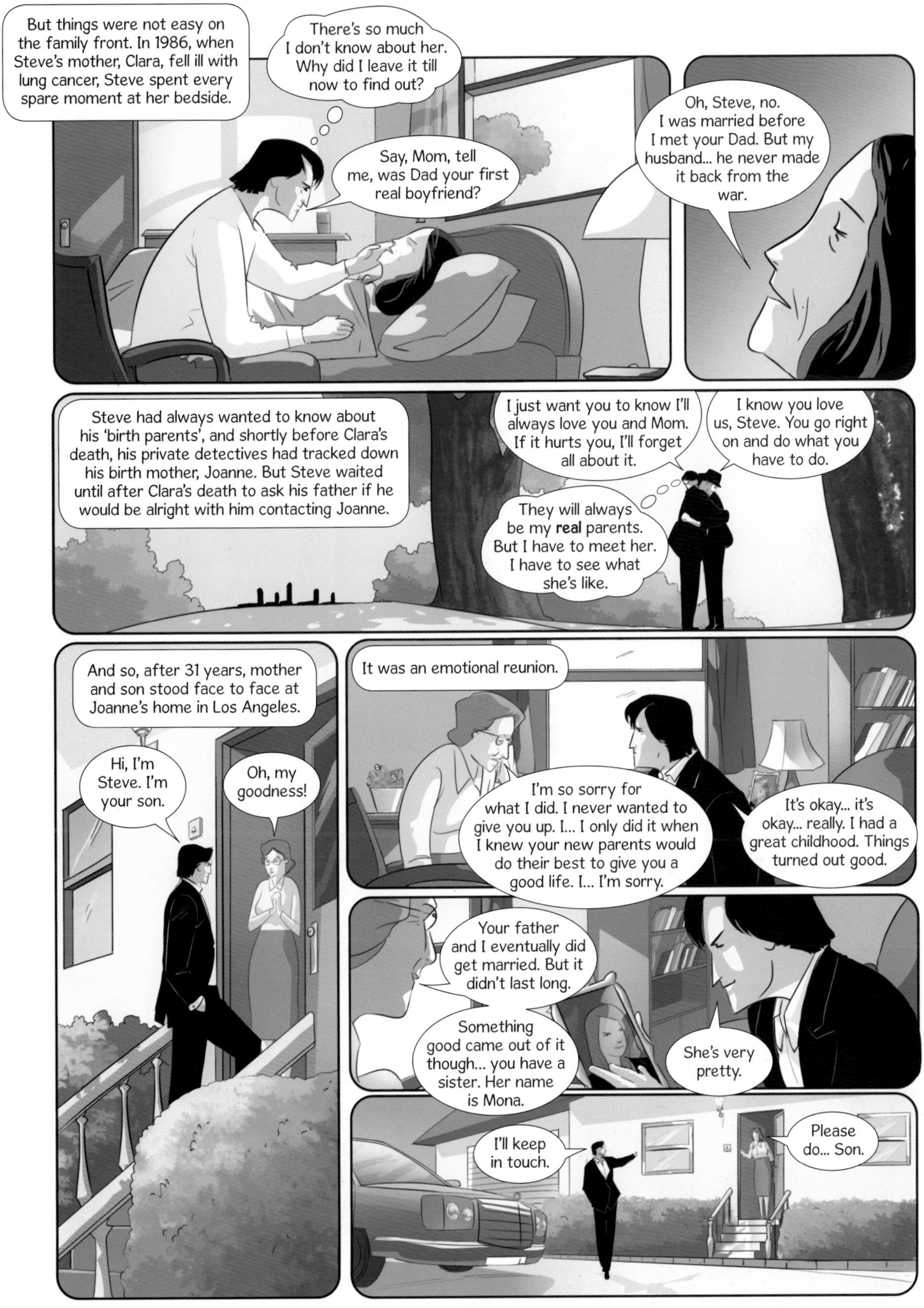

But things were not easy on the family front. In 1986, when Steve's mother, Clara, fell ill with lung cancer, Steve spent every spare moment at her bedside.
There's so much I don't know about her. Why did I leave it till now to find out?
Say, Mom, tell me, was Dad your first real boyfriend?
Oh, Steve, no. I was married before I met your Dad. But my husband... he never made it back from the war.
Steve had always wanted to know about his 'birth parents', and shortly before Clara's death, his private detectives had tracked down his birth mother, Joanne. But Steve waited until after Clara's death to ask his father if he would be alright with him contacting Joanne.
I just want you to know I'll always love you and Mom. If it hurts you, I'll forget all about it.
I know you love us, Steve. You go right on and do what you have to do.
They will always be my **real** parents. But I have to meet her. I have to see what she's like.
And so, after 31 years, mother and son stood face to face at Joanne's home in Los Angeles.
Hi, I'm Steve. I'm your son.
Oh, my goodness!
It was an emotional reunion.
I'm so sorry for what I did. I never wanted to give you up. I... I only did it when I knew your new parents would do their best to give you a good life. I... I'm sorry.
It's okay... it's okay... really. I had a great childhood. Things turned out good.
Your father and I eventually did get married. But it didn't last long.
Something good came out of it though... you have a sister. Her name is Mona.
She's very pretty.
I'll keep in touch.
Please do... Son.

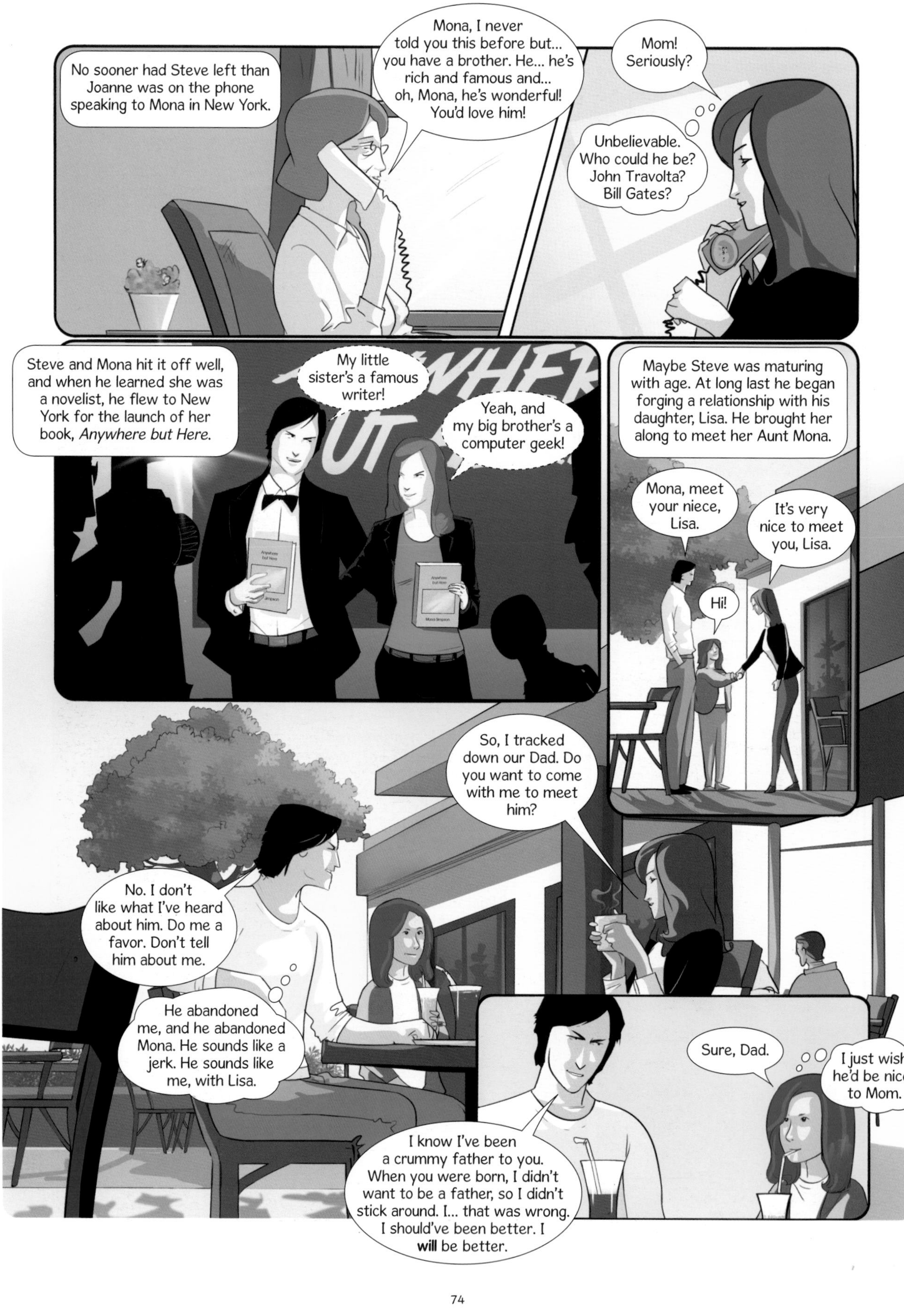
No sooner had Steve left than Joanne was on the phone speaking to Mona in New York.
Mona, I never told you this before but... you have a brother. He... he's rich and famous and... oh, Mona, he's wonderful! You'd love him!
Mom! Seriously?
Unbelievable. Who could he be? John Travolta? Bill Gates?
Steve and Mona hit it off well, and when he learned she was a novelist, he flew to New York for the launch of her book, *Anywhere but Here*.
My little sister's a famous writer!
Yeah, and my big brother's a computer geek!
Maybe Steve was maturing with age. At long last he began forging a relationship with his daughter, Lisa. He brought her along to meet her Aunt Mona.
Mona, meet your niece, Lisa.
It's very nice to meet you, Lisa.
Hi!
So, I tracked down our Dad. Do you want to come with me to meet him?
No. I don't like what I've heard about him. Do me a favor. Don't tell him about me.
He abandoned me, and he abandoned Mona. He sounds like a jerk. He sounds like me, with Lisa.
Sure, Dad.
I just wish he'd be nicer to Mom.
I know I've been a crummy father to you. When you were born, I didn't want to be a father, so I didn't stick around. I... that was wrong. I should've been better. I **will** be better.

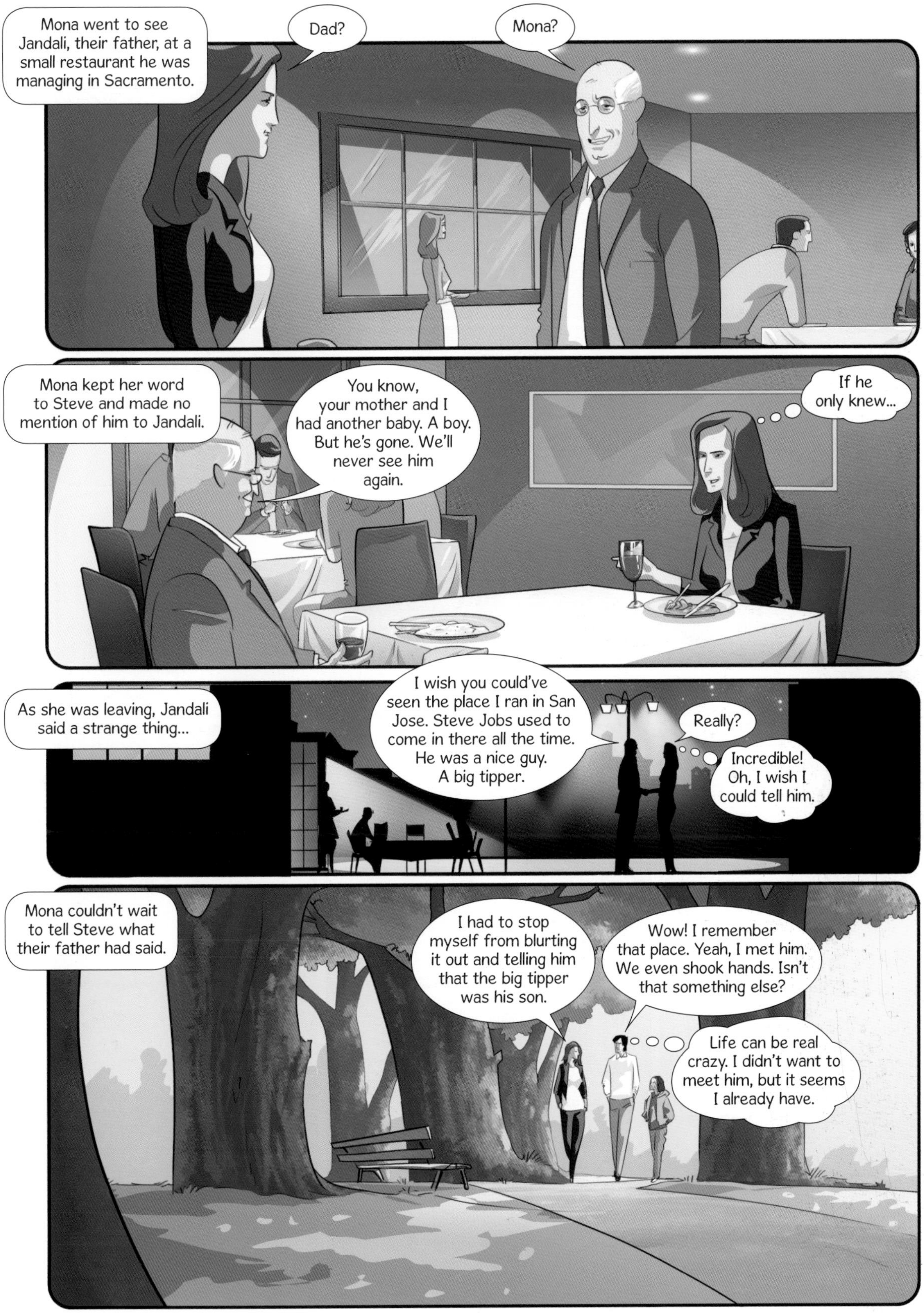
Mona went to see Jandali, their father, at a small restaurant he was managing in Sacramento.
Dad?
Mona?
Mona kept her word to Steve and made no mention of him to Jandali.
You know, your mother and I had another baby. A boy. But he's gone. We'll never see him again.
If he only knew...
As she was leaving, Jandali said a strange thing...
I wish you could've seen the place I ran in San Jose. Steve Jobs used to come in there all the time. He was a nice guy. A big tipper.
Really?
Incredible! Oh, I wish I could tell him.
Mona couldn't wait to tell Steve what their father had said.
I had to stop myself from blurting it out and telling him that the big tipper was his son.
Wow! I remember that place. Yeah, I met him. We even shook hands. Isn't that something else?
Life can be real crazy. I didn't want to meet him, but it seems I already have.

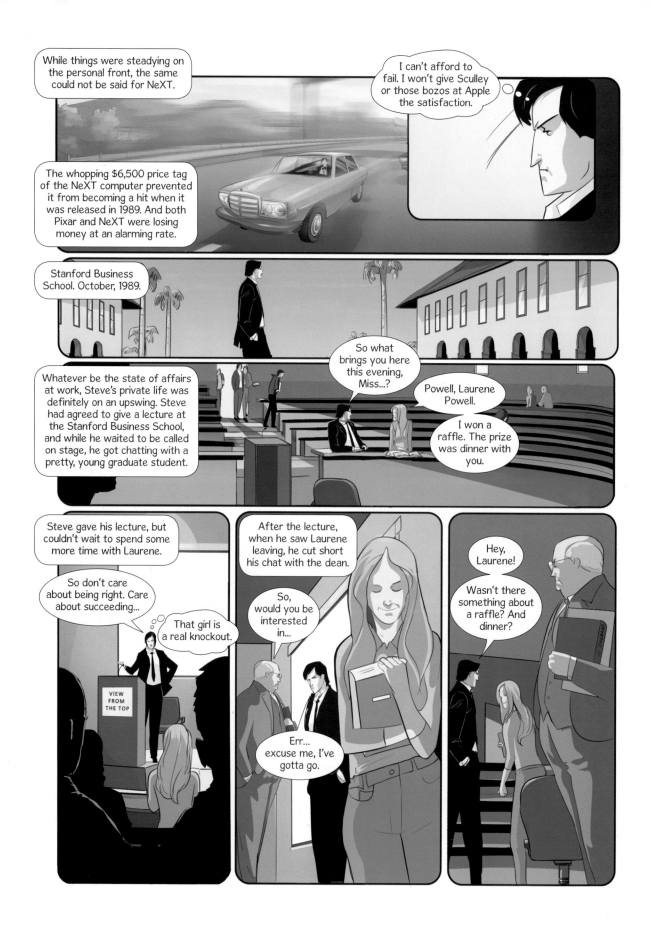

While things were steadying on the personal front, the same could not be said for NeXT.

I can't afford to fail. I won't give Sculley or those bozos at Apple the satisfaction.

The whopping $6,500 price tag of the NeXT computer prevented it from becoming a hit when it was released in 1989. And both Pixar and NeXT were losing money at an alarming rate.

Stanford Business School. October, 1989.

Whatever be the state of affairs at work, Steve's private life was definitely on an upswing. Steve had agreed to give a lecture at the Stanford Business School, and while he waited to be called on stage, he got chatting with a pretty, young graduate student.

So what brings you here this evening, Miss...?

Powell, Laurene Powell.

I won a raffle. The prize was dinner with you.

Steve gave his lecture, but couldn't wait to spend some more time with Laurene.

So don't care about being right. Care about succeeding...

That girl is a real knockout.

VIEW FROM THE TOP

After the lecture, when he saw Laurene leaving, he cut short his chat with the dean.

So, would you be interested in...

Err... excuse me, I've gotta go.

Hey, Laurene! Wasn't there something about a raffle? And dinner?

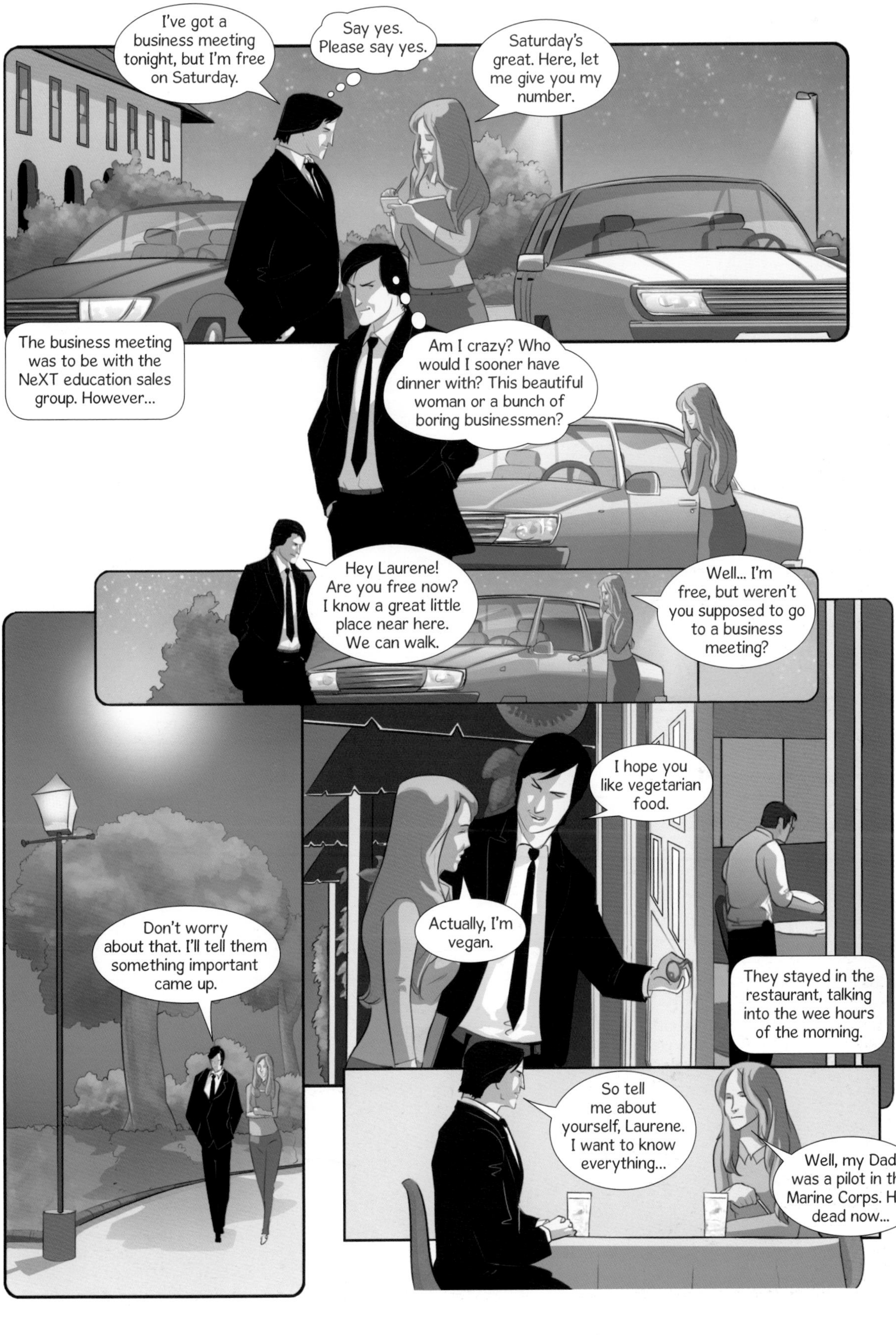
I've got a business meeting tonight, but I'm free on Saturday.
Say yes. Please say yes.
Saturday's great. Here, let me give you my number.
The business meeting was to be with the NeXT education sales group. However...
Am I crazy? Who would I sooner have dinner with? This beautiful woman or a bunch of boring businessmen?
Hey Laurene! Are you free now? I know a great little place near here. We can walk.
Well... I'm free, but weren't you supposed to go to a business meeting?
Don't worry about that. I'll tell them something important came up.
I hope you like vegetarian food.
Actually, I'm vegan.
They stayed in the restaurant, talking into the wee hours of the morning.
So tell me about yourself, Laurene. I want to know everything...
Well, my Dad was a pilot in the Marine Corps. He's dead now...

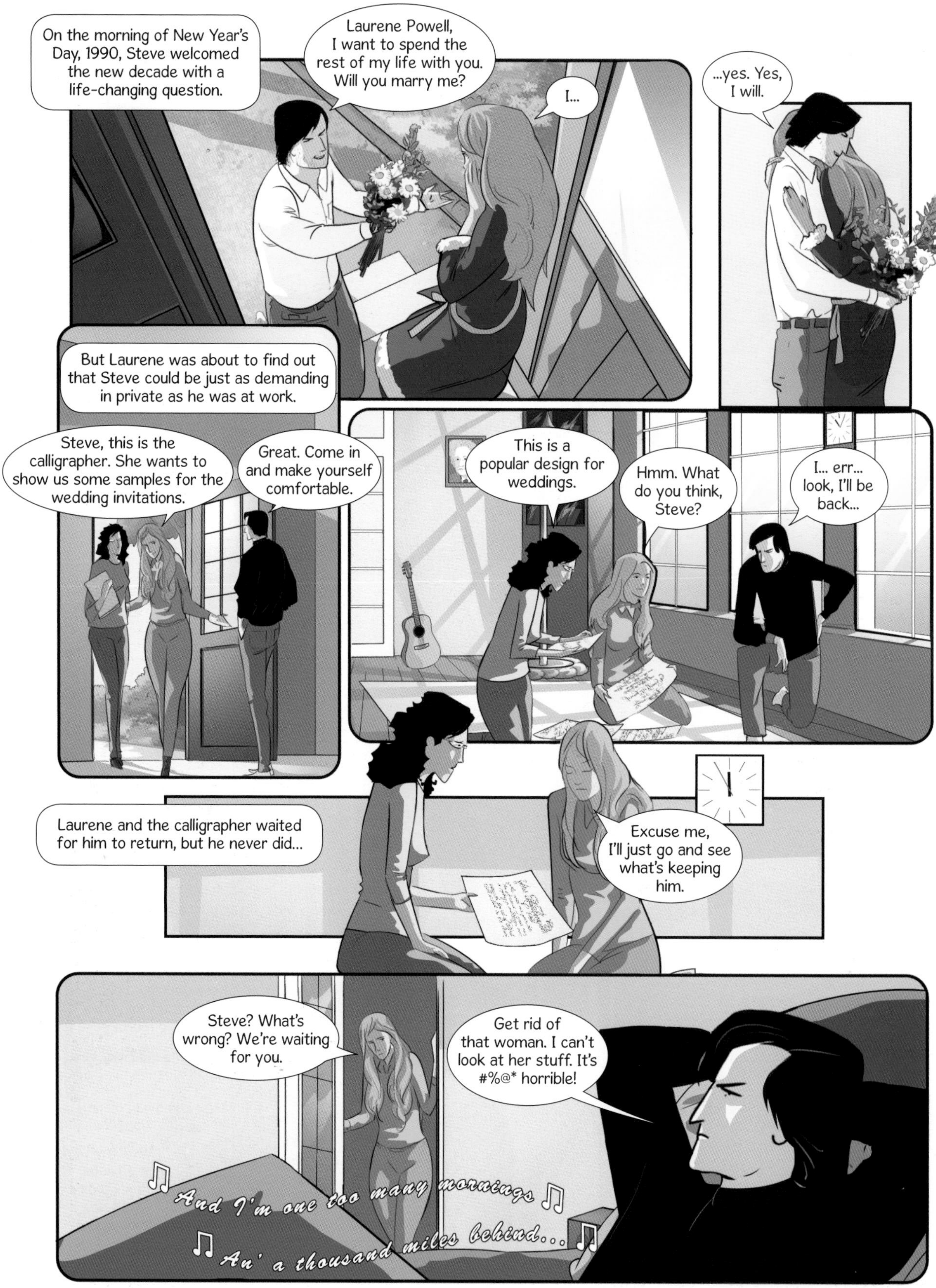
On the morning of New Year's Day, 1990, Steve welcomed the new decade with a life-changing question.
Laurene Powell, I want to spend the rest of my life with you. Will you marry me?
I...
...yes. Yes, I will.
But Laurene was about to find out that Steve could be just as demanding in private as he was at work.
Steve, this is the calligrapher. She wants to show us some samples for the wedding invitations.
Great. Come in and make yourself comfortable.
This is a popular design for weddings.
Hmm. What do you think, Steve?
I... err... look, I'll be back...
Laurene and the calligrapher waited for him to return, but he never did...
Excuse me, I'll just go and see what's keeping him.
Steve? What's wrong? We're waiting for you.
Get rid of that woman. I can't look at her stuff. It's #%@* horrible!
♫ And I'm one too many mornings ♫
♫ An' a thousand miles behind... ♫

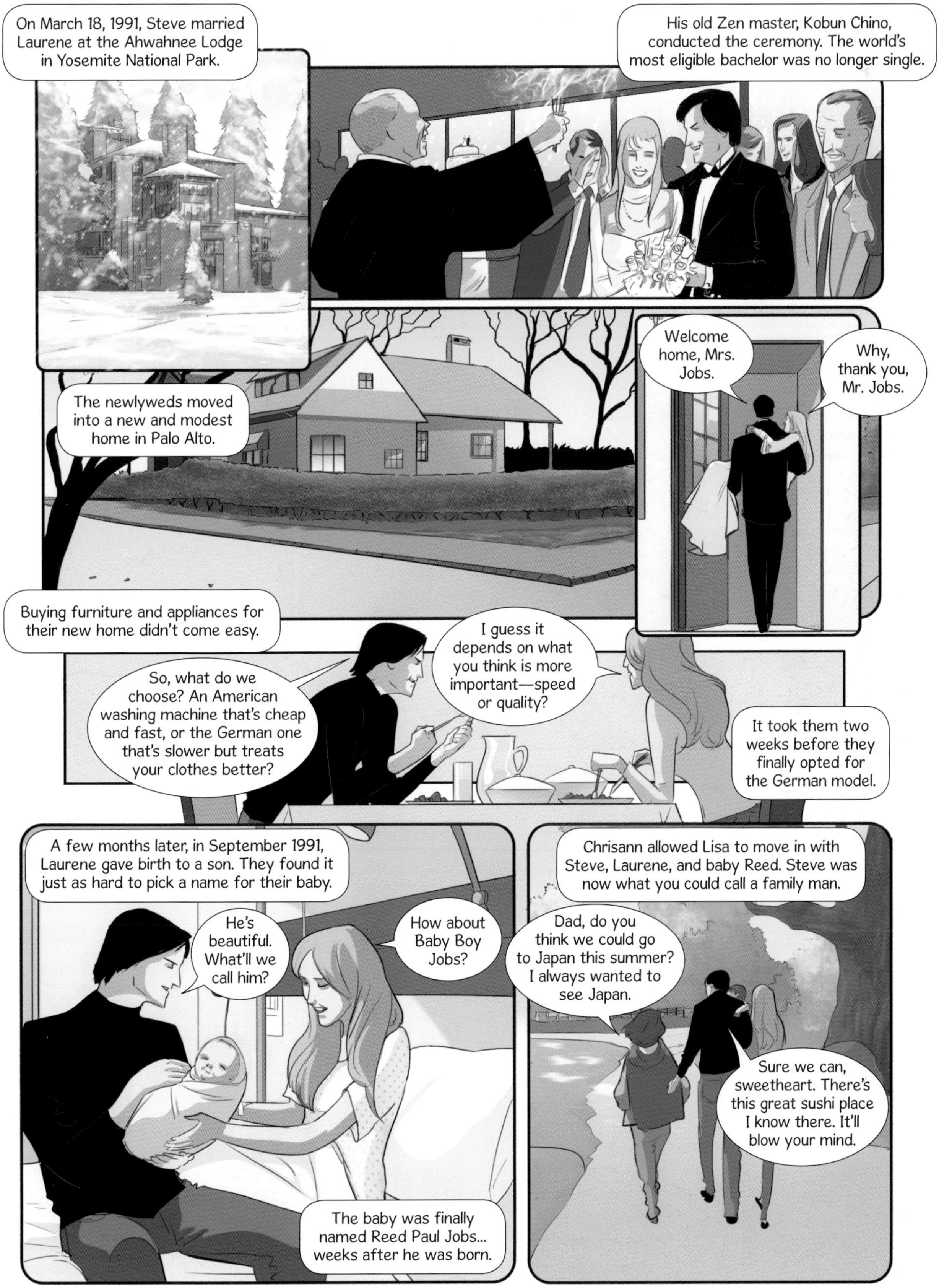
On March 18, 1991, Steve married Laurene at the Ahwahnee Lodge in Yosemite National Park.
His old Zen master, Kobun Chino, conducted the ceremony. The world's most eligible bachelor was no longer single.
The newlyweds moved into a new and modest home in Palo Alto.
Welcome home, Mrs. Jobs.
Why, thank you, Mr. Jobs.
Buying furniture and appliances for their new home didn't come easy.
So, what do we choose? An American washing machine that's cheap and fast, or the German one that's slower but treats your clothes better?
I guess it depends on what you think is more important—speed or quality?
It took them two weeks before they finally opted for the German model.
A few months later, in September 1991, Laurene gave birth to a son. They found it just as hard to pick a name for their baby.
He's beautiful. What'll we call him?
How about Baby Boy Jobs?
The baby was finally named Reed Paul Jobs... weeks after he was born.
Chrisann allowed Lisa to move in with Steve, Laurene, and baby Reed. Steve was now what you could call a family man.
Dad, do you think we could go to Japan this summer? I always wanted to see Japan.
Sure we can, sweetheart. There's this great sushi place I know there. It'll blow your mind.

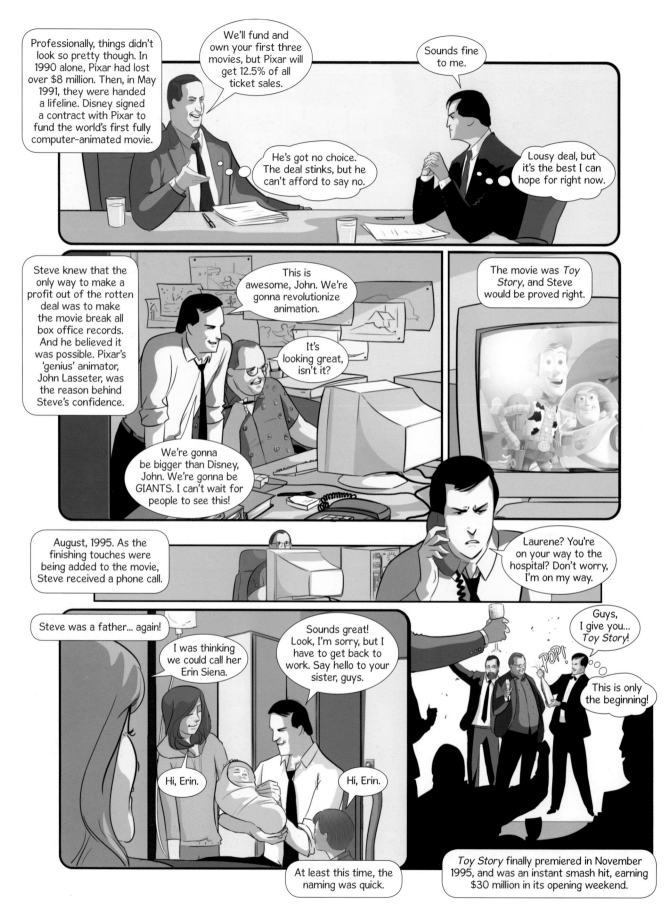

Professionally, things didn't look so pretty though. In 1990 alone, Pixar had lost over $8 million. Then, in May 1991, they were handed a lifeline. Disney signed a contract with Pixar to fund the world's first fully computer-animated movie.

We'll fund and own your first three movies, but Pixar will get 12.5% of all ticket sales.

Sounds fine to me.

He's got no choice. The deal stinks, but he can't afford to say no.

Lousy deal, but it's the best I can hope for right now.

Steve knew that the only way to make a profit out of the rotten deal was to make the movie break all box office records. And he believed it was possible. Pixar's 'genius' animator, John Lasseter, was the reason behind Steve's confidence.

This is awesome, John. We're gonna revolutionize animation.

It's looking great, isn't it?

We're gonna be bigger than Disney, John. We're gonna be GIANTS. I can't wait for people to see this!

The movie was Toy Story, and Steve would be proved right.

August, 1995. As the finishing touches were being added to the movie, Steve received a phone call.

Laurene? You're on your way to the hospital? Don't worry, I'm on my way.

Steve was a father... again!

I was thinking we could call her Erin Siena.

Sounds great! Look, I'm sorry, but I have to get back to work. Say hello to your sister, guys.

Hi, Erin.

Hi, Erin.

At least this time, the naming was quick.

Guys, I give you... Toy Story!

POP!

This is only the beginning!

Toy Story finally premiered in November 1995, and was an instant smash hit, earning $30 million in its opening weekend.

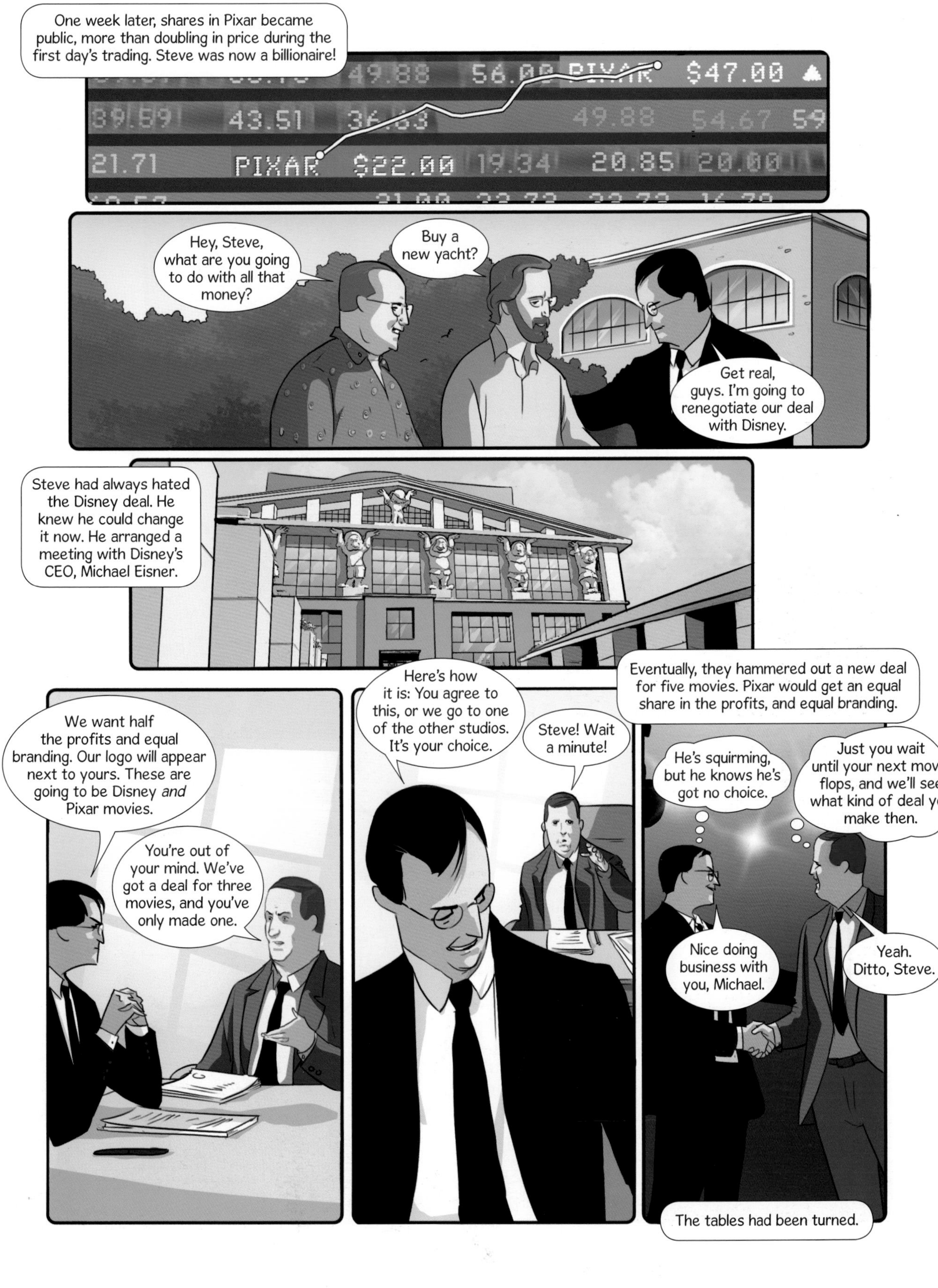

One week later, shares in Pixar became public, more than doubling in price during the first day's trading. Steve was now a billionaire!
49.88 56.00 PIXAR $47.00
43.51 49.88 54.67
21.71 PIXAR $22.00 19.34 20.85 20.00
Hey, Steve, what are you going to do with all that money?
Buy a new yacht?
Get real, guys. I'm going to renegotiate our deal with Disney.
Steve had always hated the Disney deal. He knew he could change it now. He arranged a meeting with Disney's CEO, Michael Eisner.
We want half the profits and equal branding. Our logo will appear next to yours. These are going to be Disney *and* Pixar movies.
You're out of your mind. We've got a deal for three movies, and you've only made one.
Here's how it is: You agree to this, or we go to one of the other studios. It's your choice.
Steve! Wait a minute!
Eventually, they hammered out a new deal for five movies. Pixar would get an equal share in the profits, and equal branding.
He's squirming, but he knows he's got no choice.
Just you wait until your next movie flops, and we'll see what kind of deal you make then.
Nice doing business with you, Michael.
Yeah. Ditto, Steve.
The tables had been turned.

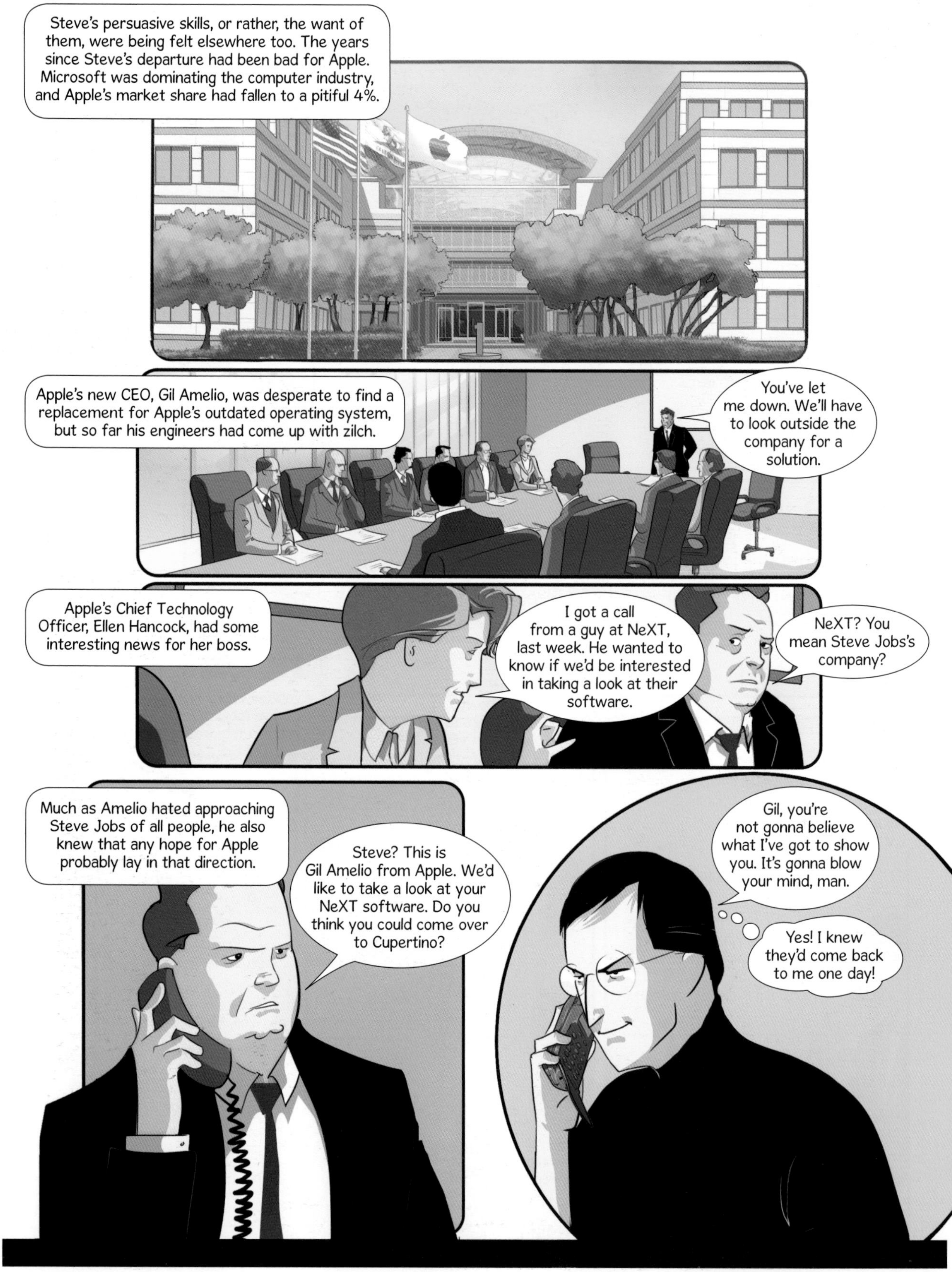
Steve's persuasive skills, or rather, the want of them, were being felt elsewhere too. The years since Steve's departure had been bad for Apple. Microsoft was dominating the computer industry, and Apple's market share had fallen to a pitiful 4%.
Apple's new CEO, Gil Amelio, was desperate to find a replacement for Apple's outdated operating system, but so far his engineers had come up with zilch.
You've let me down. We'll have to look outside the company for a solution.
Apple's Chief Technology Officer, Ellen Hancock, had some interesting news for her boss.
I got a call from a guy at NeXT, last week. He wanted to know if we'd be interested in taking a look at their software.
NeXT? You mean Steve Jobs's company?
Much as Amelio hated approaching Steve Jobs of all people, he also knew that any hope for Apple probably lay in that direction.
Steve? This is Gil Amelio from Apple. We'd like to take a look at your NeXT software. Do you think you could come over to Cupertino?
Gil, you're not gonna believe what I've got to show you. It's gonna blow your mind, man.
Yes! I knew they'd come back to me one day!

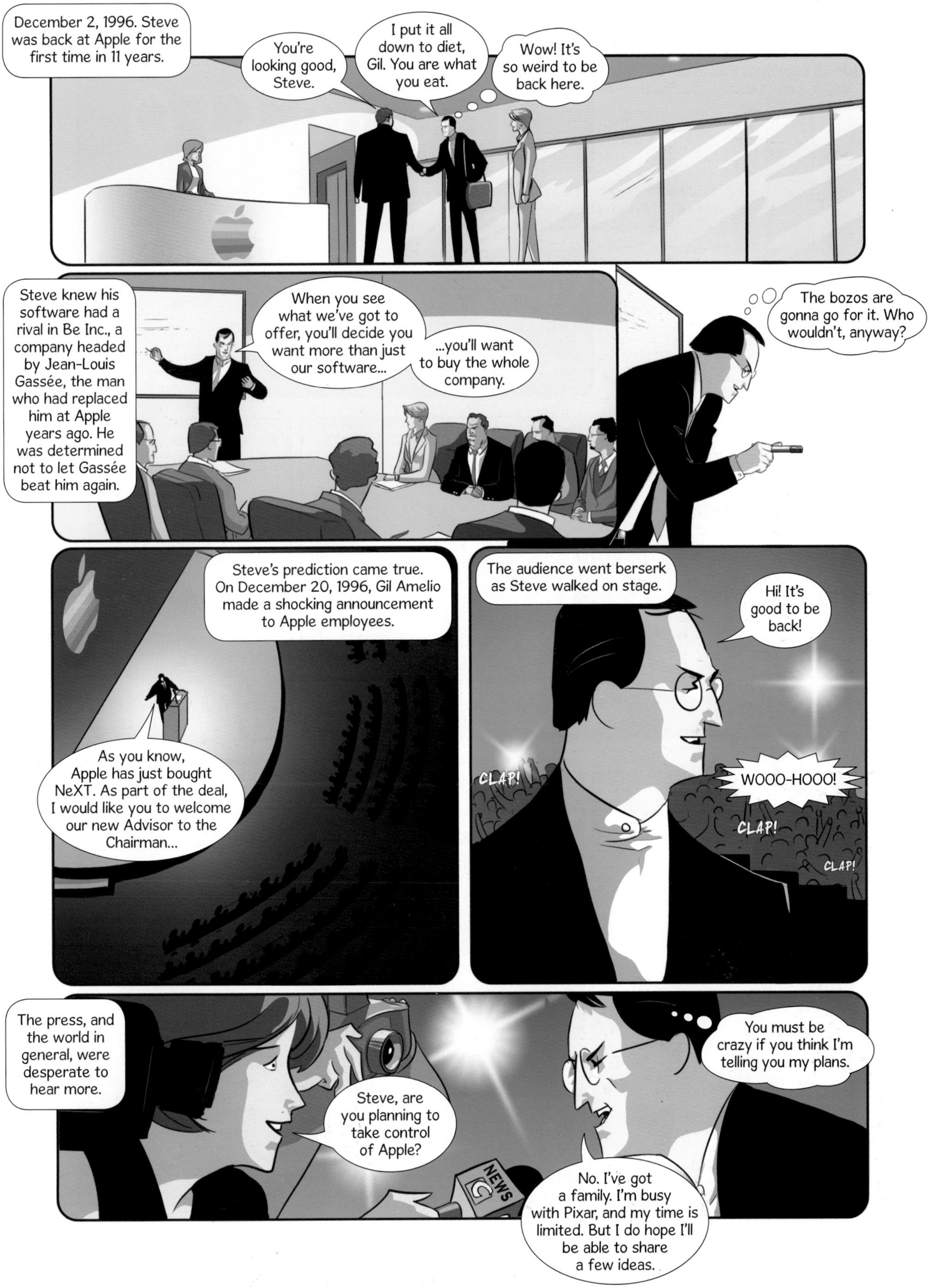
December 2, 1996. Steve was back at Apple for the first time in 11 years.
You're looking good, Steve.
I put it all down to diet, Gil. You are what you eat.
Wow! It's so weird to be back here.
Steve knew his software had a rival in Be Inc., a company headed by Jean-Louis Gassée, the man who had replaced him at Apple years ago. He was determined not to let Gassée beat him again.
When you see what we've got to offer, you'll decide you want more than just our software...
...you'll want to buy the whole company.
The bozos are gonna go for it. Who wouldn't, anyway?
Steve's prediction came true. On December 20, 1996, Gil Amelio made a shocking announcement to Apple employees.
As you know, Apple has just bought NeXT. As part of the deal, I would like you to welcome our new Advisor to the Chairman...
The audience went berserk as Steve walked on stage.
Hi! It's good to be back!
CLAP!
WOOO-HOOO!
CLAP!
CLAP!
The press, and the world in general, were desperate to hear more.
Steve, are you planning to take control of Apple?
You must be crazy if you think I'm telling you my plans.
No. I've got a family. I'm busy with Pixar, and my time is limited. But I do hope I'll be able to share a few ideas.
NEWS

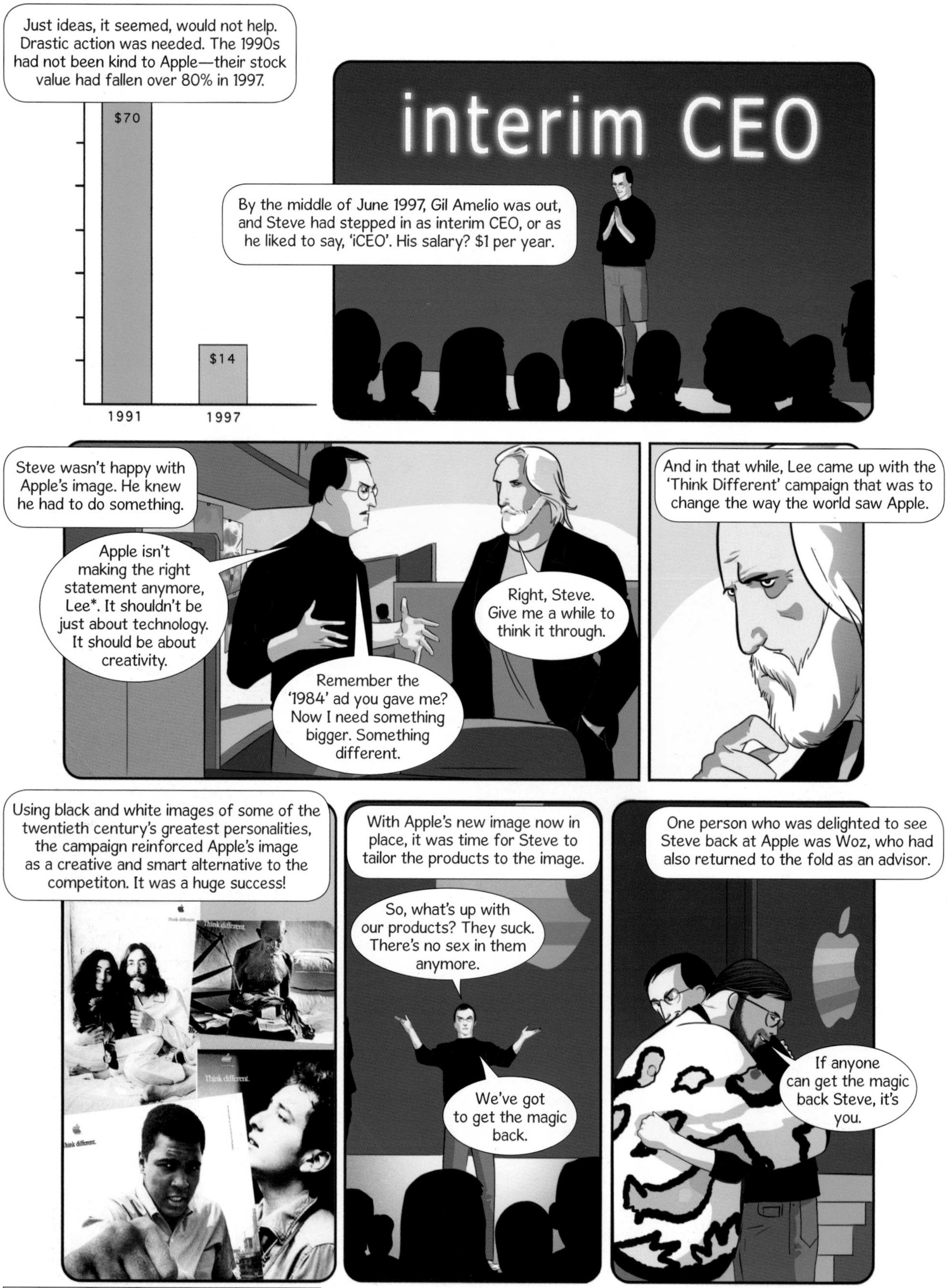
Just ideas, it seemed, would not help. Drastic action was needed. The 1990s had not been kind to Apple—their stock value had fallen over 80% in 1997.
$70
$14
1991
1997
interim CEO
By the middle of June 1997, Gil Amelio was out, and Steve had stepped in as interim CEO, or as he liked to say, 'iCEO'. His salary? $1 per year.
Steve wasn't happy with Apple's image. He knew he had to do something.
Apple isn't making the right statement anymore, Lee*. It shouldn't be just about technology. It should be about creativity.
Remember the '1984' ad you gave me? Now I need something bigger. Something different.
Right, Steve. Give me a while to think it through.
And in that while, Lee came up with the 'Think Different' campaign that was to change the way the world saw Apple.
Using black and white images of some of the twentieth century's greatest personalities, the campaign reinforced Apple's image as a creative and smart alternative to the competiton. It was a huge success!
Think different.
Think different.
With Apple's new image now in place, it was time for Steve to tailor the products to the image.
So, what's up with our products? They suck. There's no sex in them anymore.
We've got to get the magic back.
One person who was delighted to see Steve back at Apple was Woz, who had also returned to the fold as an advisor.
If anyone can get the magic back Steve, it's you.

*An art guru in the world of advertising, Lee Clow is best known for co-creating Apple's '1984' ad and the 'Think Different' slogan.

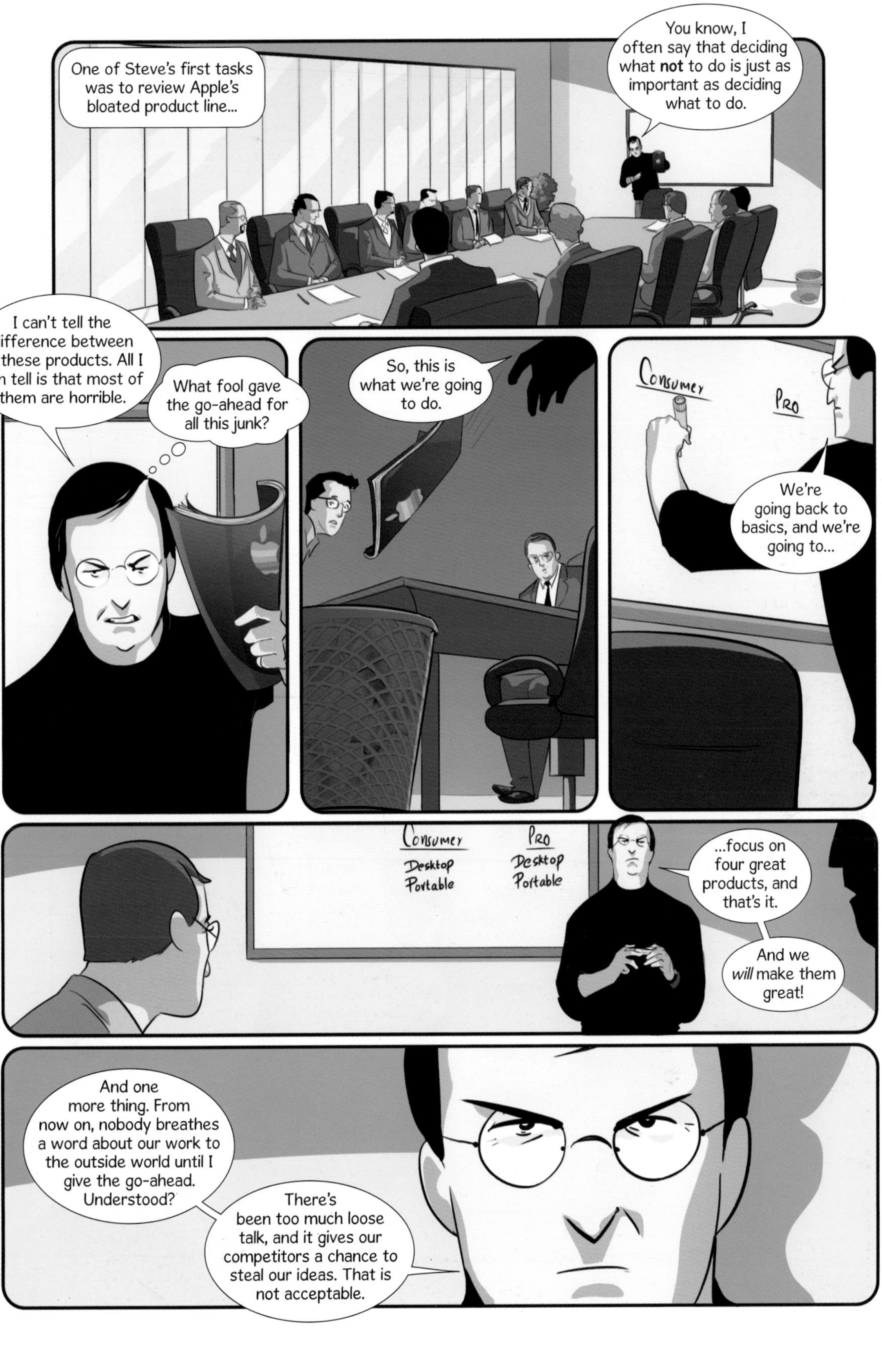
One of Steve's first tasks was to review Apple's bloated product line...
You know, I often say that deciding what **not** to do is just as important as deciding what to do.
I can't tell the difference between all these products. All I can tell is that most of them are horrible.
What fool gave the go-ahead for all this junk?
So, this is what we're going to do.
Consumer
Pro
We're going back to basics, and we're going to...
Consumer
Desktop
Portable
Pro
Desktop
Portable
...focus on four great products, and that's it.
And we *will* make them great!
And one more thing. From now on, nobody breathes a word about our work to the outside world until I give the go-ahead. Understood?
There's been too much loose talk, and it gives our competitors a chance to steal our ideas. That is not acceptable.

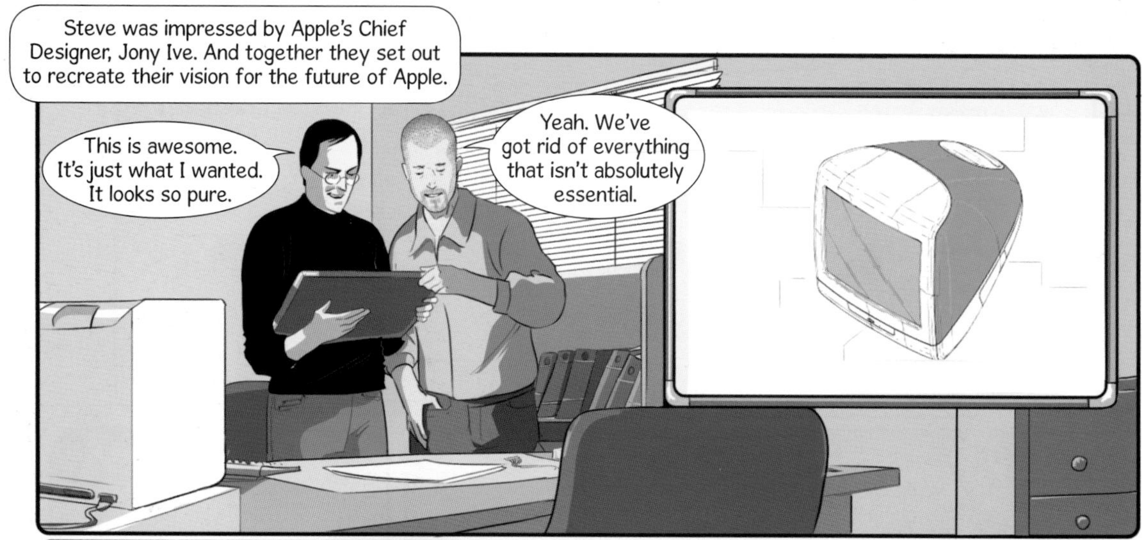
Steve was impressed by Apple's Chief Designer, Jony Ive. And together they set out to recreate their vision for the future of Apple.
This is awesome. It's just what I wanted. It looks so pure.
Yeah. We've got rid of everything that isn't absolutely essential.

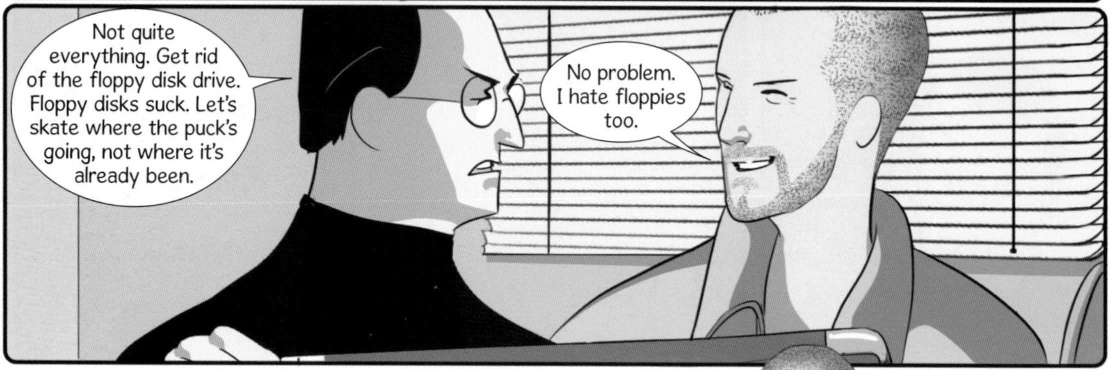
Not quite everything. Get rid of the floppy disk drive. Floppy disks suck. Let's skate where the puck's going, not where it's already been.
No problem. I hate floppies too.

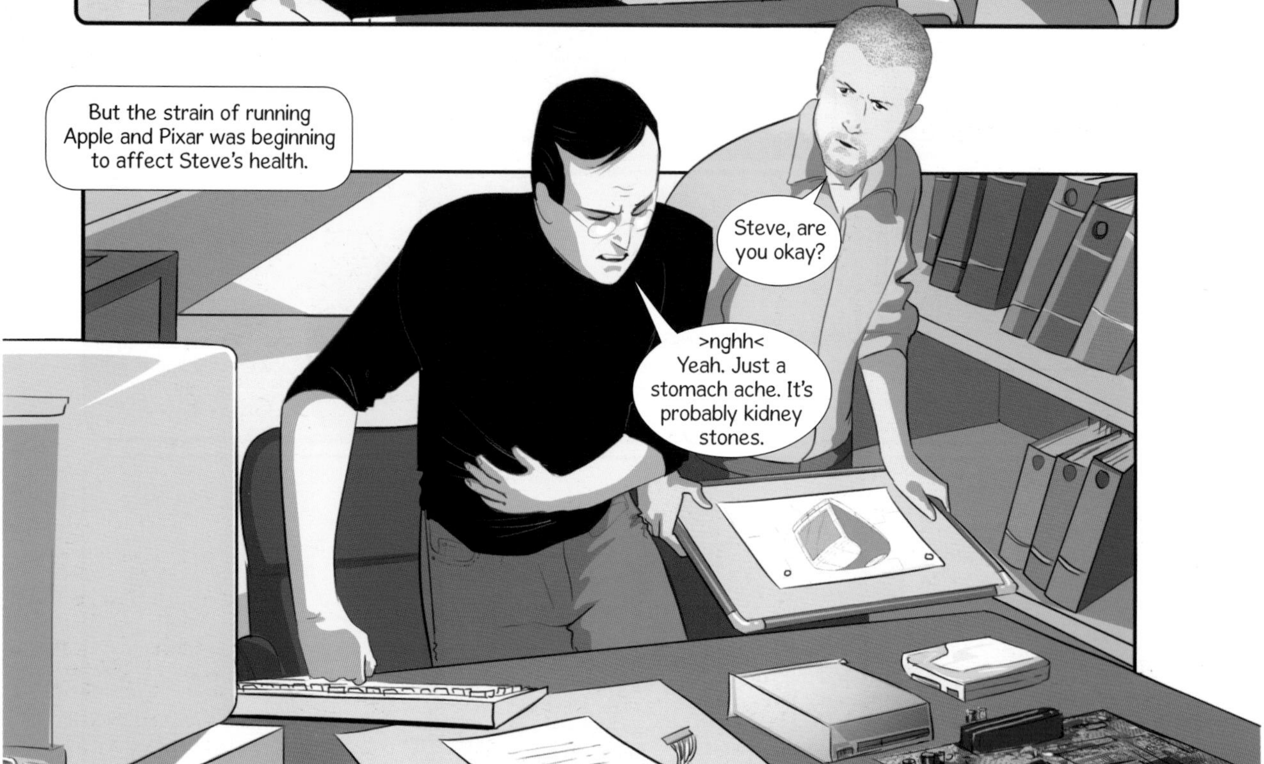
But the strain of running Apple and Pixar was beginning to affect Steve's health.
Steve, are you okay?
>nghh< Yeah. Just a stomach ache. It's probably kidney stones.

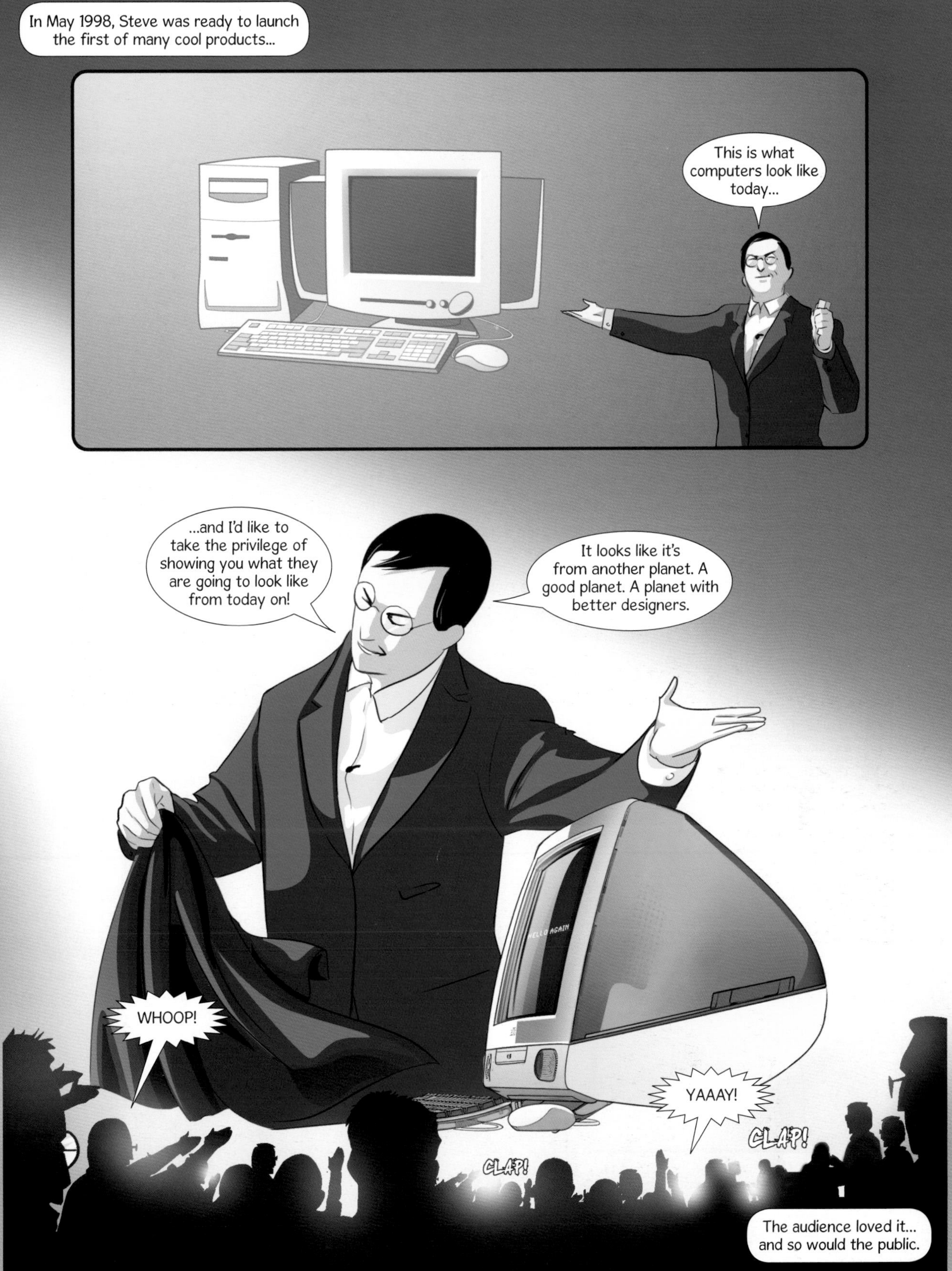
In May 1998, Steve was ready to launch the first of many cool products...
This is what computers look like today...
...and I'd like to take the privilege of showing you what they are going to look like from today on!
It looks like it's from another planet. A good planet. A planet with better designers.
HELLO AGAIN
WHOOP!
YAAAY!
CLAP!
CLAP!
The audience loved it... and so would the public.

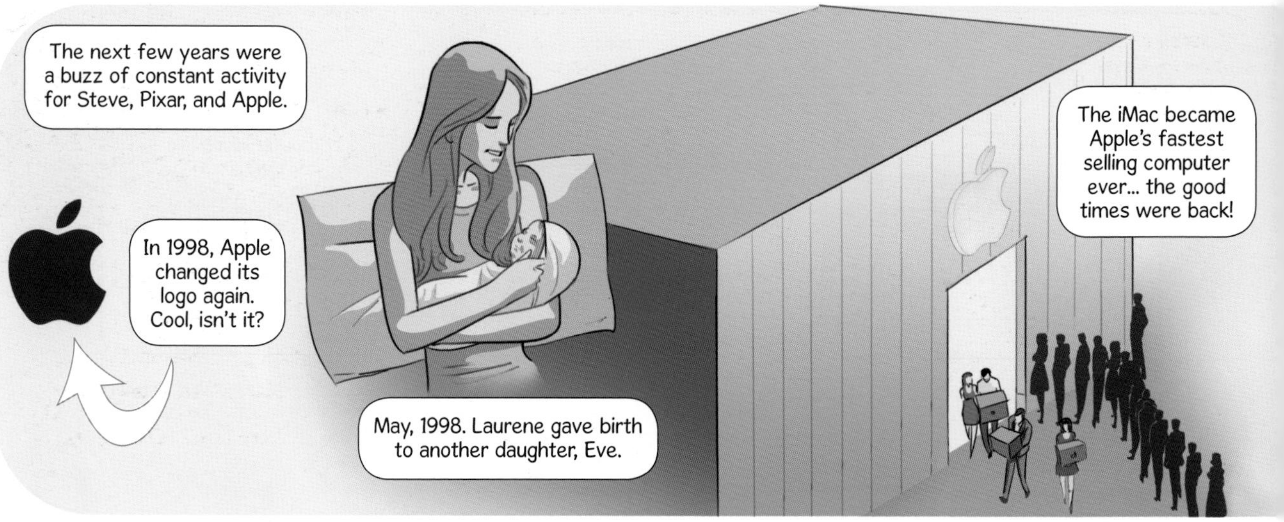
The next few years were a buzz of constant activity for Steve, Pixar, and Apple.
In 1998, Apple changed its logo again. Cool, isn't it?
May, 1998. Laurene gave birth to another daughter, Eve.
The iMac became Apple's fastest selling computer ever... the good times were back!

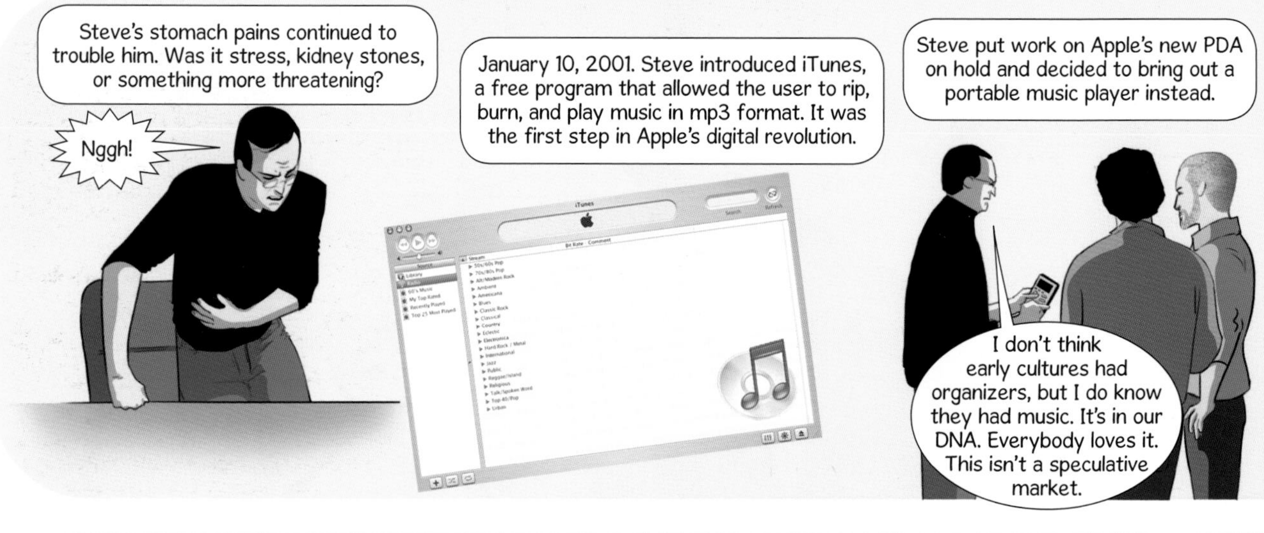
Steve's stomach pains continued to trouble him. Was it stress, kidney stones, or something more threatening?
Nggh!
January 10, 2001. Steve introduced iTunes, a free program that allowed the user to rip, burn, and play music in mp3 format. It was the first step in Apple's digital revolution.
Steve put work on Apple's new PDA on hold and decided to bring out a portable music player instead.
I don't think early cultures had organizers, but I do know they had music. It's in our DNA. Everybody loves it. This isn't a speculative market.

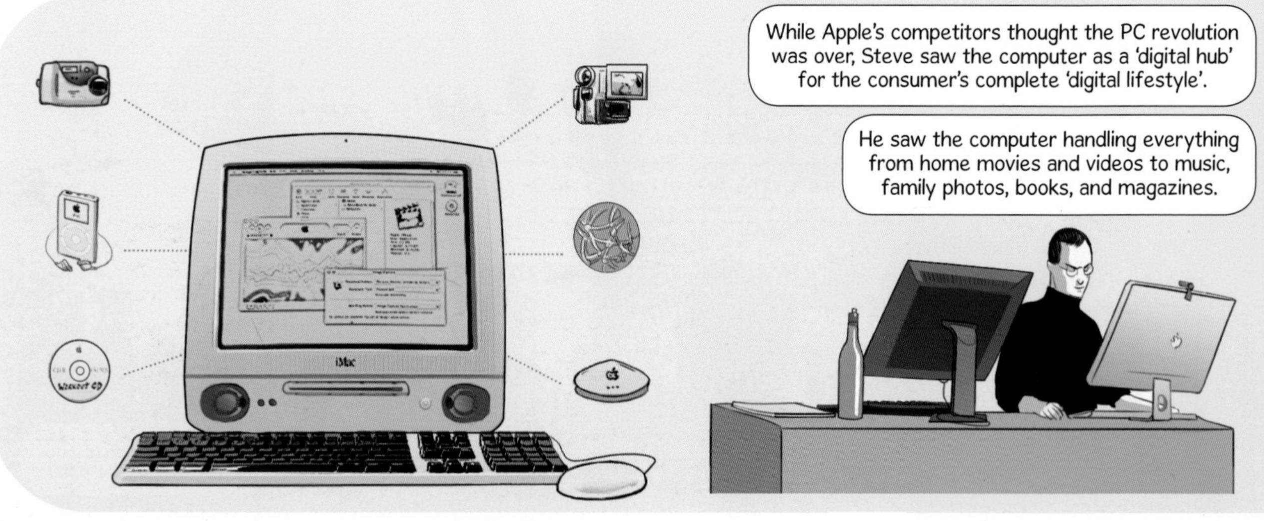
While Apple's competitors thought the PC revolution was over, Steve saw the computer as a 'digital hub' for the consumer's complete 'digital lifestyle'.
He saw the computer handling everything from home movies and videos to music, family photos, books, and magazines.
iMac

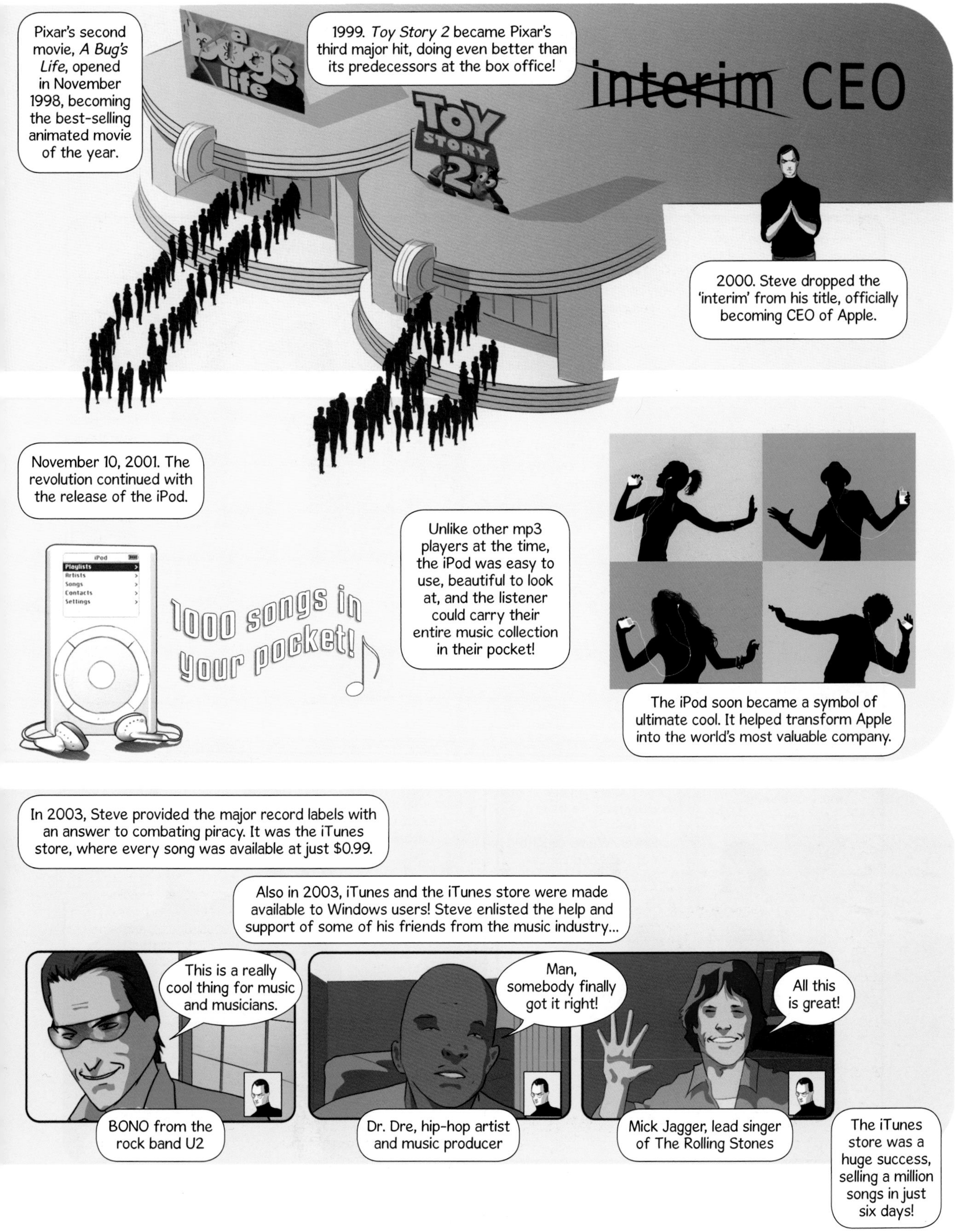
Pixar's second movie, *A Bug's Life*, opened in November 1998, becoming the best-selling animated movie of the year.
a bug's life
1999. *Toy Story 2* became Pixar's third major hit, doing even better than its predecessors at the box office!
TOY STORY 2
~~interim~~ CEO
2000. Steve dropped the 'interim' from his title, officially becoming CEO of Apple.
November 10, 2001. The revolution continued with the release of the iPod.
iPod
Playlists
Artists
Songs
Contacts
Settings
1000 songs in your pocket!
Unlike other mp3 players at the time, the iPod was easy to use, beautiful to look at, and the listener could carry their entire music collection in their pocket!
The iPod soon became a symbol of ultimate cool. It helped transform Apple into the world's most valuable company.
In 2003, Steve provided the major record labels with an answer to combating piracy. It was the iTunes store, where every song was available at just $0.99.
Also in 2003, iTunes and the iTunes store were made available to Windows users! Steve enlisted the help and support of some of his friends from the music industry...
This is a really cool thing for music and musicians.
BONO from the rock band U2
Man, somebody finally got it right!
Dr. Dre, hip-hop artist and music producer
All this is great!
Mick Jagger, lead singer of The Rolling Stones
The iTunes store was a huge success, selling a million songs in just six days!

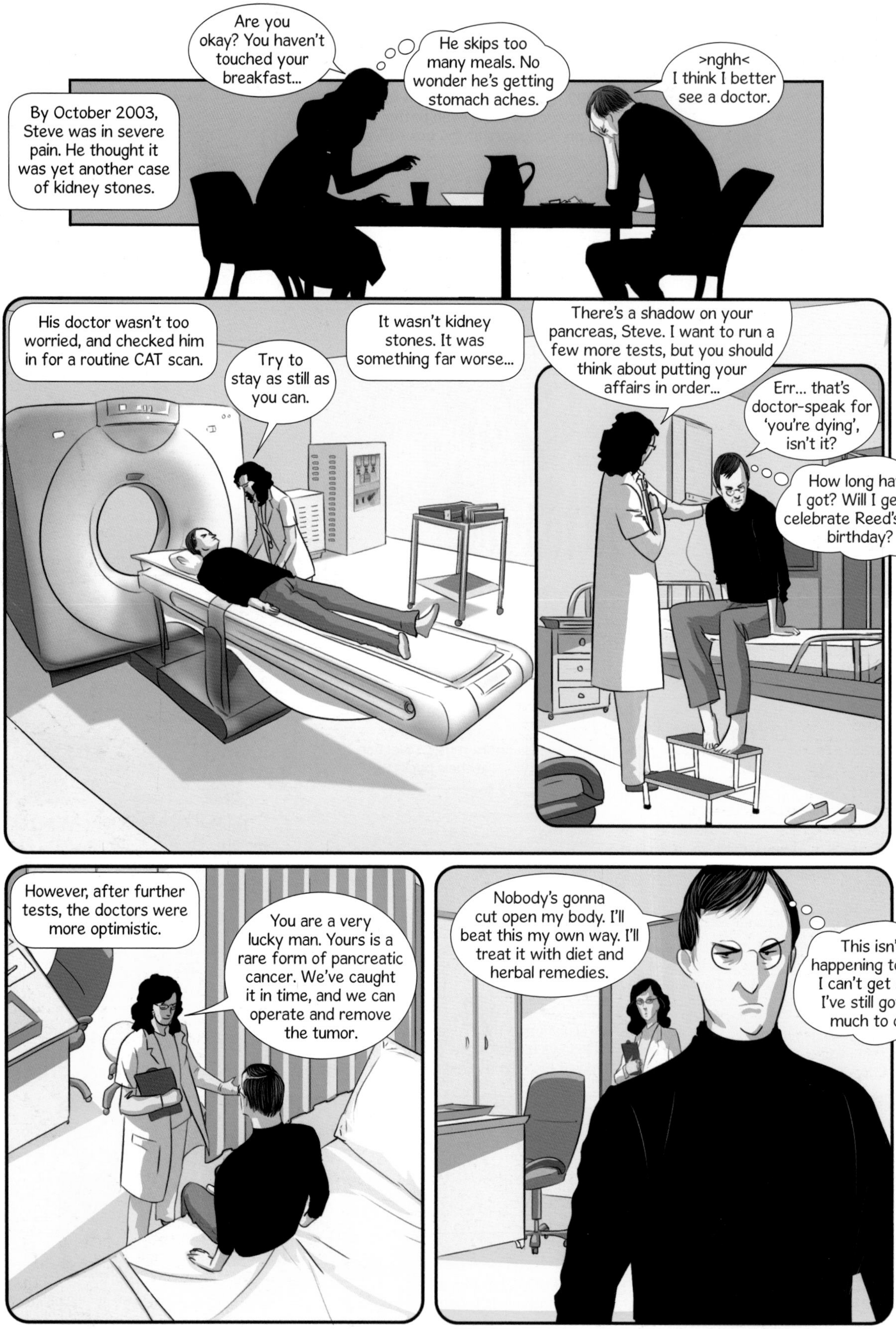

By October 2003, Steve was in severe pain. He thought it was yet another case of kidney stones.
Are you okay? You haven't touched your breakfast...
He skips too many meals. No wonder he's getting stomach aches.
>nghh< I think I better see a doctor.
His doctor wasn't too worried, and checked him in for a routine CAT scan.
Try to stay as still as you can.
It wasn't kidney stones. It was something far worse...
There's a shadow on your pancreas, Steve. I want to run a few more tests, but you should think about putting your affairs in order...
Err... that's doctor-speak for 'you're dying', isn't it?
How long have I got? Will I get to celebrate Reed's next birthday?
However, after further tests, the doctors were more optimistic.
You are a very lucky man. Yours is a rare form of pancreatic cancer. We've caught it in time, and we can operate and remove the tumor.
Nobody's gonna cut open my body. I'll beat this my own way. I'll treat it with diet and herbal remedies.
This isn't happening to me. I can't get sick. I've still got so much to do.

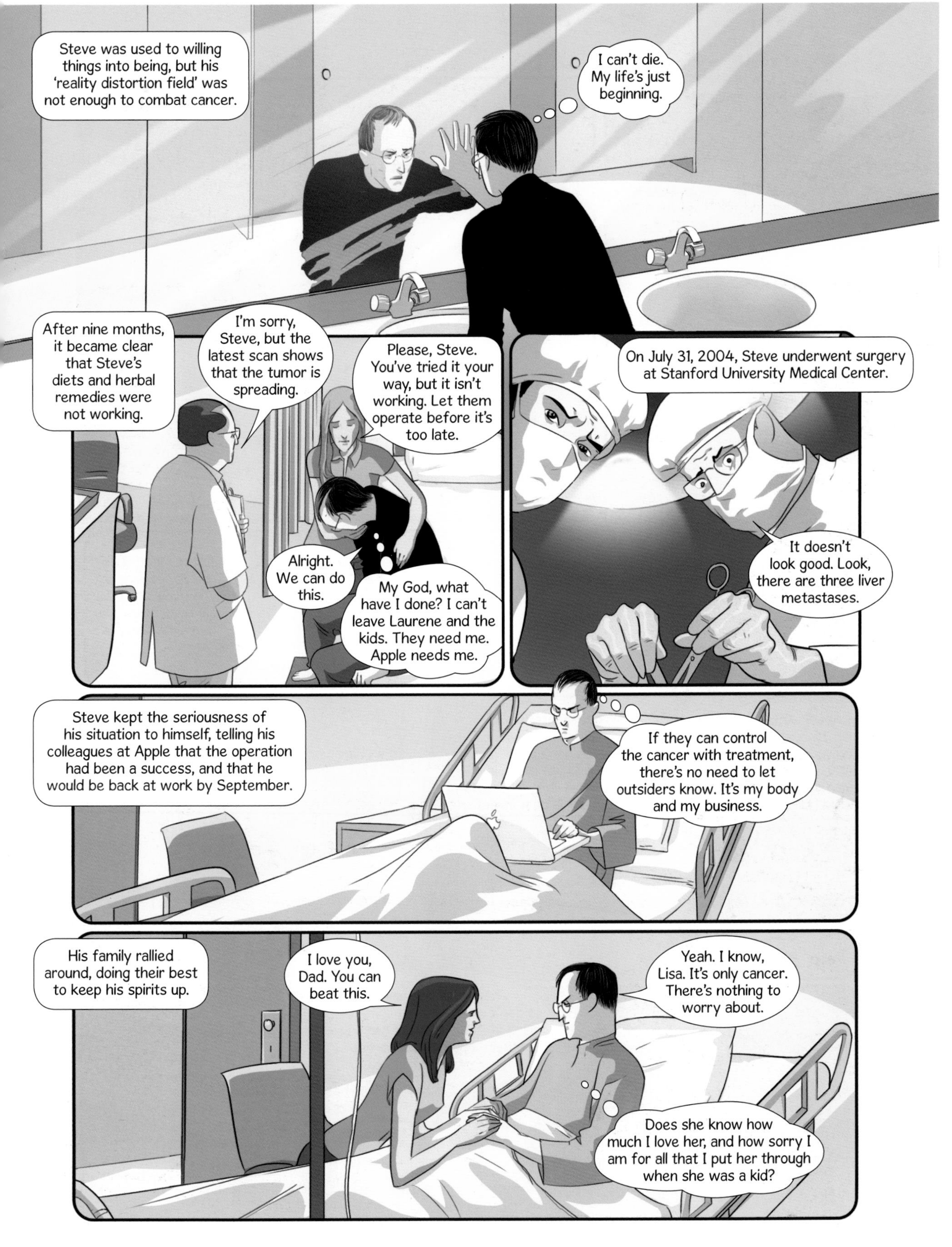
Steve was used to willing things into being, but his 'reality distortion field' was not enough to combat cancer.
I can't die. My life's just beginning.
After nine months, it became clear that Steve's diets and herbal remedies were not working.
I'm sorry, Steve, but the latest scan shows that the tumor is spreading.
Please, Steve. You've tried it your way, but it isn't working. Let them operate before it's too late.
Alright. We can do this.
My God, what have I done? I can't leave Laurene and the kids. They need me. Apple needs me.
On July 31, 2004, Steve underwent surgery at Stanford University Medical Center.
It doesn't look good. Look, there are three liver metastases.
Steve kept the seriousness of his situation to himself, telling his colleagues at Apple that the operation had been a success, and that he would be back at work by September.
If they can control the cancer with treatment, there's no need to let outsiders know. It's my body and my business.
His family rallied around, doing their best to keep his spirits up.
I love you, Dad. You can beat this.
Yeah. I know, Lisa. It's only cancer. There's nothing to worry about.
Does she know how much I love her, and how sorry I am for all that I put her through when she was a kid?

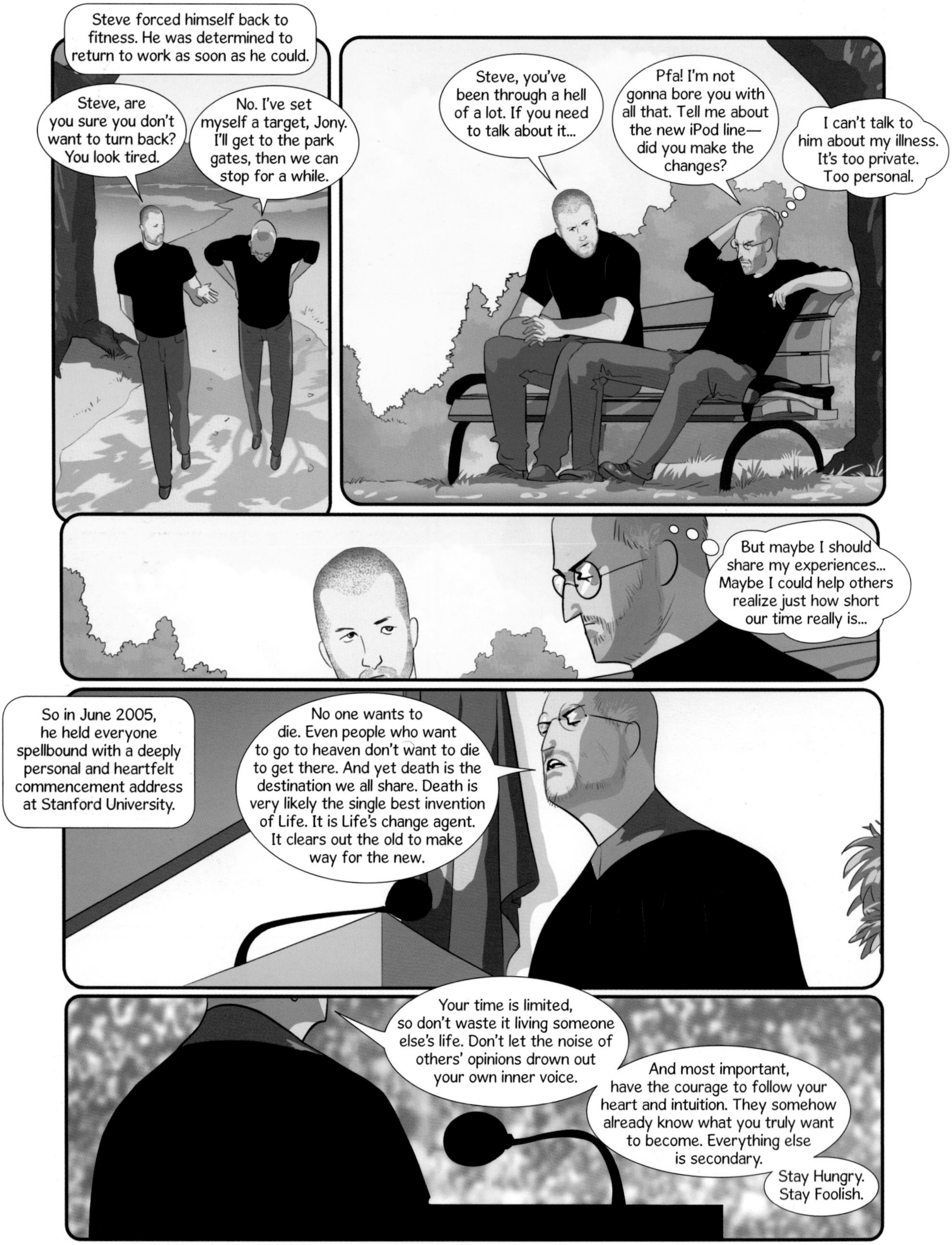
Steve forced himself back to fitness. He was determined to return to work as soon as he could.
Steve, are you sure you don't want to turn back? You look tired.
No. I've set myself a target, Jony. I'll get to the park gates, then we can stop for a while.
Steve, you've been through a hell of a lot. If you need to talk about it...
Pfa! I'm not gonna bore you with all that. Tell me about the new iPod line—did you make the changes?
I can't talk to him about my illness. It's too private. Too personal.
But maybe I should share my experiences... Maybe I could help others realize just how short our time really is...
So in June 2005, he held everyone spellbound with a deeply personal and heartfelt commencement address at Stanford University.
No one wants to die. Even people who want to go to heaven don't want to die to get there. And yet death is the destination we all share. Death is very likely the single best invention of Life. It is Life's change agent. It clears out the old to make way for the new.
Your time is limited, so don't waste it living someone else's life. Don't let the noise of others' opinions drown out your own inner voice.
And most important, have the courage to follow your heart and intuition. They somehow already know what you truly want to become. Everything else is secondary.
Stay Hungry. Stay Foolish.

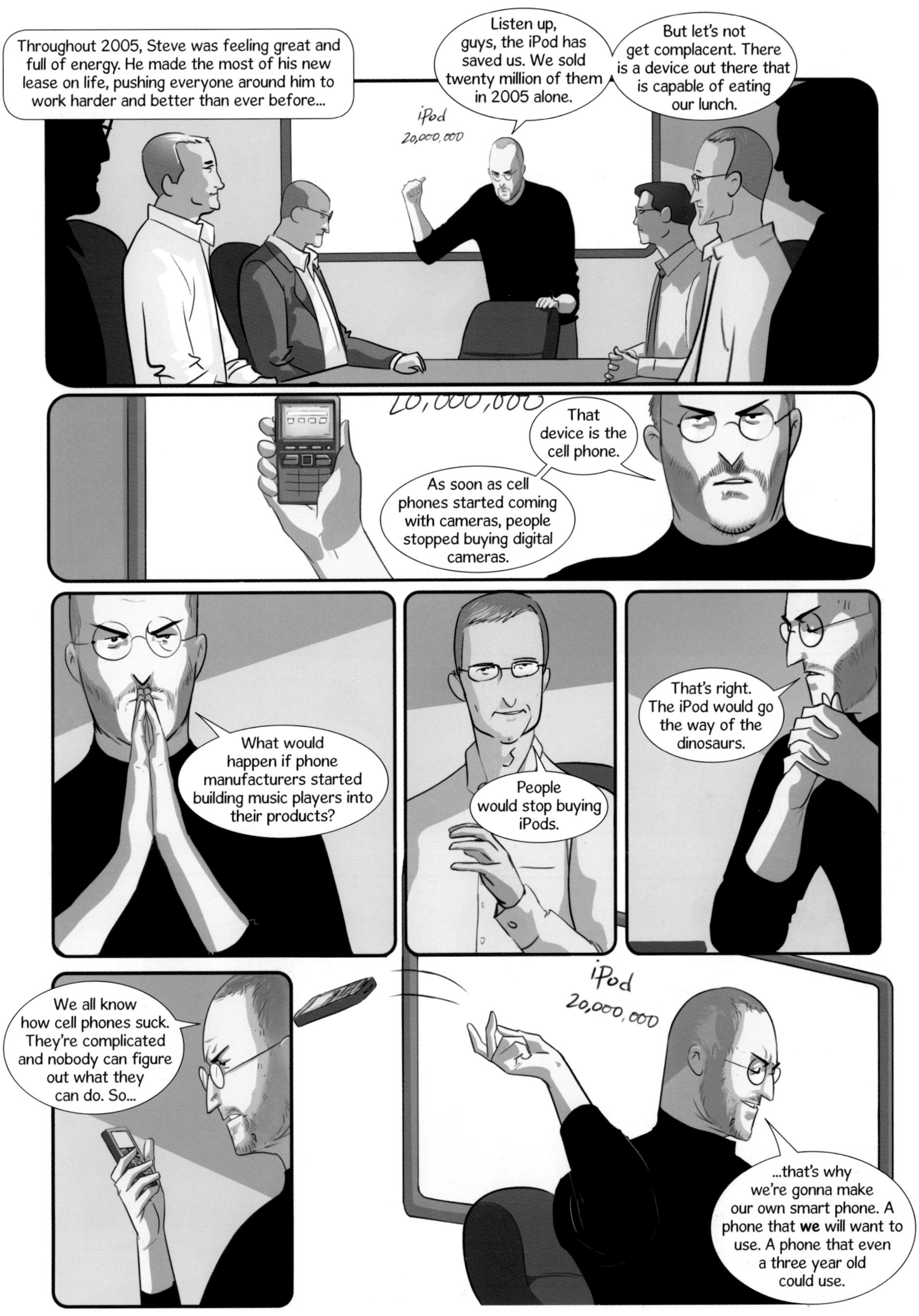
Throughout 2005, Steve was feeling great and full of energy. He made the most of his new lease on life, pushing everyone around him to work harder and better than ever before...
Listen up, guys, the iPod has saved us. We sold twenty million of them in 2005 alone.
But let's not get complacent. There is a device out there that is capable of eating our lunch.
iPod 20,000,000
That device is the cell phone.
As soon as cell phones started coming with cameras, people stopped buying digital cameras.
What would happen if phone manufacturers started building music players into their products?
People would stop buying iPods.
That's right. The iPod would go the way of the dinosaurs.
We all know how cell phones suck. They're complicated and nobody can figure out what they can do. So...
iPod 20,000,000
...that's why we're gonna make our own smart phone. A phone that **we** will want to use. A phone that even a three year old could use.

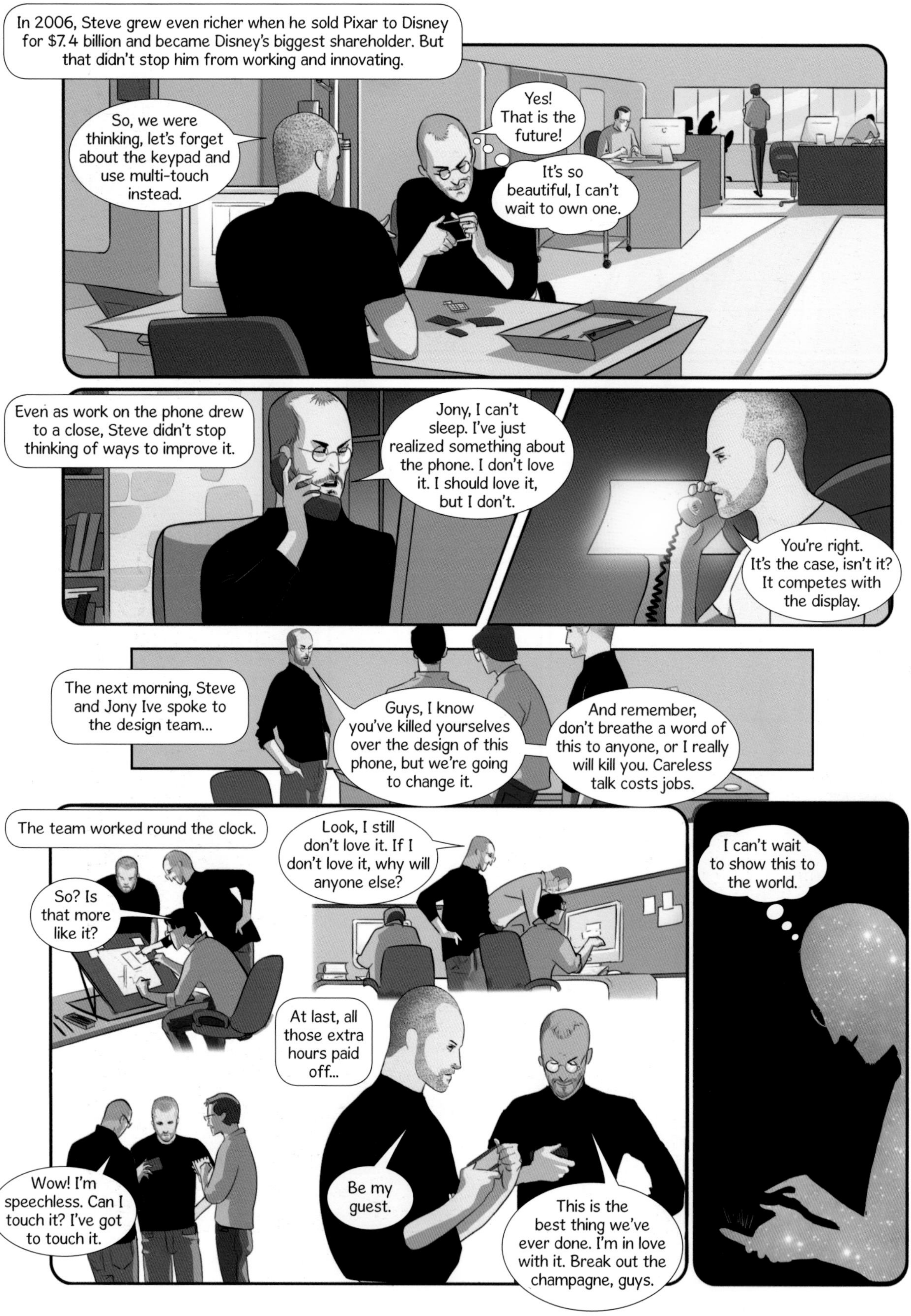

In 2006, Steve grew even richer when he sold Pixar to Disney for $7.4 billion and became Disney's biggest shareholder. But that didn't stop him from working and innovating.
So, we were thinking, let's forget about the keypad and use multi-touch instead.
Yes! That is the future!
It's so beautiful, I can't wait to own one.
Even as work on the phone drew to a close, Steve didn't stop thinking of ways to improve it.
Jony, I can't sleep. I've just realized something about the phone. I don't love it. I should love it, but I don't.
You're right. It's the case, isn't it? It competes with the display.
The next morning, Steve and Jony Ive spoke to the design team...
Guys, I know you've killed yourselves over the design of this phone, but we're going to change it.
And remember, don't breathe a word of this to anyone, or I really will kill you. Careless talk costs jobs.
The team worked round the clock.
So? Is that more like it?
Look, I still don't love it. If I don't love it, why will anyone else?
At last, all those extra hours paid off...
Wow! I'm speechless. Can I touch it? I've got to touch it.
Be my guest.
This is the best thing we've ever done. I'm in love with it. Break out the champagne, guys.
I can't wait to show this to the world.

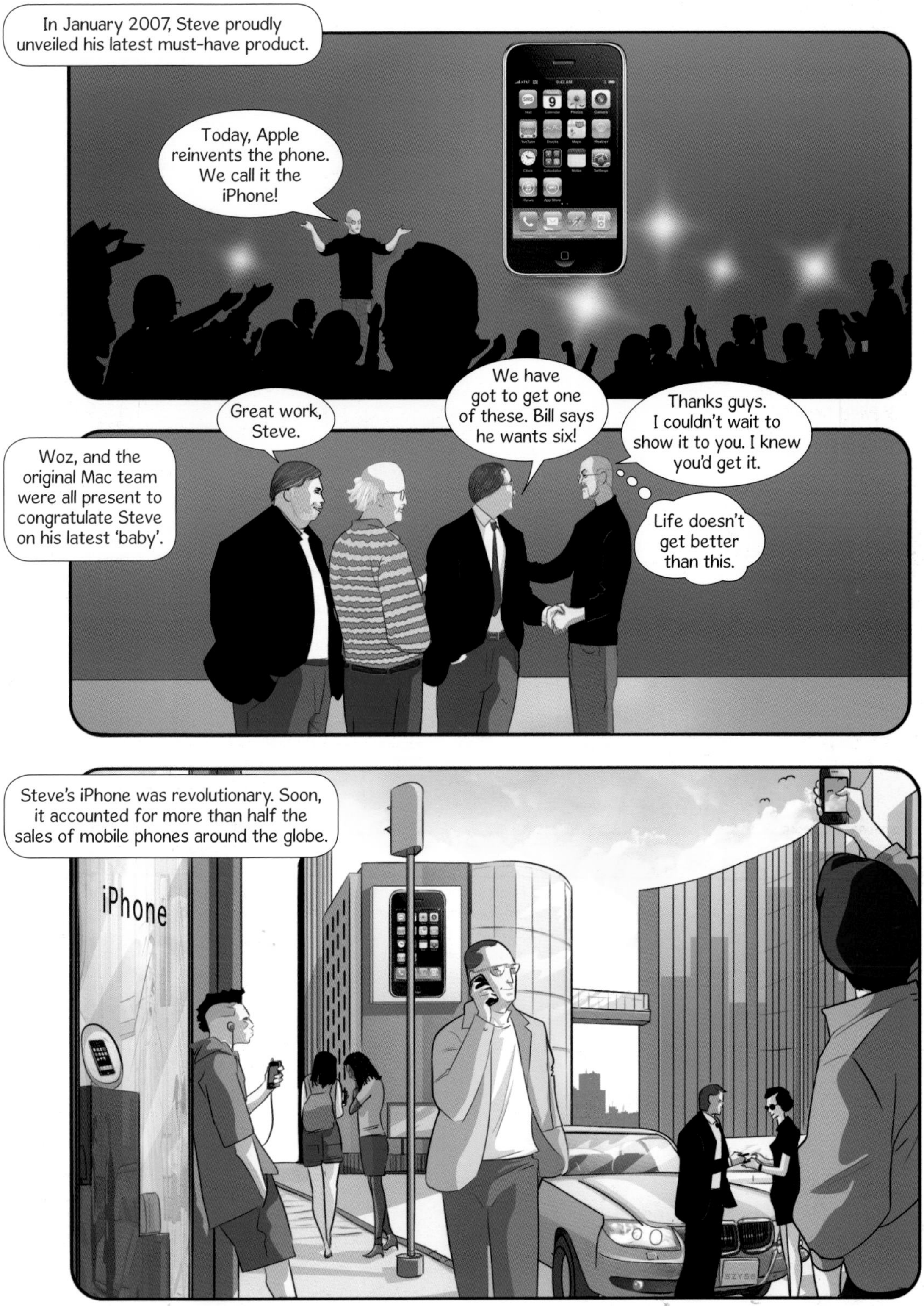
In January 2007, Steve proudly unveiled his latest must-have product.
Today, Apple reinvents the phone. We call it the iPhone!
Woz, and the original Mac team were all present to congratulate Steve on his latest 'baby'.
Great work, Steve.
We have got to get one of these. Bill says he wants six!
Thanks guys. I couldn't wait to show it to you. I knew you'd get it.
Life doesn't get better than this.
Steve's iPhone was revolutionary. Soon, it accounted for more than half the sales of mobile phones around the globe.
iPhone

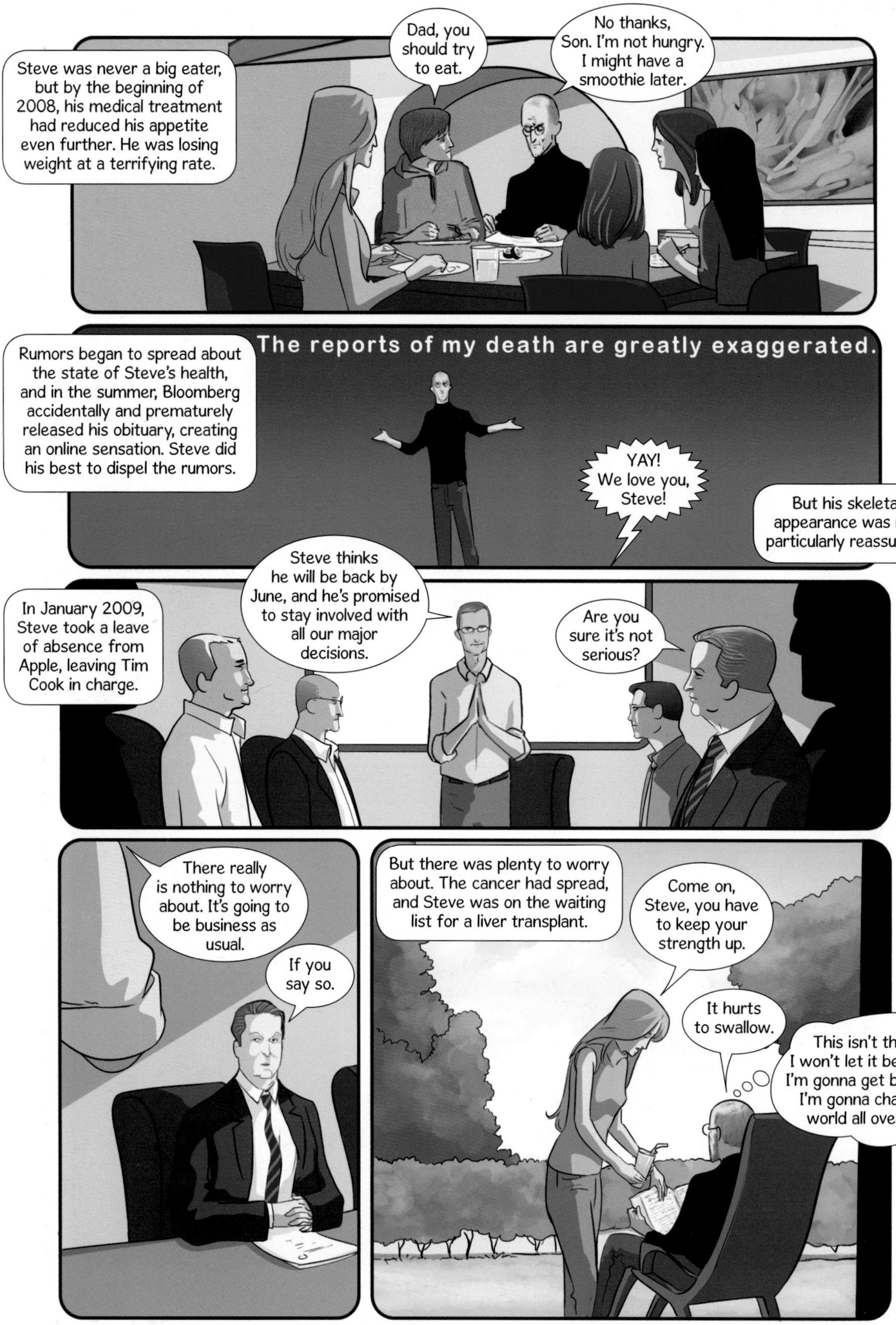
Steve was never a big eater, but by the beginning of 2008, his medical treatment had reduced his appetite even further. He was losing weight at a terrifying rate.
Dad, you should try to eat.
No thanks, Son. I'm not hungry. I might have a smoothie later.
Rumors began to spread about the state of Steve's health, and in the summer, Bloomberg accidentally and prematurely released his obituary, creating an online sensation. Steve did his best to dispel the rumors.
The reports of my death are greatly exaggerated.
YAY! We love you, Steve!
But his skeletal appearance was not particularly reassuring.
In January 2009, Steve took a leave of absence from Apple, leaving Tim Cook in charge.
Steve thinks he will be back by June, and he's promised to stay involved with all our major decisions.
Are you sure it's not serious?
There really is nothing to worry about. It's going to be business as usual.
If you say so.
But there was plenty to worry about. The cancer had spread, and Steve was on the waiting list for a liver transplant.
Come on, Steve, you have to keep your strength up.
It hurts to swallow.
This isn't the end. I won't let it be the end. I'm gonna get better, and I'm gonna change the world all over again.

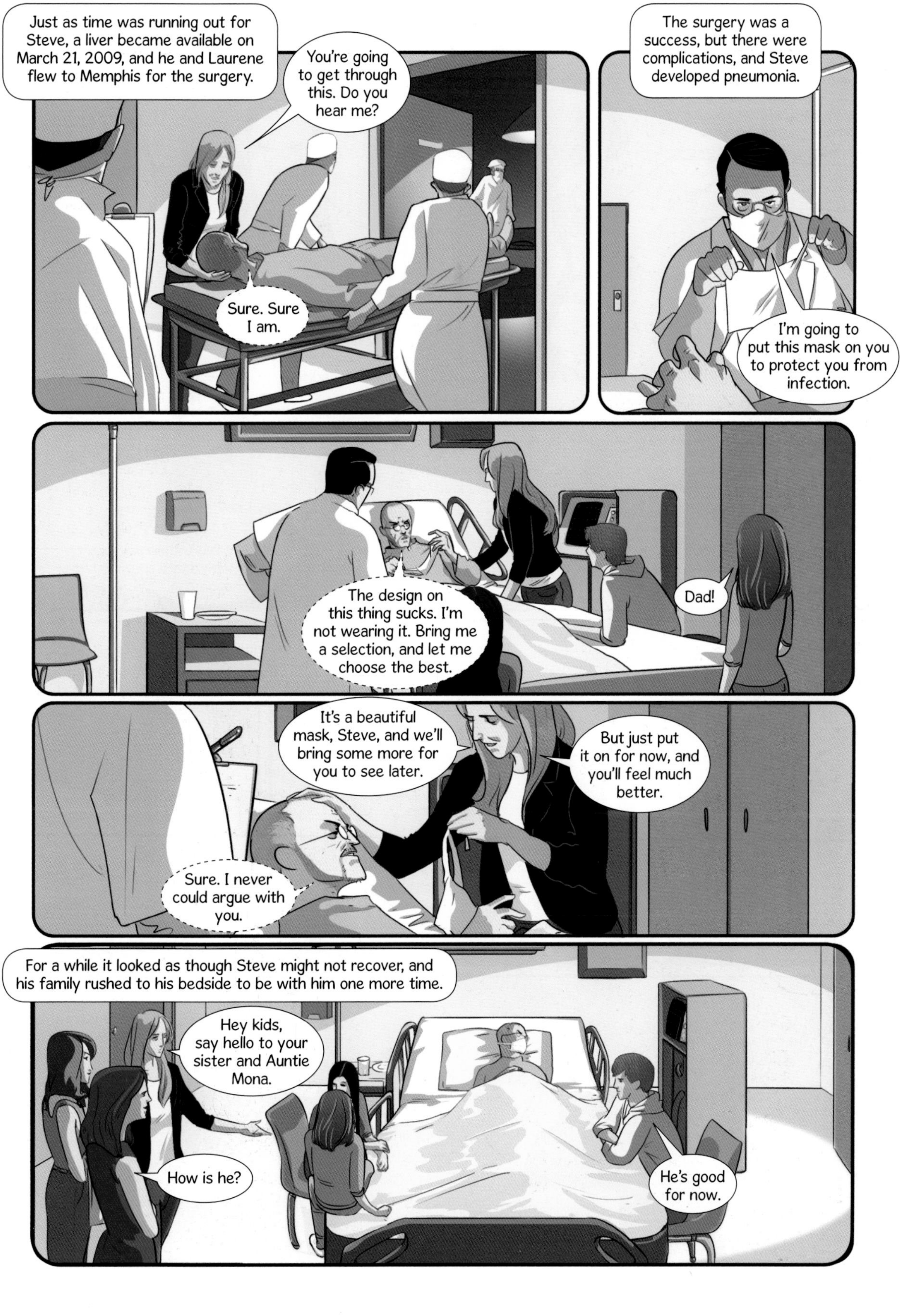

Just as time was running out for Steve, a liver became available on March 21, 2009, and he and Laurene flew to Memphis for the surgery.
You're going to get through this. Do you hear me?
Sure. Sure I am.
The surgery was a success, but there were complications, and Steve developed pneumonia.
I'm going to put this mask on you to protect you from infection.
The design on this thing sucks. I'm not wearing it. Bring me a selection, and let me choose the best.
Dad!
It's a beautiful mask, Steve, and we'll bring some more for you to see later.
But just put it on for now, and you'll feel much better.
Sure. I never could argue with you.
For a while it looked as though Steve might not recover, and his family rushed to his bedside to be with him one more time.
Hey kids, say hello to your sister and Auntie Mona.
How is he?
He's good for now.

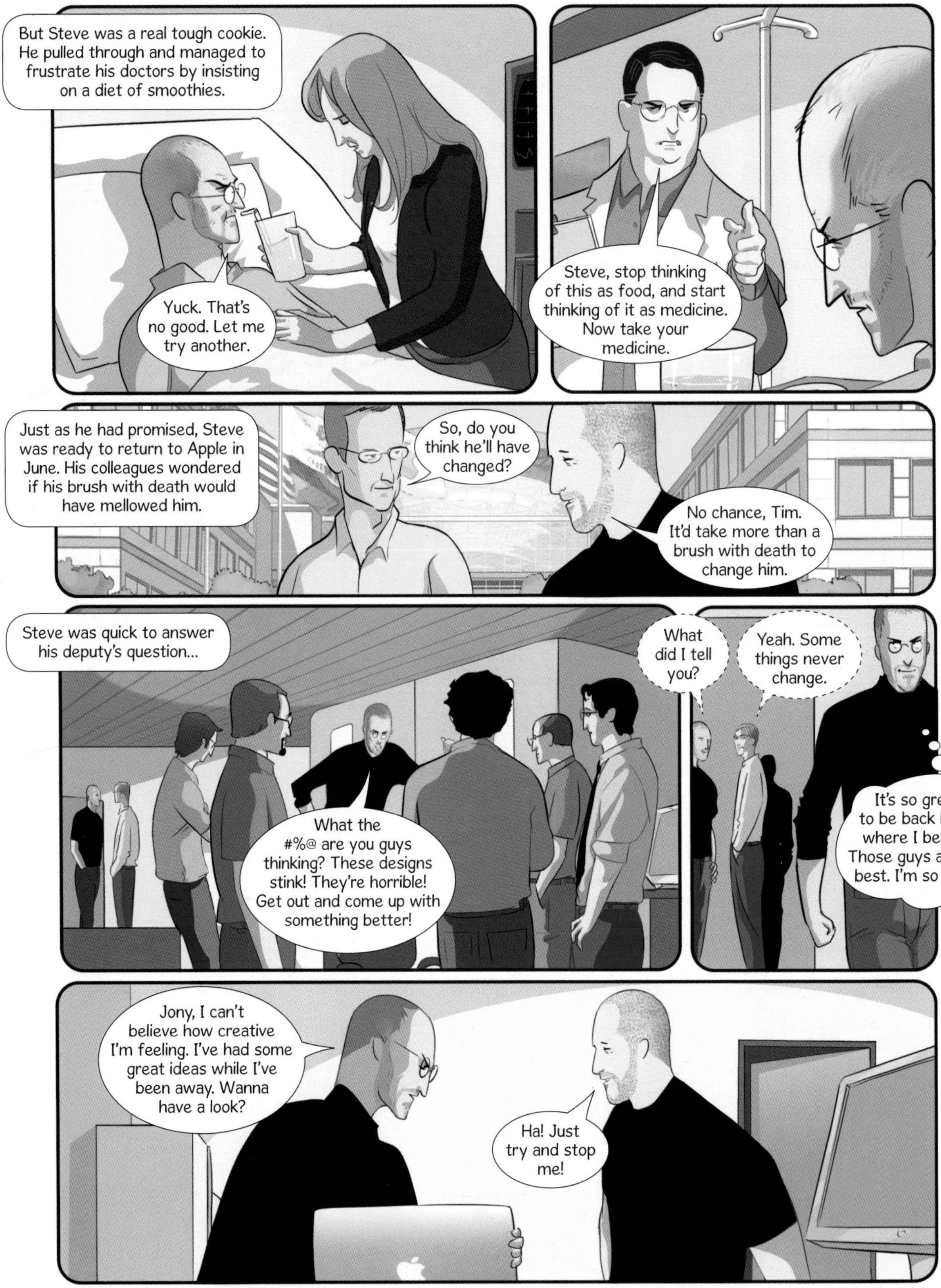
But Steve was a real tough cookie. He pulled through and managed to frustrate his doctors by insisting on a diet of smoothies.
Yuck. That's no good. Let me try another.
Steve, stop thinking of this as food, and start thinking of it as medicine. Now take your medicine.
Just as he had promised, Steve was ready to return to Apple in June. His colleagues wondered if his brush with death would have mellowed him.
So, do you think he'll have changed?
No chance, Tim. It'd take more than a brush with death to change him.
Steve was quick to answer his deputy's question...
What the #%@ are you guys thinking? These designs stink! They're horrible! Get out and come up with something better!
What did I tell you?
Yeah. Some things never change.
It's so great to be back here, where I belong. Those guys are the best. I'm so lucky.
Jony, I can't believe how creative I'm feeling. I've had some great ideas while I've been away. Wanna have a look?
Ha! Just try and stop me!

Steve threw himself back into work, and on January 27, 2010, unveiled his latest brainchild to a packed house.

The iPhone and the laptop. Is there room for something in between?

Netbooks?

Netbooks? Nah! We've got something better than that...

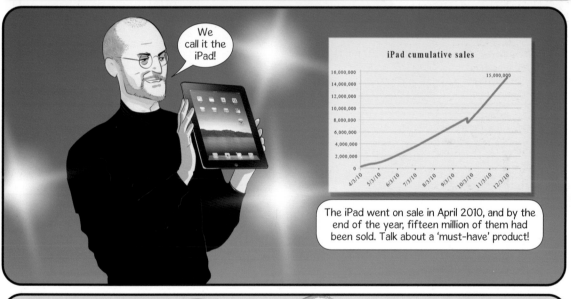

We call it the iPad!

iPad cumulative sales

The iPad went on sale in April 2010, and by the end of the year, fifteen million of them had been sold. Talk about a 'must-have' product!

But Steve was feeling unwell again.

I'm going to be taking some more time off. I know I can count on you to take care of things while I'm gone.

Sure you can. You just concentrate on getting well again.

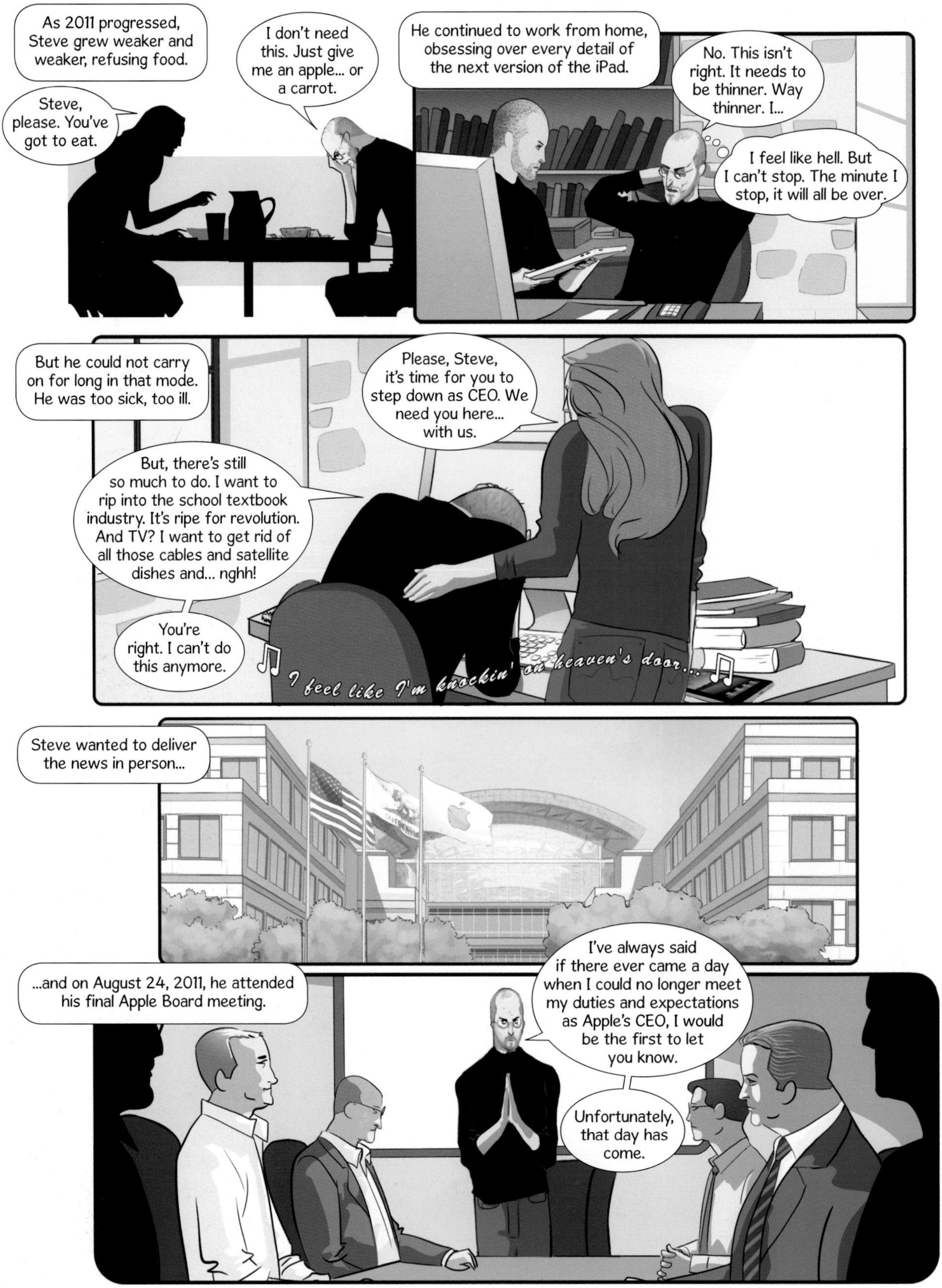
As 2011 progressed, Steve grew weaker and weaker, refusing food.
Steve, please. You've got to eat.
I don't need this. Just give me an apple... or a carrot.
He continued to work from home, obsessing over every detail of the next version of the iPad.
No. This isn't right. It needs to be thinner. Way thinner. I...
I feel like hell. But I can't stop. The minute I stop, it will all be over.
But he could not carry on for long in that mode. He was too sick, too ill.
Please, Steve, it's time for you to step down as CEO. We need you here... with us.
But, there's still so much to do. I want to rip into the school textbook industry. It's ripe for revolution. And TV? I want to get rid of all those cables and satellite dishes and... nghh!
You're right. I can't do this anymore.
I feel like I'm knockin' on heaven's door...
Steve wanted to deliver the news in person...
...and on August 24, 2011, he attended his final Apple Board meeting.
I've always said if there ever came a day when I could no longer meet my duties and expectations as Apple's CEO, I would be the first to let you know.
Unfortunately, that day has come.

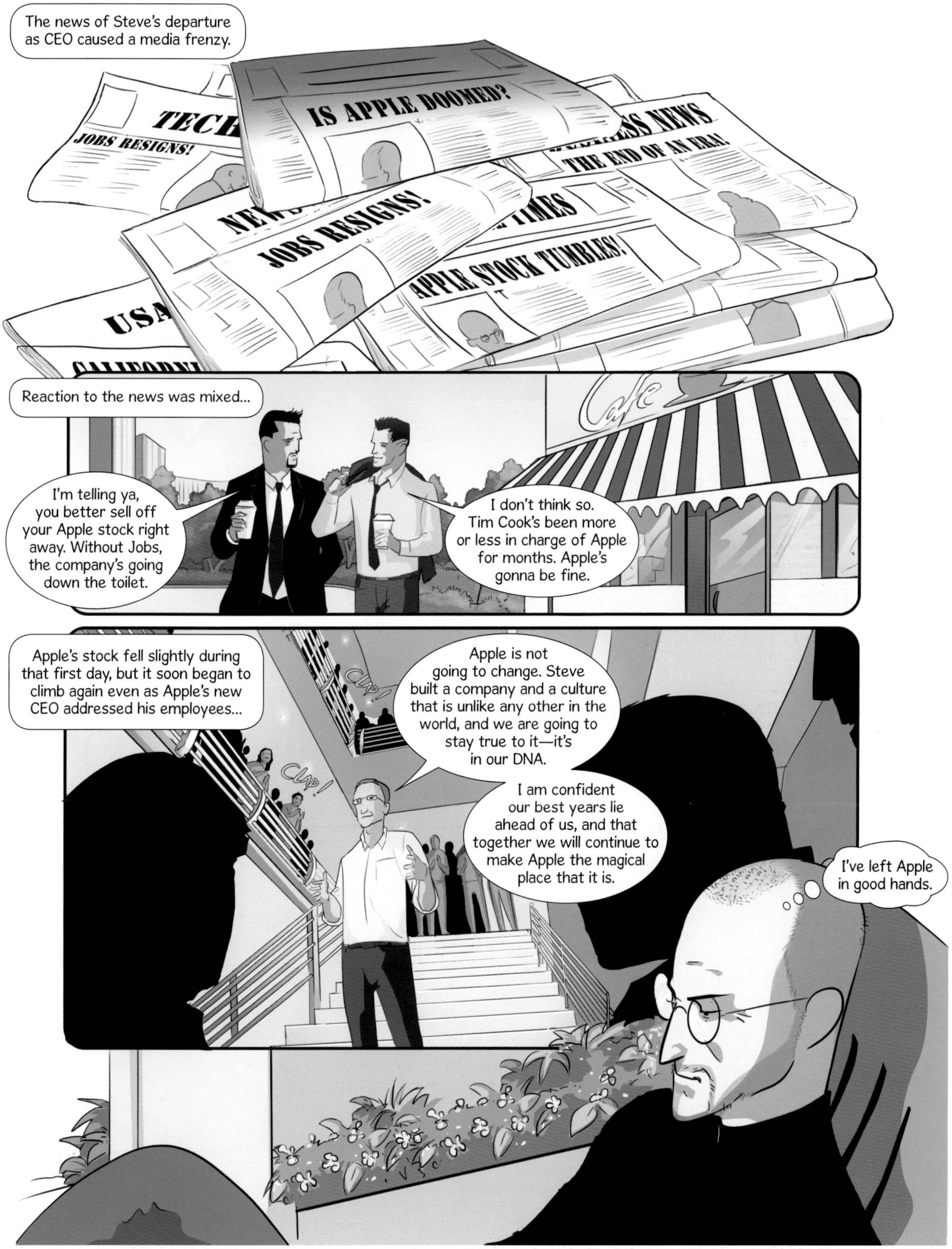
The news of Steve's departure as CEO caused a media frenzy.
IS APPLE DOOMED?
JOBS RESIGNS!
THE END OF AN ERA!
JOBS RESIGNS!
APPLE STOCK TUMBLES!
Reaction to the news was mixed...
I'm telling ya, you better sell off your Apple stock right away. Without Jobs, the company's going down the toilet.
I don't think so. Tim Cook's been more or less in charge of Apple for months. Apple's gonna be fine.
Apple's stock fell slightly during that first day, but it soon began to climb again even as Apple's new CEO addressed his employees...
CLAP!
CLAP!
Apple is not going to change. Steve built a company and a culture that is unlike any other in the world, and we are going to stay true to it—it's in our DNA.
I am confident our best years lie ahead of us, and that together we will continue to make Apple the magical place that it is.
I've left Apple in good hands.

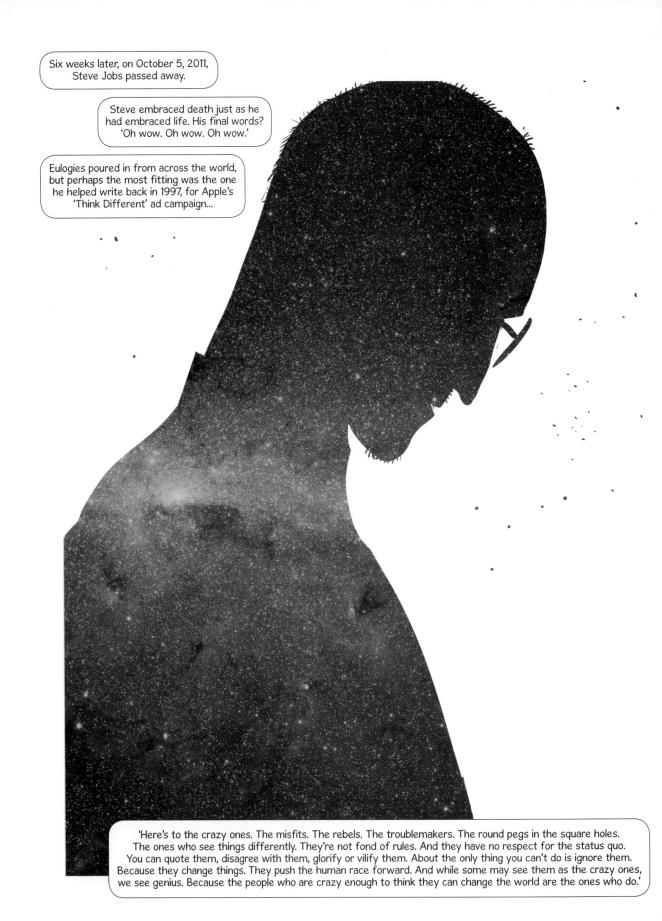

Six weeks later, on October 5, 2011, Steve Jobs passed away.

Steve embraced death just as he had embraced life. His final words? 'Oh wow. Oh wow. Oh wow.'

Eulogies poured in from across the world, but perhaps the most fitting was the one he helped write back in 1997, for Apple's 'Think Different' ad campaign...

'Here's to the crazy ones. The misfits. The rebels. The troublemakers. The round pegs in the square holes. The ones who see things differently. They're not fond of rules. And they have no respect for the status quo. You can quote them, disagree with them, glorify or vilify them. About the only thing you can't do is ignore them. Because they change things. They push the human race forward. And while some may see them as the crazy ones, we see genius. Because the people who are crazy enough to think they can change the world are the ones who do.'